Henry McBride Series in Modernism and Modernity

Eugene O'Neill and His Eleven-Play Cycle

"A Tale of Possessors Self-Dispossessed"

Donald C. Gallup

Yale University Press   New Haven and London

Copyright © 1998 by Yale University.
All rights reserved.
This book may not be reproduced, in whole
or in part, including illustrations, in any form
(beyond that copying permitted by Sections
107 and 108 of the U.S. Copyright Law and
except by reviewers for the public press),
without written permission from the
publishers.

Designed by Sonia L. Scanlon.
Set in Bulmer type by Keystone
Typesetting, Inc.
Printed in the United States of America by
BookCrafters, Inc., Chelsea, Michigan.

The paper in this book meets the guidelines
for permanence and durability of the
Committee on Production Guidelines for
Book Longevity of the Council on Library
Resources.

Frontispiece: Eugene O'Neill at Tao House.
Inscribed by Carlotta Monterey O'Neill on
verso: "Eugene O'Neill/Tao House/
California/ [July?] 1941/(When *his illness*
[i.e., his tremor] began)". (Photo: ?Oona
O'Neill, later Lady Chaplin, probably taken
between 11 and 18 July; DCG)

10 9 8 7 6 5 4 3 2 1

Library of Congress Cataloging-in-
Publication Data
Gallup, Donald Clifford, 1913–
    Eugene O'Neill and his eleven-play
cycle : "a tale of possessors self-
dispossessed" / Donald C. Gallup.
        p.cm   . — (Henry McBride series
    in modernism and modernity)
    Includes extensive summaries of the
plots of individual plays.
    Includes bibliographical references and
index.
    ISBN 0-300-07187-6 (alk. paper)
    1. O'Neill, Eugene, 1888–1953—
Criticism and interpretation.
2. Modernism (Literature)—United
States. 3. Cycles (Literature)
I. O'Neill, Eugene, 1888–1953.
II. Title. III. Title: Tale of possessors
self-dispossessed. IV. Series.
PS3529.N5Z6455   1998
812'.52—dc21   97-32718
                       CIP

A catalogue record for this book is available
from the British Library.

Pages 305–306 are a continuation of this
copyright page.

the henry mcbride series in modernism and modernity

The artistic movement known as modernism, which includes the historical avant-garde, produced the most radical and comprehensive change in Western culture since Romanticism. Its effects reverberated through all the arts, permanently altering their formal repertories and their relations with society at large, and its products still surround us in our workplaces and homes. Although modernism produced a pervasive cultural upheaval, it can never be assessed as an artistic movement alone: its contours took shape against the background of social, political, and intellectual change, and it was always bound up with larger questions of modernity and modernization and with the intellectual challenge of sifting their meanings. Henry McBride (1867–1962) became perhaps the leading American critic to write perceptively and engagingly on modern art. The Henry McBride Series in Modernism and Modernity, which focuses on modernism and the arts in their many contexts, is respectfully dedicated to his memory.

Editorial Committee

Lawrence Rainey, University of York, General Editor
Ronald Bush, Oxford University
Arthur Danto, Columbia University
Charles Harrison, Open University
Jean-Michel Rabaté, University of Pennsylvania
Jeffrey Schnapp, Stanford University
Richard Taruskin, University of California, Berkeley
Robert Wohl, University of California, Los Angeles

Suffice it that the possibilities are Gigantic, Epic, Colossal, Enormous—as the Hollywood half of the Guild Committee would probably phrase it now, lightly, in passing—and . . . this Work has the chance latent within it of making "[Mourning Becomes] Electra" & "Strange I[nterlude]." look like variety skits—provided its author can release said latent. In short, it's a challenge to carry on farther than I've carried before, and that's about the only thing that can still rouse my enthusiasm in writing for the theatre.

—O'Neill, letter to Lee Simonson
of the Theatre Guild, ca. May 1935

Contents

Note

Quotations from Eugene O'Neill's letters, as well as all "A" transcripts of his Cycle Papers, follow exactly his spelling and punctuation (or lack of it).

Words and phrases inserted by the editor in O'Neill's *Work Diary*, and therefore printed within square brackets (thus: [   ]), appear within angle brackets (thus: ⟨   ⟩) in this volume.

Acknowledgments

My first debt is to Carlotta Monterey O'Neill and Karl Ragnar Gierow, both of
revered memory, who persuaded me in 1963 that, even without knowing
Swedish, I could transform *Bygg dig allt högre boningar* into *More Stately
Mansions*. Mrs. O'Neill subsequently encouraged me to undertake the task of
transcribing the Cycle Papers and of puzzling out the story of her husband's
great-hearted attempt, from 1935 to 1939, to "carry on farther than . . .
[he had] carried before". I am also very much indebted to Yale University,
legatee under the will of Carlotta Monterey O'Neill, for authorization to publish the O'Neill manuscript materials that make up the most important part of
this book. All author's royalties will be paid into the principal of the Carlotta
Monterey and Eugene Gladstone O'Neill Memorial Fund of Yale University.

A fellowship from the John Simon Guggenheim Memorial Foundation in
1968 made it possible for me to transcribe most of the Cycle Papers.

Without Travis Bogard, whose death on 5 April 1997 is mourned by
O'Neillians all over the world, this book would probably have been published
only after my own demise, if indeed at all. I wrote the introduction at his
urging, and it contains phrasings that he suggested; his endorsement helped
persuade Yale University Press to add my manuscript to its list.

At the Beinecke Rare Book and Manuscript Library, Herman Liebert,
former librarian, Louis Martz, former director, Ralph Franklin, director,
Patricia Willis, curator of the Yale Collection of American Literature, Lynn
Braunsdorf, Phyllis Cohen, Ellen Cordes, Aldo Cupo, Maureen Heher, Joan
Hofmann, Stephen Jones, Karen Marinuzzi, Patricia Middleton, Lori Misura,
Alfred Mueller, Suzanne Rutter, Christa Sammons, Anne Whelpley, and
other past and present members of the staff have given me courteous and
willing cooperation, without which I could not have completed this book.

At Yale University Press, Ellen Graham read an early draft of this book and
gave me many helpful suggestions. Karen Gangel has improved not only the
consistency and correctness but also the readability of my manuscript.

Introduction

From 21 January 1935 until 5 June 1939 Eugene O'Neill devoted almost all of his creative energy to a Cycle of plays, finally titled "A Tale of Possessors Self-Dispossessed," that would trace the history of an American family, the Harfords, showing the corrupting influence of material things upon its members. Its theme would be the Bible's question: "What will it profit a man if he gain the whole world but lose his own soul?"

Not only was the plan for the Cycle impressive, but there were good reasons for expecting that its plays, when written, would rank with O'Neill's best. The period during which he gave them his exclusive attention ought to have been richly productive. In 1935, in the prime of life at age forty-six, he was back at home after an extended residence abroad. The success of the double-length *Strange Interlude* (1928) and the trilogy *Mourning Becomes Electra* (1931), which he considered his best plays, had relieved him of financial worries. Further, in the Theatre Guild he had a producer ready and willing to give his work the sympathetic and understanding treatment it required. His private life had at last reached an even keel. After protracted legal wrangling, his second wife, Agnes Boulton, had granted him a divorce. His third marriage, to Carlotta Monterey, afforded him great satisfaction, providing the constant loving support and the freedom from the annoying demands of everyday living that he felt he had to have in order to write.

There was, however, an increasingly serious problem: ill health. Although he had conquered an addiction to alcohol that had plagued him for many years, O'Neill had begun to pay for that and other excesses of his youth. Entries in his *Work Diary* document the frequent bouts of sickness that forced interruptions in his writing program. In February 1934, with *"Nerves—liver—digestion all shot*", he had found himself unable to work (p. 183). On 23 March, told by his physician that he was "on verge of nervous breakdown—also faint indication apex right lung—must rest for 6 mos—no work—or complete collapse", he began the first of a series of three insulin treatments in order to put on weight (p. 185) and, through the following four months, submitted, reluctantly, to the prescribed rest cure.

For a time his health improved, but early in 1935, trying to concentrate on the new Cycle while fighting off a cold, he reported that "rotten nerves continue—flying out of skin" (p. 207). In March, he began to take thyroid, and in October two months of pain sent him into Presbyterian Hospital in New York for "all sorts [of] tests—Xrays, etc.," which were inconclusive (p. 233). In desperation, from 10 November through 30 December O'Neill experimented with denying himself cigarettes, but on the latter date he gave up the experiment because it left him "inert mentally!" (p. 241). In January 1936, trouble with his teeth obliged him to return to New York to have four extracted. The next month, gastritis put him in Doctors' Hospital. In April the first of a series of bilious attacks occurred; they were accompanied by extreme depression and feelings of exhaustion that continued throughout the summer. In the fall he continued to feel "physically all shot," and on 24 October his doctor, George Draper, prescribed "absolute change—rest—forget work" (pp. 269, 270).

The consequent move from Sea Island, Georgia, to Seattle, Washington, seemed to be having a good effect until 12 November, when O'Neill received word of the not entirely welcome award of the Nobel Prize for literature. He complained on the fifteenth: "nerves all shot—hell of a chance to rest cure & forget plays!—feel I am on edge of breakdown—vitality exhausted—mental jim jams" (p. 272). Finally settled in San Francisco, he was given "medicine for bladder" and on 23 December protested: "something all wrong, I'm afraid—getting to be a god damned invalid!—it's revolting!" (p. 275). Fortunately, a new physician correctly diagnosed the symptoms, and O'Neill underwent a successful appendectomy on the twenty-ninth. But pain in his kidneys and prostate continued to plague him. A "bad sinking spell" of 12 January 1937, caused by extremely low blood pressure (p. 277), recurred intermittently, along with nervous dyspepsia, bilious attacks, and neuritis, for which various medications, treatments, and diets were prescribed. In February and March 1938, he had eight more teeth extracted, because they were either "badly abscessed" or had "bad pyorrhea," and commented on 8 March: "teeth a curse for past ten years!" (pp. 313, 315). In October he suffered a "flare-up of [the] same old infection ⟨prostate⟩" (p. 331).

Casa Genotta, Sea Island, Georgia. Built in 1932 by Eugene and Carlotta O'Neill, who lived there from 22 June of that year until 5 October 1936. (DCG)

Although there were periods of slight improvement as particular treatments seemed to bring good results, O'Neill's health gradually continued to deteriorate in the remaining months during which he concentrated on the Cycle. He managed to complete the first four plays of what had now become a nine-play Cycle; but three were of double length, and he could see no way of reducing their size without ruining them. And so, in despair, on 5 June 1939, "fed up and stale on [the] Cycle after 4½ years of not thinking of any other work", he forced himself to "forget it for a while" (p. 351).

The change had a remarkable effect. His creative mind came alive again as new ideas flooded his brain. In midyear O'Neill outlined both *The Iceman Cometh* and *Long Day's Journey into Night,* and between July and December he completed first and second drafts of the former. After his tortured attempts to get at the complicated motives of his Cycle family, the Harfords, these two autobiographical plays almost wrote themselves: *The Iceman*'s characters were drawn from associates he had known intimately in his youth; *Long Day's Journey* was part of the story of his own family, even though it had to be "written in blood" (p. 368).[1]

He returned briefly to the Cycle early in 1940 but then began to write *Long Day's Journey* and, in spite of a break of six weeks during which he could think of nothing but the war in Europe, completed first and second drafts of that play. On 20 and 21 October 1940, he analyzed the first two, overlong plays of the Cycle, acknowledging in his *Work Diary* that he had "tried to get too much into them, too many interwoven themes & motives, psychological & spiritual" (p. 391). But they were too valuable to be discarded. He awoke on the twenty-second with the idea of replacing them with four new plays in what would now be an eleven-play Cycle that traced the Harfords back to 1755. Between 23 October and 13 November, he prepared rough outlines for all four, incorporating ideas that had occurred to him for other plays, "Robespierre" and "Napoleon's Coronation."

Turning again from the Cycle, O'Neill concentrated on more new projects: a series of one-act plays to be called "By Way of Obit.," again featuring characters based on acquaintances of olden days, and *A Moon for the Misbegotten*, a partly autobiographical play that cast his brother Jamie as one of its principals. In October 1941 he again took up the Cycle long enough to read over the outlines prepared a year earlier for the new first four plays. In the *Work Diary* he described his reaction as "pleased—can be great stuff—and I mean, great—but too long, tough job to tackle now" (p. 419). And so he went on, instead, to complete *A Moon for the Misbegotten*. Fearing, with good reason, that his health would prevent him from tackling the tough job of writing the four new Cycle plays, and resolving to get at least one part of the series finished, he took up the revision of what was now Play Five, *A Touch of the Poet*, managing between February and November 1942 to make it a "much better play, both as itself & as part of [the] Cycle" (p. 451).

O'Neill had now begun to suffer increasingly from a tremor that at times affected his hands so severely that he could no longer hold a pen or pencil.[2] Although he had experimented briefly with a dictating machine the Theatre Guild had given him in 1944, he found that the only way he could create was by actually setting down words on paper. The hope that he could start writing again faded as the tremor worsened, and in February 1949 he stated to Winfield Aronberg, his lawyer, that he would "never write another play."[3] In August of that year he confided to George Jean Nathan: "As for writing, that is out of the question. It is not only a matter of hand, but of mind—I just feel there is nothing more I want to say."[4]

Travis Bogard, professor of dramatic art at the University of California, Berkeley, expressed most eloquently the regret we all must feel that the vast project was not brought to fruition:

That Eugene O'Neill could not complete the historical cycle as it was designed is one of the greatest losses the drama in any time has sustained. Goethe's comment on Marlowe's *Dr. Faustus*, "How greatly it was planned," has more relevance to *A Tale of Possessors, Self-dispossessed*. It was a work of astonishing scope and scale. Theresa Helburn rightly called it a *comédie humaine*. Nothing in the drama, except Shakespeare's two cycles on British history, could have been set beside it. The two plays that have survived reveal something of the power of life that beat in it, but they show only vestiges of what its full plan realized would have provided: a prophetic epitome for the course of American destiny.[5]

On 8 March 1938, O'Neill explained to another of his lawyers, Harry Weinberger, his difficulty in trying to write when he was not feeling well: "I only have to tear up the stuff I force myself to do when I'm under the weather. It just won't come right unless I feel reasonably fit. Rotten nerves I don't count. I've always had those. But piling other ills on top of the rotten nerves gets me groggy. I haven't yet learned to take that extra punishment and go on regardless."[6] But it was not just ill health that kept O'Neill from completing the Cycle.

Once embarked on his plans for "four or five plays," he encountered a "difficult technical problem": how to make a play "complete in itself while at the same time an indispensable link in the whole". Each play was to be "concentrated around the final fate of one member . . . but [would] . . . also carry on the story of the family".[7] As he thought about the four Harford brothers and made notes for their plays, he found that he needed to know more about their parents. Eventually he decided that the Cycle must tell of the courtship and marriage of Ethan and Sara (Melody) Harford, describing their life together and their relationship with Ethan's mother, Deborah (Deane) Harford. That earlier play expanded almost at once into two. O'Neill explained his predicament in an interview with the writer Elizabeth Shepley Sergeant in 1946. She reported his telling her that "The difficulty, after he began to go backwards, was to find the starting point in all this—[he] could never be sure of [the] place where he ought to begin. Everything derived from everything else."[8]

In June 1939 O'Neill had told his friend Richard Dana Skinner why even the outlines of the later plays were not completed:

. . . it is better not to try and finish them until I have gone on much farther with the whole thing. A matter of keeping them in their right place so they won't anticipate too much of what must appear again when the curve completes its circle. That will do for an explanation, although it doesn't tell all the story. A devilish job, this Cycle! . . . I work and work and time passes while, in relation to the whole work, I seem to stand still. Most discouraging, at times, like being on a treadmill.[9]

As the years passed and the number of plays grew to eleven, the war in Europe, too, came to have its effect. In a letter to Sean O'Casey, the Irish playwright, on 5 August 1943, O'Neill commented that "*A Touch Of The Poet* . . . is the only one of the four Cycle plays I had written which approached final form. The others will have to be entirely recreated—if I ever get around to it—because I no longer see them as I did in the pre-war 1939 days in which they were written."[10] On 24 March 1945, referring to the Cycle by its final title, "A Tale of Possessors Self-Dispossessed," O'Neill admitted to the critic Frederic I. Carpenter that he would never write the last play, the old "Bessie Bowen."[11] "The Great Depression caught up with its prophecies, for one thing."[12]

After turning his attention from the Cycle, on 15 June 1940, during a period of depression brought on by ill health and news of the war in Europe, O'Neill had written to George Jean Nathan: "My main selfish worry is that now the Cycle recedes farther and farther away, until I cannot imagine myself going back to it. . . . And if I become finally convinced it is not in me to go on with it, I shall destroy all I have done so far, the completed plays and everything else down to the last note. If it cannot exist as the unique whole I conceived, then I don't want it to exist at all."[13] Although he eventually decided against this drastic course, on 21 February 1944, just before he and Carlotta left Tao House, in California, he did destroy the manuscripts of the first two plays of the nine-play Cycle—in order not to be too much influenced by them in writing the four plays he had outlined in 1940 to replace them in an eleven-play Cycle. A detailed scenario, completed 9 November 1935 for act one of the old second play, escaped destruction and was eventually printed in the fall 1992 issue of the *Eugene O'Neill Review.*

Of the new first four plays there were still only outlines, along with notes prepared for revision of Plays Five to Eleven. Play Five, *A Touch of the Poet,* in the new version of November 1942, was complete and could stand by itself. Published posthumously in 1957, it was first produced in Swedish that year and in English in the United States a year later. Play Six, *More Stately*

Mansions, had been one of the double-length plays, but O'Neill had sufficiently cut, revised, and rewritten the first three acts so that he could describe
his typescript as a "3rd Draft", even though it was still too long.[14] He took the
precaution of labeling that script "*Unfinished Work . . . to be destroyed in case
of my death!*"[15] Preserved by accident, it was produced in 1962 in a shortened
Swedish version prepared by Karl Ragnar Gierow, director of the Royal
Dramatic Theatre in Stockholm, and was published in the United States in an
equivalent English text in 1964. A variant shortened version prepared by José
Quintero was produced here in 1967. O'Neill's original draft was published
in its entirety in 1988.

Play Seven, *The Calms of Capricorn*—the starting point for the whole
series—existed only in a detailed scenario written in May and June 1935. It
was printed, along with my "development" in conventional play form, in
1981 and 1982; that script was given a staged reading at the University of
Wisconsin-Madison in those years. Of Play Eight, "The Earth Is the Limit,"
Play Nine, "Nothing Is Lost but Honor," and Play Ten, "The Man on Iron
Horseback," there were only the rough outlines O'Neill had prepared in
1935. For the eleventh and final play, "The Hair of the Dog," O'Neill had
assembled various notes and partial scenarios.

In the years immediately following his death, in 1953, it was generally
assumed that O'Neill had destroyed all of the Cycle material save for the one
completed play and a few miscellaneous notes. This impression was reinforced in an interview with Carlotta Monterey O'Neill conducted by Seymour Peck and printed in the *New York Times* on 4 November 1956. Her
account as reported by Peck was dramatically convincing:

> O'Neill was always working on three or four plays at a time . . . . Even
> while he was doing *Long Day's Journey,* he was also occupied with a cycle
> of nine plays covering an American family from the Eighteen Twenties to
> modern times. *A Touch of the Poet,* the first play in the cycle, was com-
> pleted, but six others, which needed revision and cutting, were destroyed
> by the O'Neills in the Boston hotel where they were living before his death.
>
> "He didn't want to leave any unfinished plays and he said, 'It isn't that I
> don't trust you, Carlotta, but you might drop dead or get run over or
> something and I don't want anybody else finishing up a play of mine.' We
> tore them up, bit by bit, together. I helped him because [of] his hands—he
> had this terrific tremor, he could tear just a few pages at a time. It was
> awful, it was like tearing up children."[16]

Peck's typed transcript of his interview with Mrs. O'Neill included even more vivid detail and provided embellishments for the account in Arthur and Barbara Gelb's *O'Neill* (1962):

> On a dark winter afternoon in the early part of 1953 O'Neill and Carlotta sat before their living-room fire. A while before O'Neill had been talking . . . of his own death. . . . Suddenly he said:
> "Nobody must be allowed to finish my plays."
> He was speaking of the six cycle plays, which still existed in scenario or rough draft. He asked Carlotta to fetch all the manuscripts so that he could destroy them. . . .
> O'Neill began tearing the manuscript pages into pieces.
> "He could only tear a few pages at a time, because of his tremor," Carlotta said. "So I helped him. We tore up all the manuscripts together, bit by bit. It took hours. After a pile of torn pages had collected, I'd throw it into the fire. It was awful. It was like tearing up children."
> O'Neill did not ask for, or destroy, the sheaf of notes he had made, outlining the cycle families' genealogy and planned changes in the various plays; and somehow, a typed, unedited draft of the sixth play in the series, *More Stately Mansions,* was overlooked—probably because another version of the play was on hand to be torn up. This manuscript, five times the length of a conventional play, was later sent to Yale, along with other papers and documents.
> With the destruction of the cycle, O'Neill gave up his last feeble pretense of a hold on life.[17]

There are problems with details in these accounts. Both George Jean Nathan and Elizabeth Shepley Sergeant quote O'Neill as having spoken in 1946 of a Cycle of eleven plays. Hamilton Basso, in late 1947, has O'Neill referring to a nine-play Cycle, as does Seymour Peck, here, in 1956, in his interview with Mrs. O'Neill. The context of Basso's reference proves that the plan was still for eleven plays, beginning during the French and Indian War (1755–60).[18]

Nicholas Gage, in his *A Place for Us* (1989), pointed out that there was no fireplace in the apartment occupied by the O'Neills in the Hotel Shelton and that the scene of the actual burning of the manuscripts must have been the incinerator in the basement.[19] But which were the plays so laboriously torn up and burned? Writing from the Shelton on 4 March 1954, Mrs. O'Neill gave Dale Fern a significantly different account: "One of the most ghastly half-hours in my life was when (about a year ago, in this very room) I helped the Master destroy 4 plays out of the 'Cycle'—I thought I would die—& he looked as if he had!"[20] Two and a half years later, in 1956, the burning seemed to Mrs. O'Neill to have lasted not just a half hour but "hours," and the number of manuscripts destroyed had grown from four to six. The *four* plays were most probably the outlines of Plays One and Two of the nine-play Cycle, "Greed of the Meek" and "And Give Me Death," and the original manuscripts of *A Touch of the Poet* and *More Stately Mansions*. O'Neill himself recorded the destruction of the original *manuscripts* of the first two in February 1944.[21] Of *A Touch of the Poet,* a fourth draft, typed, with many manuscript revisions, is the earliest at Yale. The typescript of *More Stately Mansions*—which O'Neill himself referred to only as more than *double* length—was not overlooked: it had already been sent to New Haven in 1951. There is no documentary evidence that any other Cycle play was ever completed in first draft.

Although some Cycle notes and starts that O'Neill had decided were "n[o]. g[ood].",[22] were torn up, all the outlines, scenarios, and drafts referred to in the preceding pages, save for the two first drafts destroyed in 1944 and the two outlines and two manuscripts burned in 1953, were preserved, along with a great many notes and drawings. In 1942 O'Neill gave most of the manuscripts of his published plays to three libraries: the early ones went to the Museum of the City of New York; those of the middle period to Princeton; and the late ones to Yale. Because many in the last group had already been given to Carlotta and were technically her property, both O'Neills tended to think of the Yale collection as hers. In the fall of 1950, through Norman Holmes Pearson, an instructor in English and a friend and classmate of Eugene O'Neill, Jr., at Yale, the university received the original manuscript of *Long Day's Journey into Night,* sealed, not to be opened until twenty-five years after O'Neill's death. Then, in 1951 when the Marblehead cottage, the O'Neills' last home together, had to be sold, Yale was again the recipient of the remaining manuscripts. These included the original, corrected typescript of *Long Day's Journey,* along with *A Touch of the Poet, Hughie* (the only completed unit of the "By Way of Obit." series), *More Stately Mansions,* the scenario for *The Calms of Capricorn,* and other such Cycle Papers as had not been destroyed. Of all the Papers, only the partly revised typescript of *More Stately Mansions* was specifically marked by O'Neill for destruction in the event of his death.[23]

In 1951, when both O'Neills were ill and Mrs. O'Neill was about to sell the

Marblehead cottage, she had by mistake included the revised typescript of *More Stately Mansions* in a large box of papers sent to Yale. Five years later, at her request, I returned the typescript to her, having first photographed it and removed and retained in the collection the instruction leaf that O'Neill had laid into it, directing that the script be destroyed. In the spring of 1957 Mrs. O'Neill gave Gierow permission to prepare his version of the play for production in Swedish translation. There was at that time no question of its publication, either in Swedish or in English. In the printed program for the first production Gierow assured the audience that "there is not a scene, not a passage, not a line in the drama which is presented tonight that is not by O'Neill himself."

Although the Swedish production was not an unqualified success, Mrs. O'Neill decided, a year or so later, that the English text could be made available for students of her husband's work. Because Gierow had made his version by shortening a translation that he and Sven Barthel had prepared of the complete play, the equivalent in O'Neill's words had to be established by comparison of the two scripts. Mrs. O'Neill and Gierow asked me to be responsible for this work. I had a photocopy made of the English script and, with the help of a Swedish dictionary, compared Gierow's version with O'Neill's original, deleting on the copy all words and phrases not represented in the Swedish text. I subsequently restored O'Neill's stage directions and his descriptions of characters and sets, since ours was to be a reading version rather than an acting script. And I included a few short passages primarily to restore references to the American scene and to make certain transitions less abrupt for the reader. Although publishing the play was undeniably a violation of O'Neill's expressed wish, Mrs. O'Neill, Gierow, and I felt that our text was one that he himself might have authorized.[24]

Pleased with my editing of *More Stately Mansions,* Mrs. O'Neill authorized me in 1967 to see what I could do with the other Cycle materials extant in the Yale collection. Both she and Gierow endorsed my successful application to the John Simon Guggenheim Memorial Foundation for a grant that enabled me to spend the academic year 1968-69 free of teaching and curatorial duties.

Attempting to do anything at all with these fascinating materials without violating the dramatist's injunction against anyone's finishing his plays seemed doomed from the outset. At least I could, and did, transcribe these hundreds of pages of his almost microscopic handwriting.[25] But fears of antagonizing O'Neill's ghost made it difficult to fix upon a scheme for publishing the notes, and I extemporized by dealing with two detailed scenarios (for *The Calms of*

Capricorn and act one of the second play of the nine-play Cycle) and the fully sketched original epilogue for *A Touch of the Poet*.[26]

But printing those documents brought me no closer to a solution of what to do with the Cycle material as a whole. Eventually, I decided that I had to find answers to three basic questions: What had O'Neill attempted to do? How had he set about doing it? And why had he failed? I would then have to put together an account of the project, using, wherever I could, the dramatist's own words. Without the *Work Diary,* this would not have been possible: its entries, along with the dates inscribed on many of the notes, provided a basic, chronological outline. In the last years of his life, after he had given up hope of being able to complete the Cycle, O'Neill had talked about it in detail with George Jean Nathan, Elizabeth Shepley Sergeant, and the novelist Hamilton Basso. Nathan and Basso published accounts of their conversations; Sergeant made elaborate notes and preserved them with her papers, which she bequeathed to the Yale Collection of American Literature.[27] O'Neill also made occasional, invaluable references to the Cycle in letters to various friends. From these materials I constructed the account presented here.

The Cycle Papers must be approached with understanding. On 7 April 1936, at an early stage in his work on the project, O'Neill had warned Theresa Helburn, one of the directors of the Theatre Guild, the principal producer of his plays in the United States since 1928: "I hate letting anyone see first drafts. Mine are intolerably long and wordy—intentionally so, because I put everything in them, so as not to lose anything, and rely on a subsequent revision and rewriting, after a lapse of time with better perspective on them, to concentrate on the essential and eliminate the overweight."[28] It is easy to agree with the author in downgrading the readability of these materials. But they *do* exist, and in them we find O'Neill analyzing characters, outlining settings and scenes, and writing often extensive passages intended for eleven plays, only one of which he was ever able to complete to his own satisfaction.

To appreciate the significance of the documents quoted, summarized, and referred to in the following pages, the reader must keep in mind O'Neill's intentions in creating them. We cannot expect the notes and outlines—even the scenarios—to have automatic claim to literary distinction: they were, after all, written for no other audience than the dramatist himself.[29] Even the first drafts are just the bare bones of the dramatic works that the author planned, without the appeal that flesh and muscle would have given them. And yet many of these Cycle Papers provide evidence of O'Neill's skill. The detailed scenario for act one of the second play of the nine-play Cycle gives a telling picture of the domestic life of a genteel but impoverished New England clergyman, widowed and the father of four daughters, and precious insight into O'Neill's plan for that play, written in 1935 and 1936 in double length but subsequently destroyed. In the epilogue for an early draft of *A Touch of the Poet* O'Neill writes with economy and force a scene that with very little revision could have taken an honorable place in the finished play. The final act of *More Stately Mansions* contains what is potentially one of the most dramatically effective scenes O'Neill ever wrote.[30] The scenario for the play includes a first, variant plan for the climax of the tragedy. Sara (Melody) Harford's address to the dead body of her husband in the second scene of the first act of *The Calms of Capricorn* is a high point for O'Neill in dramatically effective poetic writing. These and other such passages afford the reader tantalizing intimations of what the Cycle might have become.

Certainly none of the Cycle Papers is without its significance for the student of O'Neill's work. The plan was, as Travis Bogard points out, unique in the history of American, if not English, literary endeavor, and even ideas that the author thought better of and canceled have their importance for the scholar attempting to form some concept of the "prophetic epitome for the course of American destiny" that O'Neill had hoped to create. For the general reader as well, these surviving fragments are valuable for the light they shed on the most significant American dramatist of his time.

The Papers tell us a great deal about his method of composing his plays. Here, for example, we find him first setting down notes describing his characters in great detail—their mental and physical traits, their interests and activities. Gradually he individualizes them, making further notes on their interrelationships. Through repeated analyses he gets to know his people so intimately that, for him, they become in effect life-and-blood human beings: while he is writing a play, that is his reality. *Mourning Becomes Electra* opened at the Guild Theatre in New York on 26 October 1931, and the following day O'Neill noted in his *Work Diary* that the "Trilogy [was] splendidly received—Carlotta & I overjoyed!" But on the twenty-eighth the entry reads: "Reaction—sunk—worn out—depressed—sad that the Mannons exist no more—for me!" (p. 111). As Carlotta expressed it on 26 February 1944, "Gene working—Thank God his mind, heart & soul are in his work—he is not interested in the living or the dead!"[31] He finds himself occasionally confronting the situation about which he wrote George Jean Nathan: "I never know how closely the characters, when they begin to live, will follow my plans for them."[32]

As O'Neill became more intimately involved with the Harfords, his attempt to disentangle their motives gradually became all-consuming. At the same time, his brain was often dulled by illness and medication. The attempt to express dramatically such highly complicated psychology eventually proved self-defeating. In *More Stately Mansions* and in the first two double-length plays of the nine-play Cycle, his fascination with the motivation of his characters grew almost morbid. The notes of 18 May 1937 (given in their entirety below) mention "Double characterization—two planes of dramas— . . . or on three planes—as Curtain rises—darkness—unconscious assertion—then half-light—characters dimly perceived—solil[oquy]. of conscious struggle living in part—then full light, realism, play begins in terms of surface life".[33] These comments indicate how impossibly difficult of execution the plans had become. O'Neill's acknowledgment, in his *Work Diary* in October 1940, that the first two plays were "too complicated . . . [with] too many interwoven themes & motives, psychological & spiritual" (p. 391) implies that he would have made every effort to avoid these excesses in writing the four plays that would replace them in the eleven-play Cycle. Unfortunately, he never experienced the improvement in his health that might have enabled him to carry out his plans.

The Cycle Papers are our primary source for information about the Cycle itself. Along with references in the *Work Diary*, a few letters in which O'Neill reported his progress to various correspondents—notably representatives of the Theatre Guild—and some interviews, these documents tell the story of his great project. Cumulatively, the various notes make it possible to reconstruct a surprisingly full, though still sadly incomplete, outline of the plots of the Cycle plays as they developed in the mind of their creator. The establishment of the plot outline of the destroyed double-length Play Two of the nine-play Cycle is made possible by purely fortuitous circumstances: O'Neill happened to write the scenario for its first act in a special notebook that Carlotta had given him; he also failed to destroy the elaborate notes for revising the later acts of that play.

The Papers also show how O'Neill made use of his reading and his life experience. In August 1936 he warned Lawrence Langner that the Cycle would not be " 'an American life' in any usual sense of the word":

I'm not giving a damn whether the dramatic event of each play has any significance in the growth of the country or not, as long as it is significant in the spiritual and psychological history of the American family in the plays. The Cycle is primarily just that, the history of a family. What larger significance I can give my people as extraordinary examples and symbols in the drama of American possessiveness and materialism is something else again.[34]

This attitude toward historical background in his work is further clarified in a letter O'Neill wrote on 8 April 1921 to his friend and associate Kenneth Macgowan about O'Neill's play on Ponce de León, *The Fountain:* "I am afraid too many facts might obstruct what vision I have and narrow me into an historical play of spotless integrity but no spiritual significance. Facts are facts, but the truth is beyond and outside them."[35] Yet in the mid-1930s O'Neill explained to his Spanish translator that his writing involved "a tremendous amount of reading and note-taking—for even if I find it beside my point to use much historical-fact background, still I wish to live in the time of each play when writing it."[36]

The Papers include many notes of the reading O'Neill had done as he went about the process of learning how to "live in the time of each play." Each would reflect, however obliquely, the momentous developments of the period in which it was set. *The Calms of Capricorn,* eventually Play Seven in the eleven-play Cycle, would tell the story of Captain Ethan Harford and his attempt to make a record run from New York to San Francisco in his ship *Dream of the West.* Fully developed, it would dramatize—far more effectively than its scenario—the excitement of one of the most romantic eras in the history of American expansion. In Play Eight, "The Earth Is the Limit," the post-Gold Rush days in California would become the setting for the tragic tale of the life and death of the gambler Wolfe Harford. Play Nine, "Nothing Is Lost but Honor," would describe the rise and fall of Honey Harford, a politician, against a background of graft, corruption, and commercial triumph. Play Ten, "The Man on Iron Horseback," featuring Jonathan Harford, a railroad man, would trace the steps by which he, like so many of his fellow American capitalists, rode the iron horse roughshod over all competition to ultimate success, for his own and his country's benefit. Play Eleven, "The Hair of the Dog," bringing the story up to the present, would tell of the development and popularization of the automobile in the United States, with experimentation on rockets as a portent of the future. Its conclusion, summing up all that had gone before, would present for the Harfords the ultimate truth about life, liberty, freedom, and the pursuit of happiness.

For the most part, O'Neill seems to have planned to introduce specific historical events in the course of revision. In *A Touch of the Poet*, for example, there is no mention of the anniversary of the battle of Talavera (1809) in the scenario for the play. It is only in the revision of the first scene of the third act that the commemoration of the event provides the occasion for Con Melody, Sara Harford's father, to don his old uniform and relive with his crony Cregan the glorious repulse of the French attack. O'Neill's notes, taken from one of the first-person narratives of the Peninsular War, include a number of details that are used almost verbatim in the play.[37]

As an example of how O'Neill would have developed his outlines into full-fledged plays, some notes of June 1937 for the writing of "Nothing Is Lost but Honor" demonstrate how he planned to fill out the character of that wily politician Honey Harford:

> Honey brazenly builds up a legend of his heroic [Civil] War record—when Jonathan [his brother] and Sara [his mother] point out that his story of having marched to the sea with Sherman can be easily refuted by facts & dates, he laughs—they don't know their voters—voters want to believe in heroes—don't reason, or no politician would ever be elected— . . .
>
> But the irony is that in succeeding plays Honey begins to believe his own lie—so does Sara—at last he believes it implicitly—and so does she—he has an imaginative narrative of the march to the Sea which is a real feat of tall lying—Georgia becoming a tropic wilderness infested with all manner of wild beasts & ferocious serpents—his tale is a sort of victorious tropical retreat from Moreno & Sherman a Napoleon—[38]

As another example of O'Neill's use of historical background, the Cycle Papers include his pencil notes on Van Wyck Brooks's *The Flowering of New England* (1936), made, presumably, soon after the book was published, just as O'Neill was engaged in writing *A Touch of the Poet*. The section on Thoreau's philosophy would have had strong appeal, especially in its reference to the passage in the Bible that O'Neill had chosen as the theme for the entire Cycle: "[Thoreau] could not help taunting his fellow-Yankees. Seek first the kingdom of heaven! Lay not up for yourselves treasures on earth! What does it profit a man! Think of this, Yankees, think twice, ye who drone these words on the Sabbath day and spend the other six denying them! 'Doing a good business!'—words more profane than any oath, words of death and sin. The

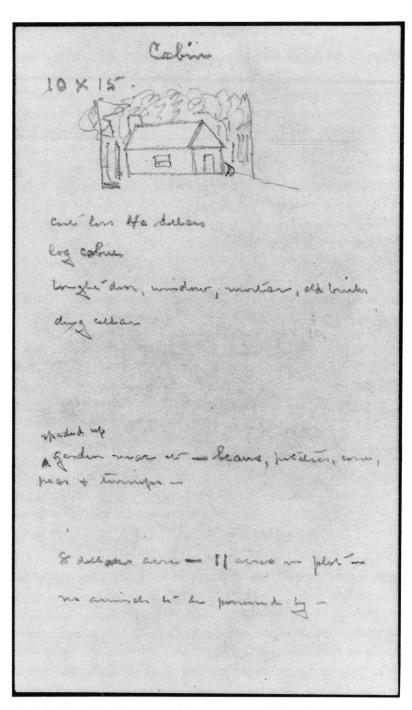

The Log Cabin. O'Neill's notes on Thoreau's cabin at Walden Pond, used for Simon Harford's cabin in *A Touch of the Poet* and *More Stately Mansions,* Plays Three and Four of the nine-play Cycle. (YCAL, 12.7 × 7.6 cm.)

children should not be allowed to hear them." The hut at Walden Pond becomes Simon's log cabin, of exactly the same ten-by-fifteen-foot dimensions and with the same patch of beans, potatoes, corn, peas, and turnips nearby, in the same order.[39]

A sheet entitled "*General Dope On Empire Builders*," taken from Matthew Josephson's *The Robber Barons: The Great American Capitalists, 1861–1901* (1934), provides a further example of how O'Neill acquired the information enabling him to outline the action for the plays in which first Honey and then Jonathan Harford were to take the principal parts. O'Neill set down the details he needed of the complicated processes by which the "barons" gained control of their various railroads and used incidents involving them in the outlines for Plays Nine and Ten.[40]

It was to be expected that in writing about the Harfords O'Neill would draw upon his own experiences. Evidence provided in the Cycle Papers includes descriptions of various male characters that bear an unmistakable resemblance to the author himself, as though he, subconsciously, was creating them in his own image. Carlotta O'Neill's notation in her diary on 9 October 1943 that her husband was trying to persuade her to come out of retirement as an actress in order to appear as Deborah Harford in *A Touch of the Poet* indicates that he had her in mind as at least one of the models for that enigmatic character.[41] The various mother-son encounters, especially between Deborah and Simon Harford in *More Stately Mansions,* reflect the agonized relationship of O'Neill with his mother. In that same play, the competition between James, Jr., and Eugene for the love of their mother seems to be reflected in the rivalry of Simon and Joel for the affection of Deborah Harford.[42]

The Cycle Papers show O'Neill seeking to extend the limits of what was possible in the presentation of dramatic works on the stage. An example is the choreo-cinematographic linkage of scenes during the calms in *The Calms of Capricorn.* The scenario directs that they are to have "the feeling of running simultaneously, a subject being picked up from one to another", and that "the sentences and exclamations come from both groups at first, then a topic is taken up by one group, then by the other".[43] Worked up fully, the convergence of many voices and many actions on a common thematic center would have been both innovative and startling. Other examples of this cinematic cutting and overlap of scenes occur elsewhere in the Cycle, especially in the outlines for "The Earth Is the Limit" and "Nothing Is Lost but Honor."

Although O'Neill resisted dealing with what would obviously be difficult production problems until he had finished plays to work with—and therefore never really faced up to them—still there are among the Cycle Papers various plans, especially for the presentation of the necessary expository material linking the individual plays. An example is the detailed notes for drop curtains for all eleven plays that would be symbolic of the action in each play. Scenes played before those curtains would give the comments of a chorus of townspeople about the Harfords, using either masked actors or, even, life-sized marionettes to emphasize their "type nature in contrast to [the] living characters of [the] plays".[44]

The Papers include various statements by the author of the principal themes of the plays. As one example of the meditative considerations that characterized this preparatory work, the nine-play Cycle Papers contain detailed plans for the "Three Sisters," daughters of the Harford progenitor. These women come to provide a mythic background for the tale to be told, serving emblematically as the Fates. On 3 February 1940, in some thoughts about the "*Cycle as [a] whole* / mythological background—Sisters as Fates," O'Neill elaborated on his basic underlying theme of "the frustrated meek to whom greed becomes a fate which they pass on as a destiny to the family":

> At the opening of the first play ["Greed of the Meek"], the fate goes back to their own dispossession and that of their mother (with whom they identify themselves) by their father's second marriage to Janet [later Naomi]. . . . Janet brings them, through identification with her, love of flowers, garden as willful greedy cultivation—love versus lust—dream versus material reality—God versus Satan—meekness versus pride—free will (will to freedom) versus acceptance of predestination).
>
> . . . they . . . come to realize through their own slavery to the past in themselves that the secret is that there is no present except in the past as it moves on: the past is the future. Those who know the past in others can use it to control the future. They deliberately resolve finally to identify themselves with the past, to be its agents and use it to be fate to others. . . .
>
> There is a struggle throughout the Cycle of free will versus destiny (the past which is oneself) and therefore to conquer oneself in order to be free, to conquer outside one the symbols of the past that are in one (or evade, escape them).[45]

In his plans for the eleven-play Cycle, the three strong women become stepdaughters of a much younger Harford progenitor.

O'Neill elaborated upon the spiritual undertheme at various times after December 1940, when work on the entire eleven-play project had to all intents and purposes ceased. He set down ideas that he had attempted to express or planned to develop more fully in the new first four plays, in revising Play Five (*A Touch of the Poet*) and Play Six (*More Stately Mansions*), and in writing Plays Seven through Eleven from the various outlines and notes that he had prepared for them. An example of such a statement is that of 8 October 1941:

> The admiration and longing for the Leader of the Meek who takes possession of the earth—Robespierre, Napoleon, all or nothing Caesarism—is part of a recurrent overtheme for the whole Cycle: in Robespierre, Napoleon, Brahma, the fanatic idealist, the cynical opportunist and realist, the escapist into non-life; in the United States Napoleon dispossesses Christ. At the end of the eleventh play, the Harfords, in their defeat and bewilderment and faithlessness, again want a leader to save them—Christ, Stalin, Hitler; that is part of the Hair of the Dog symbol. It is women who always yearn for the ruthless possessor who sets them free from themselves by enslaving them; and in a time of the collapse of faith in life's meaning, the feminine in men becomes dominant; it is the spur to their manly, warrior virtues.[46]

A final example of what the Cycle Papers tell us about O'Neill's intentions is provided by some notes for the conclusion of the final play, "The Hair of the Dog." On 1 October 1941, O'Neill describes it as the "prayer for a Savior to lead them [the Harfords] out of Wilderness & debacle."[47] Later that year, on 18 December, he outlined a characteristic ending:

> In the last play comes the complete realistic divorce from all sanctions, with religion, morals dead. There is no feeling of need for any justification or goal for success except success. At the end, the hophead son [Honey Harford's grandson] sees the truth, but he cannot believe that he or anyone else can believe in it. It is too late; they've gone too far along the wrong road; there is no turning back: "we must destroy ourselves so a few survivors, reminded by ruins of the wrong way, can start again". But they deny, grope for hope. Honey's ironic dying comment: "it's a hair of the dog you need".[48]

It is these Cycle Papers that form the basis of the narrative that follows.

chapter one

June 1931 to January 1935

On 20 June 1931, at Beacon Farm on Eaton's Point, near Northport, Long Island, Eugene O'Neill set down in his *Work Diary* an *"idea for Clipper Ship-around-Horn play"* (p. 103). Probably on that day he wrote this brief description: "Play whole action of which takes place on clipper ship bound round the horn and winds up in Shanghai Brown's boarding house in Frisco—what year best (?)—look up data on Shanghai Brown, if any."[1] Although he did some reading on the subject of the clipper ships, he allowed this idea to germinate for almost a year. He made a few notes in March 1932, recorded "new conceptions" in the *Work Diary* in May, and added further jottings in October (pp. 127, 141, 142). He found the "right" title for the play—*The Calms of Capricorn*— in March 1933 and made some additional notes in April and May of that same year (pp. 155, 158, 160).

When the plan next surfaced, in December 1934, it had become the " '*Calms Of Capricorn*' series", to be made up of four plays, the first of which would be *The Calms of Capricorn* (p. 204). The series would deal with the four sons of Enoch (later Simon) and Sara (Melody) Harford, each play featuring one of the sons as its central character. O'Neill made notes of "grand ideas for this Opus Magnus [*sic*] if [I] can ever do it—wonderful characters!" on 1 January 1935, and set down "grand new ideas for 1ˢᵗ two plays" on the twenty-first. That same day he decided to "chuck" another project "out of further present consideration" and to concentrate on the Cycle (pp. 206, 208).

Since his days at Harvard in Professor George Pierce Baker's "47 Workshop," it had been O'Neill's practice to begin each play with a note of an idea, to develop it into an outline (often containing

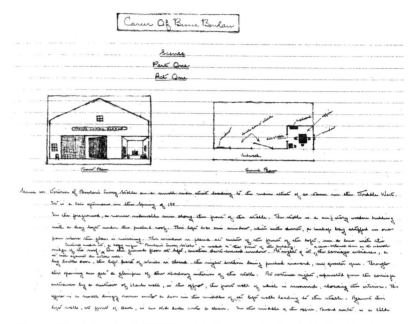

"Career of Bessie Bowlan." O'Neill's original manuscript (top half of leaf 5) of an early version of "The Hair of the Dog," the final Cycle play. (YCAL, 14.5 × 20.5 cm.)

passages of dialogue), and then to sketch characters, acts, and scenes and draw sets. This method of composition, especially the drawing of sets, meant that he could, as he wrote, visualize his characters taking part in the action. His stage directions almost invariably describe the scene with a wealth of detail supplied by an imagination grounded in a thorough understanding of the possibilities of the stage. O'Neill's setting for the opening of what eventually became the Cycle's final play (titled the "Career of Bessie Bowlan" in December 1934) illustrates how minutely the dramatist visualized the scene. It is further realized by small pencil sketches of both *"Front Plan"* and *"Ground Plan."*

Scene—Exterior of Bowlan's Livery Stable on a small side street leading to the main street of a town in the Middle West. It is a late afternoon in the Spring of 189[-.]

In the foreground, a narrow sidewalk runs along the front of the stable. The stable is a one [and] ½ story wooden building with a hay loft under the peaked roof. This loft has one window, white with dust, a burlap bag stuffed in one pane where the glass is missing. The window is placed at center of the front of the loft, in a line with the ridge of the roof. Centered under it, a long sign, "Bowlan's Livery Stable", is nailed to the front of the building. On the ground floor at left, another dust-covered window. At right of it, a cane-bottomed chair on the sidewalk, its back against the stable wall. The carriage entrance, a big double door, the left part of which is closed, the right section being pushed inward, one quarter open. Through this opening one gets a glimpse of the shadowy interior of the stable. At extreme right, separated from the carriage entrance by a section of blank wall, is the office, the front wall of which is removed, showing the interior. This office is a small dingy room with a door in the middle of its left wall leading to the stable. Against this left wall, at front of door, is an old desk with a chair. In the middle of the office, toward right, is a table with cane-bottomed chairs at left, right, and in front of it. In the middle of the right wall, a window. Against the rear wall, at left, is an old cupboard. A brass cuspidor is on the floor by the table.

The stable is painted yellow but this has faded to pale lemon. The big doors are a faded green—also the window frames. The sign is a dusty white with black lettering. From the appearance of exterior and interior of the office, one gets the impression of lazy contentment with things "as is" over a period of years, a contentment which has drifted unconsciously into neglect and slovenliness.

From nearby along the street, off left, comes the sound of hammering in a blacksmith shop—a leisurely sound emphasizing the sleepy quiet of the beautiful Spring afternoon.[2]

Only after all this preliminary work was completed did O'Neill begin to write the detailed scenario, which was in effect a first draft. He later wrote to Theresa Helburn concerning his drafts:

There is a word of warning in regard to planning ahead that I feel bound to repeat now, in justice both to the Guild and me. Don't begin to plan for the production of the Cycle, except in a very general way, until you receive finished plays from me to plan on. Don't expect first drafts. I hate letting anyone see first drafts. Mine are intolerably long and wordy—intentionally so, because I put everything in them, so as not to lose anything, and rely on a subsequent revision and rewriting, after a lapse of time with better perspective on them, to concentrate on the essential and eliminate the overweight. . . .

And don't rely on receiving the first plays at any definite future date, for though I may do some speculating about the matter, I cannot honestly even tell myself just when it will be. . . . I might find myself in a surge of creative energy where I could keep going on, in first draft, from one to another until . . . all . . . were written. In which case, as you will appreciate, I would be insane to pause for any interruption—especially such an exhausting interruption as production is for me, followed always by a long period of blank uncreativeness. . . .

All of which sounds like handing you a large package of uncertainty to go on with. But the ill of uncertainty is inherent in authorship—at least, my kind of authorship.[3]

Many years earlier, on 8 April 1921, in a letter to Kenneth Macgowan, O'Neill had discussed his method of play construction:

As for act or scene divisions, I have no rule either one way or the other. I always let the subject matter mould itself into its own particular form and I find it does this without my ever wasting thought upon it. I start out with the idea that there are no rules or precedent in the game except what the play chooses to make for itself—but not forgetting that it is to be played in a theatre—("theatre" meaning my notion of what a modern theatre should be capable of instead of merely what it is). I usually feel instinctively a sort of rhythm of acts or scenes and obey it hit or miss.[4]

And so, in January 1935, as he began work on the Cycle, O'Neill followed his accustomed writing habits. Some of his earliest "*General Outline Notes*" already show the importance he placed upon a thorough understanding of the motivation of his characters:

Father Enoch [later Simon Harford] has kept general store, small town, New England. He goes broke, insists he must pay off all creditors in full. He becomes a tin peddler, with wagon. His eldest [later third] son, Jonathan, goes with him on the wagon. The second son, Wolfe Tone, takes a job in a store which his father gets for him (and which Wolfe hates). The third [later eldest] son, Ethan, goes to sea. The fourth son, Brian Bone ["Honey"], remains at home to help his mother with the house, the chores, and the vegetable crops on their small barren farm, to which they have moved after the bankruptcy and the father's selling their small but comfortable house in town.

The mother, Sara Melody, had been a second girl in Enoch's father's house. He had been disinherited for marrying her, although she had married him as a Protestant and agreed not to bring up the children as Catholic. Her reasons for this are a queer mixture: love for him and the desire to prove it by giving up her everything for him who had given up so much for her, and her own pride in giving up more, raising his bet, her eternal salvation, going to hell for him; and, at the same time, a shrewd material reason: her desire to rise in the world, her resentment against "No Irish need apply."

She is always (except with her husband, with whom she lives as his ideal of her) naively frank about these contrasts in her nature. For example, re religion, she wonders shrewdly if it isn't all priests' fairy tales, and the next second is crossing herself with superstitious guilt at her blasphemy, and is reflecting comfortingly that God understands her and doesn't blame her.

It is her husband, astonishingly enough, who, with his idea of justice, had insisted that half the children have Irish names and [at first?] be brought up Catholic (Wolfe and Brian). He has a sentimental view of the Irish, the race oppressed by England as America had been. It is the American view of the Irish as romantic belligerent-poetical impractical people. He has an interest in Irish history, a love for the sound of Irish names. There's a "touch of the poet in him. He was more in his heart what he believed the Irish to be than any Irishman ever was." She scorns this view of his with the practical shrewd side of her nature, which keenly sees the fake in the Irish. At the same time, the other side of her nature encourages it; and besides, she concludes wisely, it helps make her romantic in his eyes.

At Harford's death (1850), Sara is 40, Jonathan is 22, Wolfe 21, Ethan 20, Brian 19. Harford had been 47.

Incident of her brogue: in spite of his sentimental romantic attitude toward the Irish, her husband had not liked it: to him it had a connotation of vulgar jibes, peasant origin, and was unworthy of a descendant of Irish kings, as she had told him she was. In speaking of him, she laughs about his inconsistency. She had tried to break herself and succeeded, but she is always conscious of restraining the brogue. After his death, she feels relief: she can talk now as she wants; but she discovers that she doesn't want to talk brogue out of respect and love for his memory. But it keeps breaking through her New England speech, in moments of joking, self-revelation, or passion, as does her Rabelaisian vulgarity. Her husband had rebuked her for this, but she knows that he was tickled by her coming out with it now and again, so she feels free to now, but at the same time guilty.[5]

In his planning for the four-play Cycle, O'Neill made detailed notes on the "Character of [the] Sons":

Jonathan—is the most N[ew]. E[ngland]. of the four, takes after grand-father—tricky, Yankee trader—cold, sparse in speech, slow to action, calculating—religious (Congregationalist) in outward observances because he feels it is good business to conform, a good disguise to make people unsuspicious of his shifty schemes—greedy for money—his mother sees his weakness, a fear of change, a tendency to stay in a familiar rut, to be content with small cheatings & small profits—to stay in the town, con-fident of his ability to become big frog in this small puddle, but not sure of his ability to deal with bigger world and cheat it—

He loves his mother—she shocks, amazes & fascinates him—and domi-nates him even while he is disapproving of her most strongly—he knows she always sees through him—he feels a secret resentment because he knows she loves all his brothers more than him, although he appreciates that, in her justice, she fights against this and leans over backwards in being fair to him—and he, on his part, is determined to the end to super-sede his brothers in her affection—

In appearance he resembles his father & grandfather—is skinny & under medium height—N[ew]. E[ngland]. boney face—no resemblance to mother—neat, respectable in dress—light brown hair, hazel eyes

He marries Irma [later Elizabeth Warren]

Wolfe is a mixture of father & mother—tall and thin, pale aristocratic face—has the least practical ability of any of the brothers, the least will power & ambition—nervous volatile temperament covering a cold reserve and detachment—a dry cynical sense of humor—full of get-rich-quick schemes, yet lazy—no ability to concentrate long on anything—easily ex-cited to extreme optimism or pessimism—Cal[ifornia]. means gold to him, easy gold—when he finds it hard to get, he takes to gambling which immediately becomes his absorbing passion[.] He loves mother & she loves him as a black sheep—until gambling becomes his mistress, he lets himself be dominated by her in everything, is conscious of this but accepts it as easiest way—hates to make decisions—attracted to dangerous life

He believes in nothing and makes no pretence to—he sees through his elder brother and despises him for his pretence and hypocrisy—he admires Ethan for the driving ruthless power of his personality but at same time feels no affection or envy for him—for the peasant, Honey, he has a fastidious contempt for his commonness but at the same time, an amused liking for him where he resembles mother, and a tolerance for his sins.

In his prosperity, he has mistress (principally for display, as he might have fine dog or horse) but he cares little for women; he is man's man.

Ethan is, like Wolfe, a mixture of father & mother—under medium height but with powerful, muscular body which later on becomes fat and dumpy Napoleonic—full of intense, nervous vitality and driving ambitious will—"a bit of the poet in him"—a sense of serving a higher force for betterment & progress which makes him ruthless & unscrupulous—he justifies murder of Captain on grounds of "for the ship's sake—not getting enough out of her"—a religious nature—superstitious—

Straight light brown hair, a visionary's intense blue eyes—at first a square handsome hawk-nosed face which later becomes fat

He marries

He kills himself from overwork

Honey is all his mother—tall & heavily-built, running early to fat—curly black hair, blue eyes—joking, grinning, Rabelaisian nature concealing real peasant shrewdness in judging character—lazy, a heavy drinker—his mother's pet—likeable, irresponsible, without ambition except for food, drink & women, his success is wholly due to his being figure head for mother

He never marries—his mother remains his only love—but plenty of promiscuity with whores, which Sara reproves but understands, just as he reproves but understands her philandering with lovers.[6]

In early January 1935 O'Neill outlined the action of the first play, *The Calms of Capricorn,* having decided to make Ethan rather than Jonathan the eldest son:

The first act, at the Harford farm, ends with the decision that they shall all go to California on Ethan's clipper.

The second act is on the clipper in the Calms of Capricorn during the first part of the calm. Among the passengers are Hull [later Warren], the owner, a widower, and his daughter, Irma [later Elizabeth]. He is taking her on this voyage for her health. [There are also a company of gold-seekers and a defaulting banker, Graber, and his mistress, Goldie (later Leda).] Others are Captain Paine [later Payne] and his wife, whom he has just married. This is their honeymoon trip. There is also a minister—the first mate, Sturgess. It is the death (natural) of the first mate that puts the captain's death in Ethan's mind (?).

The tension of the continued calm gradually brings out the real natures of all of them. The owner, Hull, had hoped for a record on this second voyage of his new clipper, for purely commercial reasons, advertisement and freight. He frets and stews and blames the captain and the designer as if the continued calm were their fault. Jonathan, from the first, ingratiates himself with him. The ship is to him nothing but profit and loss. Sara, also, cultivates Hull and impresses him with her shrewd common sense. She immediately sees his daughter as a wife for one of her sons, Ethan primarily, for it's in the line of his job. But her distrust for the sea as an occupation increases as she sees it as a business at the mercy of Nature, just as the farm had been.

The calm drives Wolfe to the company of the gold-seekers, to gambling. He is indifferent to the ship except as a gamble.

To Honey the calm is a relief from sea sickness, but at the same time it postpones the day he longs for when he'll set foot on dry land never to go on a ship again. He gets drunk whenever he can and sings well for them.

The captain's wife falls in love with Ethan; the owner's daughter is attracted to Jonathan. Both these women fall under the influence of Sara and form an alliance with her against Goldie, for whom two [i.e., three] of the four sons have fallen. Jonathan hides this, but lusts for her in secret; Honey hides it because afraid of mother; Ethan hides it because afraid of the owner. And Goldie herself falls for Wolfe, who likes her as a pal, as a mistress, but remains inwardly cold and incapable of love.

In the strain of the continued calm all these relationships reveal themselves in naked primitiveness. Goldie is worshipped by all the men except

Dream of the West. O'Neill's set design for *The Calms of Capricorn,*
Play Five of the nine-play Cycle. (YCAL, 27.7 × 21.5 cm.)

the captain, who has an old-fashioned conservative honor and responsibility, and the designer, who is in love with the ship.[7]

The final scene was not outlined in detail until March 1935: to be free to drive
the ship and try for a record run to California, Ethan murders the captain. But
the attempt fails, and Ethan commits suicide.

Ideas for the play took an ever stronger hold on O'Neill's creative imagination, with Goldie, the defaulting banker's mistress, assuming an increasingly
important role as a kind of Earth Mother. He worked out detailed "*Interrelationships*/(men toward Goldie) [and] (women toward Goldie)",[8] and then
sketched an outline for parts of the next play, "The Earth Is the Limit,"
devoted to the second son, Wolfe:

> The play ends with the suicide of Wolfe after he has lost Goldie in
> gambling to Honey. She had fallen in love with him and he had found
> himself falling in love with her. He hates himself for this, feeling that it
> drags him into the gutter from his remote pedestal of superior indifference.
> She begins to get in the way of his passion for gambling; she changes its
> spirit into a game for gain; she spoils its appeal as an art for art's sake to

him. He grows to hate her as he desires her more and more. She goads his jealousy by an affair with Honey, to which she asks his consent, since he never wants to possess her; and he agrees—to prove his indifference, although it tortures him. His betting her with Honey is his last insult to drive her from him.

Then when he has lost her, he immediately is madly in love with her. He frantically offers to stake all he's got against her, the mining stock in Gould & Curry. She then says she's glad Honey has won her; she won't be staked any more; Honey sees her as a woman. She turns on Wolfe: "You never saw me as a woman." She finally says: "Honey, we'll go to my room. We'll leave him to his red, white, and blue chips." Wolfe pulls out his pistol: "No, I'll kill him first." She steps between them. They go.

Then scene outside their bedroom door where Wolfe grovels on his knees and pleads, finally shoots himself.

Then scene where Mother bawls out Goldie, then justifies her. She knows the insult, had felt that herself—Wolfe keeping scornfully aloof and away as if denying her womb which bore him.

Then scene with Mother and Jonathan. Mother has decreed that all of Wolfe's possessions are to go to Goldie. Jonathan expostulates: the sale of Wolfe's stock would enable him to enter a railroad combine, realize his dream of spanning the Sierras. He goes into details. Sara sees the practical profit, immense. "Of course," he says, "but that's not the main point: I want to step up, then get control."

Goldie refuses Wolfe's money. Mother refuses to accept it. Finally she sees a way out if Honey marries Goldie: "And anyway, he ought to marry her, we owe her that. Simon would want justice done her. Besides, she's afraid of him; marriage will make both her and Honey settle down." She tells Honey of her solution. He says blithely: "Why not?" And Goldie accepts him, seeing through everything but wanting peace now.

At the end, they are all drinking to the luck of the new company. Goldie is attracted by Jonathan's enthusiasm. He is reckless, lawless, and, like his mother, confident of knowing Honey, being sure of him. Their mother is silent, after the toast, then she utters a sudden wild keen of grief for Wolfe. Goldie goes crazy: "Stop her! Stop her! I can't bear it." Then she grovels on her knees before Sara: "Forgive me! Forgive me!" Sara stops her outburst, and says calmly: "Of course I forgive you. Didn't I tell you I understood? Didn't I live for years with his father away off lonely, and my love for him beating the air and crying? And wasn't Wolfe his father's son, with that same touch of the poet in him, and didn't I bear him a stranger from my womb? Why wouldn't I understand you and forgive? We'll never speak a word of it again, Goldie. And do you and Honey forget and be happy. And we'll leave Wolfe to rest with Ethan in the lovely peace of God where they'll both feel at home at last."[9]

On 23 January 1935, O'Neill set down a general idea for the third play, "Nothing Is Lost but Honor," probably part of the following:

There is hatred between the two women, Goldie and Irma. Irma, socially ambitious, mother of children, severely respectable, regards Goldie's coming into the family as a disgrace. She has always regarded Honey as a disgrace, but has been forced by Jonathan to tolerate him, as Jonathan needs him politically in his railroad scheming. Irma (the motherless daughter of a widower) has always felt attracted to Sara, in spite of the fact that her peasantness, her Irishness etc. repel her. It is her desire to reform Sara, make her socially fit (Jonathan, of course, encourages this). And she succeeds in this to a certain extent, forces her to build a grand house, to give and go to parties, etc. For Sara, after Wolfe's suicide, has tended to become melancholy and listless, to give up her own will and let herself be led. Also she has tended to turn away from Honey and Goldie to Jonathan and his wife and children, thus falling under their influence. But, finally, as she recovers herself and as they demand more and more of a conformity that is irksome to her (in spite of the fact that she appreciates its practical position- and money-making value), she rebels and turns naturally back to Honey and Goldie. (For Goldie she feels a secret, horrified affinity; she loves her.)

Underneath, the great reason for the hatred between Irma and Goldie is deep and primitive. Irma feels strongly and is jealous of Goldie's "It," a superiority where men are concerned. She hates Goldie for her ability to give herself and thus to possess men. Irma has remained cold, and feels that it is her fault that Jonathan has never given himself, that she can never feel the security of possessing him, of owning him. Of course, the irony of this is that the "touch of the poet" which is in Jonathan, too, is just what, in Wolfe, foiled Goldie for so long. On the other hand, what Goldie hates in Irma is that social belonging—the fixed, preordained place in the world which her uprootedness longs for obscurely, although she pretends to scorn it—and Irma's detachment from passion, her seeming ability to remain detached, superior, never to be enslaved by herself or by others, to use everything and give nothing in return (which is Goldie's hard ideal that she is never able to live up to).

Goldie is attracted to Jonathan by his "touch of the poet," which she senses in him and which to her is Wolfe, the only man she has ever really loved. She is afraid of this attraction he has for her, fights against it, tries to hate him and antagonize him, until in the end she is forced to use it as a last resort in her battle with Irma. Jonathan also feels the attraction, the longing to spend himself recklessly in love as he does in his career. And, of course, at the same time he has good surface practical reasons to get her on his side and use Honey.

In the fight between Irma and Goldie for Sara, Goldie wins, and corrupts her into a scandalous, disreputable lovable character. Sara is socially successful in this way in a measure she never would have achieved as Irma's protégée. She becomes a news figure beloved by the public and, as such, shrewdly helps Honey.

It is Goldie who tempts Honey to go too far and be forced out and disgraced, and thus disgrace Irma through Jonathan. Then, conscience-stricken, Goldie runs to tell Jonathan. But she finds that, cold-bloodedly, he has taken his precautions: legally he is untouchable, let people suspect his implication as much as they like. And his scheme has gone through: he controls the western part of the transcontinental line. His big ambition now will be a whole system of his own, coast to coast. Then, feeling an interlude, Jonathan gives way to passion, calls on Goldie to give herself to him, as a reward to the dreamer for having realized part of his dream. (Honey, of course, is to be thrown to the wolves. Goldie is shocked. But Jonathan knows Honey: "He won't be hurt, he's got the money. I'll take care of him.") Goldie repulses Jonathan at first in horror: she won't be made the whore of his dreams, as she was to Wolfe; but she finally succumbs.

In the meantime, Irma has gone to Sara to plead, ostensibly for her to keep Honey from disgracing Jonathan, but really to keep Goldie from taking Jonathan from her. She is terrified by what she feels.

In the next scene, Honey has resigned from the Senate, is glad of it, there was no fun there. He has got his dream—10,000,000 dollars: "Nothing is lost but honor." Irma, and even Goldie, are appalled, but Sara understands. Honey begins to plan for her, but laments that he will miss the fun of politics, the speeches, and singing, and reciting. Maybe he'll have to open a saloon again. He dreams of one with a floor of silver dollars, gold foot-rails, etc. He sings or recites. Sara says: "Ah, that's poetry, Honey. I've always loved that one—and you're a beautiful man." (She sees how hurt he is deep down inside.)

Honey knows of Goldie with Jonathan—or, conscience-stricken, Goldie tells him. He is at first in a rage, but his mother says that those with a touch of the poet in them are not to blame. She knows now that Goldie, for all the hard show she puts up, has the touch. Honey is wounded: "And I? Haven't I it—with my working all these years for a mountain of gold to give you so you can tell them all to go to hell?"

Jonathan comes in. He talks to Honey in a practical, terse fashion, then reveals that he has been prepared for Honey's disgrace all the time, that he has contempt for Honey as a man who wants money for money's sake. He speaks his dream aloud to himself.

The two women are appalled, burst into tears, then fall into each other's arms. Their love for each other trends toward the homosexual.

The scene ends when Jonathan gets up, gives terse practical orders. He can't be seen associating with Honey or come to Sara's when Goldie or Honey is there, etc. He suggests that Sara, Goldie, and Honey go on a couple years' European tour. Irma asks if she can go with them? Jonathan answers: "Of course." Irma says with vindictive malice: "Goldie can teach me the things I need to know—to help you put your arms around America." Goldie says: "Irma can teach me to be a lady and help you in realizing your dream."

Jonathan relapses again into his dream. Irma and Goldie comment mockingly: "He's in the arms of his dream again." Sara says: "He looks like his father now, doesn't he, Honey?" Honey answers: "Ay, the same damned fool look in his eye."[10]

On 24 and 25 January 1935, O'Neill similarly summarized the fourth play, eventually called "The Man on Iron Horseback":

The play is located in New York and concerns Jonathan primarily and his struggle on the Stock Exchange to get control of the Central Atlantic, the road he needs to complete his transcontinental system.

The play opens with the return of Honey, Goldie, and Irma after a couple of years spent abroad. Sara has been taking care of her grandchildren

(Bessie and Brad, Irma's children, and Bette, who is Goldie's(?)), and Jonathan has been living with her. During the time abroad the strange morbid
relationship between Goldie and Irma, each now in her change-of-life
period, has become fixed. Irma now has a passionate love for Goldie, and
she has come entirely under her immoral destructive influence. The two
women have become inseparable, and Irma, encouraged by Goldie, has
one lover after another. Goldie participates in this only vicariously. Although she will not admit it to herself and thinks she hates Jonathan and is
revenging herself on him by corrupting Irma, she has really been in love
with him ever since their affair. He is Wolfe reincarnated for her, and she
takes a queer inner pride in being true to him, while at the same time
making Irma betray him. Irma almost unconsciously suspects this. It is a
hate-love passion for Goldie on her part. She wants to possess Goldie, to
make herself Goldie in order to possess her attraction for men, that is, for
Jonathan. But, in spite of herself, she remains cold, she cannot give herself;
her lovers always feel this; she can never hold them; they cast longing eyes
at Goldie.

In this experience abroad, Honey is left to his own devices; for him it is
a drinking tour combined with women and song. He wrongly suspects that
Goldie is deceiving him all the time, but he is resigned and closes his eyes,
content if she only mothers him a bit now and then. She does this, feeling a
sort of contemptuous, amused, maternal affection for him and encouraging
him to have a good time and drink himself to death.

In New York, in this interim, Sara is a fond, respectable grandmother.
She plays the grand lady as hostess for Jonathan and becomes very popular
with his business associates. But the two parts are strains on her: she is
bored; she looks forward to Irma's return to relieve her of her duties so that
she can relax again, living with Honey and Goldie. With them she can be
herself. She continues to speculate shrewdly in real estate, cunningly prying information out of her guests without their ever suspecting.

As before, Jonathan is always cash poor and in debt to the hilt at the
banks in order to swing his operations, and he calls upon Sara to pledge all
her real estate to the limit to help him. She is full of misgiving, but he is so
like his father she can no more hold out than she could against Simon.

When Irma comes back, hoping Jonathan may now desire what she has
become, she finds him unaware of her and starts out to lead the same

scandalous existence she has led abroad, throwing money away, etc. Goldie also finds Jonathan entirely unaware of her, and eggs Irma on.

Honey wants to open his bar in New York but Jonathan objects for practical reasons and gets his mother to dissuade him. Sara is only too glad to, for she wants to get away from New York herself and go back to Frisco. So it is finally arranged that she and Honey will go. Goldie stays.

In a scene with his doctor, Jonathan is warned of heart—overwork. He is not afraid of death, but is angrily impatient with the idea. He repudiates it as if he were refusing an invitation from the doctor for a trip. The doctor is awed and stunned into silence by Jonathan's attitude: "Very well, then; I have nothing to say. Good day." Jonathan says: "Good bye, Doctor. I'm sorry I can't consider it just at present. Later, perhaps."

Jonathan is aware of Irma's affair with the man he is fighting, but is unmoved and uses this. When she pumps him for information with which to ruin him, he gives her wrong facts. Then when in triumph she taunts him, he tells her that the information was false. He explains, indifferently, rebuking not angry. This drives her into a frenzy, but he asks kindly: "Why not go back to the old basis? You've had enough, haven't you? It's not your fault: I know that it's Goldie's doing. I don't care how many lovers you have, but you must be discreet and not have affairs with my enemies." She makes a last broken appeal to him: "But you did love me once—in the first years of our marriage?" He replies contemptuously: "Oh, those days! I was weak then, weak and selfish. I was thinking only of comfort and security. I was a coward, money-saving. I had no dream." He turns on her: "Don't you betray my dream or by God I'll kill you!" (Or this when he hears about her and his rival, but conceals from her that he cares at all.)

She is finally crushed by this, frozen. She will live apart with the children for the rest of her life, will do her duty: "Goodbye." Then, as soon as she is gone, Jonathan begins to doubt his dream. He feels a frightful loneliness, a confusion about business. He forces himself back into concentration. And then a message comes that Sara, in California, is mortally ill. . . .

Jonathan leaves everything, takes a train to Frisco to be with his mother. Before he arrives, Honey, drunk, cheers their mother with reminiscences of the old political days, his speeches. Sara has recurrent fits of pathetic fears. Honey asks her if she wants a priest and she answers: "No, I wouldn't insult God's intelligence by pretending at the end. He knows that my sin was for love, and I'm not afraid of that. I'm afraid I'll find when I come to Simon, he'll have forgotten me, be entirely lost in his loneliness and his dreams. Glory be to God, I hope it's a land without dreams over there and he'll be awake in his love for me!" Then she reminds herself that the habit of her brogue has grown on her again since she has been relaxing with Honey after playing the grand lady for Jonathan.

Jonathan arrives just in time. With her last breath his mother reassures him about the worth of his dream. And he begins to dream again, even as his mother dies. Oblivious of her, he starts out, and Honey stops him: "She's dead." Jonathan, vaguely, repeats: "Dead?" Honey, in a rage, grabs him by the throat. Goldie stops him. Jonathan is badly shaken, then realizes that his mother *is* dead. He and his dream collapse totally. He pleads with his dead mother, then he himself dies.

Honey, in his despairing loneliness and drunken rage at fate, at the very end swears an oath: "I'll never draw another sober breath till the day I die, so help me God. I'll puke in the face of life!"

The two women, Irma and Goldie, turn to each other, drained of emotion: "There's nothing left now to hate or love each other for. We can be friends."

But the final curtain falls on the note of the children. Irma says that she will go back to live in the home town of her mother's people in the Middle West. She wants to get away from all the scenes connected with her married life, doesn't want the children contaminated by dreams. She asks Goldie why she doesn't come too. She, Irma, will be lonely there, out of touch with people. It's a quiet, little town. They can find peace there. But Goldie says no; Honey will want to remain. The only comfort for him will be the old scenes. She foresees that he won't live long, now that his mother is gone, but she can't join Irma until he dies. Afterwards she'll come; she too wants to get away from dreams.[11]

As he outlined the action of the four plays, O'Neill became increasingly interested in the Harford parents, and he set down further facts concerning Sara and Simon:

> Sara [Melody] at the start of the first play is forty-five, but looks much younger, more like an elder sister to her sons than a mother. She is above medium height, has a fine sturdy, healthy peasant-female figure, is very active, strong. Her hands and feet are small but broad, her ankles rather

thick and her legs a bit too chunky. Her face is pretty and full of character; she has clear fair skin, pink cheeks; a mass of coarse black hair (a bit untidy); a short sensual retrousée nose; a strong, full-lipped humorous wide mouth, fine white even teeth, a charming merry smile that lights up her whole face; fine large blue eyes, intelligent; a long rather heavy jaw, and a short strong neck.

In character, there is a strange mixture of Irish peasant, ignorant, but full of a shrewd, acquisitive practical intelligence, merry (with a strong common flair toward Rabelaisian jokes), melancholy by turns, capable and energetic. Her peasantness is overlaid by the veneer of the lady she has tried to make herself for the love of Simon Harford.

She is inclined to a carelessly dirty slovenliness. The small things to her don't matter, but she has determinedly, to please Simon, made herself over into a scrupulously neat and efficient New England housewife.

Simon Harford is under medium height, thin and small-boned, with brown hair, dark eyes, and a dark complexion. He has an aristocratic small-featured, handsome face, a bit weak. He is a dreamer and an impractical enthusiast, with a bit of the stubborn fanatic about him underneath, a scrupulously honorable gentleman, a believer in the innate goodness of human nature, of the God in everyone. He is trustful and unsuspecting, a sucker for every schemer who can clothe his scheme with a humanitarian mask. He is a great reader and an idealist, has a poet's feeling for kinship with nature. There is something childlike, helpless and lonely about him, appealing for affection and protection. He is gentle, considerate, well-bred in manner, a friend of Emerson's and Thoreau's, a first admirer of Whitman's. Underneath a self-effacing, mild and silent exterior, there is a passionate nature.[12]

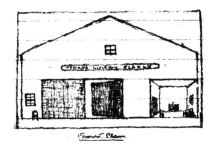

chapter two

January to February 1935

Up to this point O'Neill had projected a Cycle of four plays, but as he had once admitted to George Jean Nathan, his characters, when they began to come alive, did not always follow the plans he had made for them.[1] As he thought about Simon and Sara Harford, the two indeed began to have an existence of their own. He noted in his *Work Diary* on 27 January 1935: "story of Harford & Sara before 1st play opens—this may develope [*sic*] into additional 1st play, making five in all" (p. 208).

The next day he outlined the "*Spiritual Undertheme*" of the Cycle:

> Simon Harford—The lonely soul, longing but unable to "belong"—an alien in his family, misunderstood & thought a queer stranger—longing for love, yet unable to communicate this, is rejected—same at school & college with comradeship and friendship—afraid advances will be rejected, defense of aloofness—then makes defiant gesture of himself rejecting, makes virtue of his solitude, a philosophy—belong to Nature—[like Thoreau at] Walden Pond—but unable to give himself to Nature either—is rejected solitary in solitude—
>
> Then love comes—but leads him back into rejected world—away from his dream to the counting-house—thus, in spite of great love for Sara, something of him remains always solitary within his dream—His thwarted desire is ever to give himself, to be possessed and thus to "belong"—but even in love he never can completely give himself—his dream remains lonely—
>
> Sara—Her "belonging" is by possessing to be possessed—to be possessed in order to possess—her thwarting is that she can never feel she possesses all of Harford—that he never can take

all of her—there is that "touch of the poet" in him which remains forever solitary—her resignation in love is because she knows his love for her and his longing to belong wholly to her—that it is not his fault, that he suffers bitterly in his solitude—and because of this, in spite of her sorrow & frustration, she blames herself and loves him all the more because of what she feels is her failure to give him enough, to be enough of a gift to break through to his soul.

The Sons—In varying degrees, elder three all a mixture—the mother's will power & possession, the father's longing & inability to be possessed, "the touch of the poet". In "Honey" is the deterioration of both ideals. His touch of the poet appears obviously in his Tom Moor[e]ishness. His will to possession is a material acquisitive greed; as applies to women, a frank animal lust.

Ethan—must have power over sea, possess her in order to be possessed.

Wolfe—his father's withdrawal into solitude, without father's love of life—replaced by disdain—his gambling the passionate symbol of this disdain for all possession & being possessed.

Jonathan Edwards—Possess the land, conquer it,—vague social service dream, combined with ruthless acquisitiveness[2]

Now, in the very last days of January, O'Neill drew plans for the sets of the clipper-ship play, still referring to it in his *Work Diary* as the first of a four-play Cycle. But early in the next month he recorded some fresh developments: " '*A Touch Of The Poet*' Cycle (get this title for Cycle & like it—'Calms Of C⟨apricorn⟩' having always been title for particular 1ˢᵗ play—clipper ship. Also decide new first play of Sara—Harford—marriage—parents, etc.)" (p. 209). This new play soon divided itself into two, one centering on Sara and Simon, and Sara's parents, Con (Cornelius) and Norah (later Nora) Melody, the other on the relationship between the young couple and Simon's mother, initially given the name Abigail but finally called Deborah (Deane) Harford. During a three-week period in February, O'Neill did the preliminary work for the new first play, tentatively titled "The Hair of the Dog" (finally *A Touch of the Poet*), finishing the scenario on the twenty-fourth. A summary follows:

> The play opens around ten in the morning of a fine day in June 1829 at Melody's Inn, a roadhouse on a post road on the outskirts of Boston. Sara Melody, only daughter of Cornelius Melody, the proprietor, is finishing

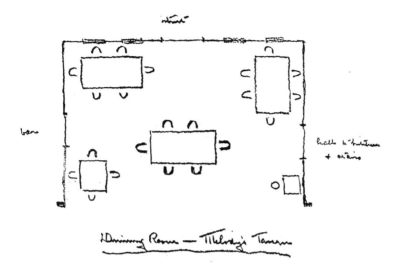

Dining Room, Melody's Tavern. O'Neill's diagram for the set in *A Touch of the Poet* and *More Stately Mansions,* Plays Three and Four of the nine-play Cycle. (YCAL, Size of original: 13.5 × 17.8 cm.) Manuscript notes: (*at top*) "street"; (*at right*) "hall to kitchen / & stairs"; (*at left*) "bar."

setting the tables for dinner and cleaning up the restaurant. Mickey Maloy, the barkeep, tries to kiss her and, when she is coldly and insultingly disdainful of him, accuses her of being stuck-up, of taking her father's pretensions seriously. Everyone knows *his* father was only a shabeen [i.e., saloon] keeper in Ireland who, by cheating and stealing got control of a rich squire's estate and set himself up, then put on airs, sending his sons to Trinity College, Dublin. Cornelius soon ran the estate into ruin with his drink, gambling, and women. The priest saved him from prison on condition he marry her mother, only five months before Sara was born. She is no better than he and she has no reason to object to his courting her since Melody himself has given his blessing, with or without marriage. She says that her father must have been drunk, not knowing what he was saying. Mickey argues that she could do worse than marrying him, thus escaping the life of drudgery Melody makes her and her mother lead, while he plays the gentleman, loafing and drinking up all the profits. But Sara again refuses him disdainfully.

He asks her tauntingly if she's thinking she'll catch young Simon Harford, the world's prize jackass, who, even if willing, hasn't a cent of his own and no brains to make one. His family, the Harfords, damned stuck-up Yanks, would as soon welcome a pig in the family as an Irish saloon-keeper's daughter. She tells him haughtily it's none of his business: she's not discussing her private affairs with their barkeep. Stung, he says, "And aint you the waitress and dishwasher, and aint your mother the cook? Sure, it's I am lowering meself to you!" He curses her and goes into the bar, slamming the door behind him.

Norah Melody comes out of the kitchen. She is prematurely old, worn out by hard work. She asks whether Melody has come down yet; she has his breakfast ready. Sara doesn't think he'll want any breakfast. Her mother asks dully, because he had too much to drink last night? Sara replies bitterly, "*Last* night? *Every* night since I can remember!" Norah excuses him; liquor is his only comfort.

She complains of the bills: the grocer has threatened to stop their credit. She had money put by, but Melody took it to pay for feed and stable bills for his trotting horse. Sara angrily protests the idea of her father keeping a horse when they can't pay their bills. They ought to sell her. Norah answers that the horse is Melody's greatest pride and love; he'd be heartbroken if he lost her. Sara comments bitterly that her father cares more for his horse than for his family. Norah replies, "Oh, no, he has great love for you, although you do provoke him by putting on the brogue. You shouldn't; you know how he hates it. And there's no excuse. You're not an ignorant woman like me: didn't he send you to school so you could learn to read and write like a gentleman's daughter?" Sara says, "Yes, but he took me out of school on the grounds that I had to help you. We can't afford a waitress, but we do keep bartenders when Father could very well tend for himself." Norah protests, "Oh, no, that would be beneath his station." Sara laughs scornfully, "What station?"

She tells her mother about her conversation with Maloy, but Norah defends Melody: "He doesn't mean what he says in liquor; it's the drink talking." Sara answers, "No, it's the truth. Look at the way he treats you. I don't see how you stand it; have you no pride?" Her mother, aroused, says proudly, "I love him! What do I care what he is or what he does? But it's no use talking of love to you. What do you know of love? There's a hard lonely pride in you that'll keep you from ever giving the whole of you to anyone." Sara protests, "I can give myself in love—if I want to." Her mother answers scornfully, "Want to? It's when you don't give a damn for all the want-tos in the world—that's love—and don't I know the sorrow and joy of it!" Sara is impressed, but insists that she'll give herself in love when it's time. "But I'll do it to gain freedom, not to put myself in slavery for life." Norah says there's no slavery in it at all that matters. She breaks down: "Don't try to take love from me, Sara, for without it what am I at all but an ugly fat woman, getting old?" Sara is all tenderness and contrition, begs her forgiveness.

Her mother changes the subject: she's run into Father Flynn on the street and he's advised her to warn Melody about denouncing the faith when he's drunk. The priest has blamed her for letting her husband make heathens out of her and their daughter. Sara is indignant, comforts her mother. But Norah admits miserably that it's true. She's damned unless Melody returns to the faith. Sara says he never will; he hates the priests because they made him marry. But for Norah, damned or not, her love comes first. She did it for Melody, who cheated the priests while giving way to them.

The talk comes round again to love, and her mother asks Sara about Simon Harford. Does she love him? Sara doesn't know: "I don't want to love him too much, only enough so he won't feel cheated when I marry him, not too much so I can't be free." Norah repeats, "When you marry him?" and Sara replies, "Yes, you didn't think I'd stay here as a waitress for Father forever, did you? No, I've made up my mind I'll get on in the world, Mother." Norah protests, "But his family?" Sara vows she'll win them 'round or she'll make Simon defy them. Money doesn't matter. What she wants first is to be raised from a drunken Irish liar's daughter, and then she'll raise her mother. Norah says angrily, "I'll not let you! Won't your father be the first to be proud of your marrying into the swell Yankees?" Sara replies bitterly, "I don't think you know him, Mother. There's nothing he'd hate worse. He'd rather I married Mickey the barkeep, so he could keep on looking down on me." Norah defends Melody, then asks if Sara is sure about Simon's intentions. Sara answers that Simon is a real honorable gentleman born, not the son of a shabeen-keeper pretending to be a gentleman like her father.

She changes the subject abruptly, thinks she'll go for a walk along the beach. Norah asks if she expects to meet Simon. Sara confesses that she wants to surprise him, do a bit of tidying up for him. Her mother asks what he is doing, and Sara explains that he has wanted to get away from the world, to live close to Nature, think great thoughts, and write a book. But he does little writing and spends his days and nights dreaming and observing the sun, the sea, and the stars. He's a disciple of Mr. Emerson of Boston. The only thing she has against him is that she sometimes thinks he cares more about his queer dream than he does for her. Her mother nods smilingly, "He sounds the queer creature entirely. He's a bit of the poet in him—like your father himself." Sara scorns the comparison, but agrees that Simon does have a touch of the poet. Maybe that's why she loves him. Her mother wonders if it is wise for her to go alone to Simon's shack. "You can't trust a man with a touch of the poet." Sara replies: "I *can* trust him, or if I can't then I can trust myself not to do anything I'd not want to do." Norah warns: "People may see you and start talking." She replies defiantly, "Let them for all I care. Simon wouldn't care either." The scene ends when they hear Melody coming down stairs. Sara goes to get ready for her walk.

Melody enters, the wreck of a once handsome man, sick, nervous, and tormented. Norah flutters around him, offering breakfast, finally a drink. At first he guiltily curses the liquor, then accepts. He admits he was drunk the night before, afraid he said some bitter things to her, asks her forgiveness. There is a love-hate relationship with her on his part: he bursts out against her brogue, the smell of stale cooking in her hair. She breaks down and cries. He again begs her forgiveness. She goes into the kitchen.

Gradually the drink brings him back to normal. He goes to the mirror, arranges himself fastidiously, squaring his shoulders. Sara comes in quietly and he puts on a front, but she sees through him. He asks her where she is going, all dressed up. "For a walk along the beach." "And if you should meet young Mr. Harford, that would be all the better, I suppose?" But she has her father's blessing: he has made inquiries about the Harford family and finds them suitable. He supposes he can expect a visit to talk over arrangements for her dowry, although his financial situation is a bit difficult at present. Sara expresses amazed scorn at this fantasy. She'll thank him not to interfere. Her father's manner changes and he casts doubt on Simon's intentions. They exchange insults, and she warns she's not the slave to him that her mother is.

Melody's cronies enter the bar, greet the barkeep, and exchange boisterous comments about last night and Melody's fancied exploits in Galway. They drink on credit. The barkeep signs them to quiet down so that Sara and her father won't hear.

Meanwhile she tells her father, contemptuously, not to let her keep him from his gentleman friends. She goes out. Melody turns contrite, makes a motion to call her back; but a burst of laughter from the bar causes him to go again to the mirror, compose his face, and then enter the bar, where he is welcomed enthusiastically. He offers drinks and will take a drop himself, "to be sociable." Norah, coming in from the kitchen, overhearing, sets the breakfast tray down on a table, sinks on to a chair, and begins to cry miserably.

Act two opens at Simon's boatshed, later in the morning. He is sitting outside in the sun, notebook in hand, dreaming. His thoughts keep returning to love and Sara. But his meditations are interrupted by the arrival of his mother [here Abigail, later Deborah], bringing a basket of provisions. Her first reaction is to Nature, the dunes and the sea, a joyous abandon to it, then awe and fright. It possesses her, and she has always been afraid of being possessed. She prefers her garden to this. She has lightning changes of mood, from mockery to searching her son's face, trying to draw him out. She wants to know what has happened to him; but he evades her questioning, asks after his father and brother. She replies that they are always the same, and describes the daily routine. His father rarely speaks of Simon, and has forbidden her to write to him. But she has managed to send him supplies weekly by their coachman without letting her husband know. Simon agrees that he could not have continued to live at the cabin without her help. His father is certain he will eventually come around.

Abigail asks Simon about his recent decision. He has just been writing a letter to her about it, and reads her what he has written. He has come to feel that Nature has rejected him. He has felt the lack of human warmth, and now sees his flight from life and society as a selfish, cowardly thing. He must go back and learn to live unselfishly among men as his brothers. She asks how he plans to get along. He answers that there is enough of his father in him to enable him to make a living at some business. She wants to know his *real* secret: is he sure he's in love with this Irish girl? He is flabbergasted that she knows he has fallen in love with Sara Melody during his week at Melody Inn (when a storm had blown the roof off his shack). He asks if his father suspects. She warns of the price he'll have to pay: his father will disinherit him. Simon says that unless Sara is welcomed as his wife, he'll accept nothing from his father. Abigail professes to be happy in his happiness, has investigated and had good reports of Sara. Simon tells her that Sara is coming to see him this morning, and his mother at once prepares to go: she can't bear to meet Sara; she would be jealous of her. But she advises him to marry at once so that he can confront his family with a fact accomplished. She foresees that his father will scheme to prevent the marriage and work through the weakest link— Melody. She goes.

Left alone, Simon begins to doubt himself: if only he could have both Sara and his mother. He finally breaks down and sobs, then hastily dries his tears as he sees Sara coming. He welcomes her passionately. She asks about his mother's visit, and he insists that she approves of their love, has only asked him to be very sure. He *is* sure, and he'll ask Melody for her hand. Sara replies that her father doesn't count, but Simon insists. She asks why he's been crying, but he denies it: it's only the wind and sun in his eyes. He goes inside to set the table for the food his mother has brought. Sara, alone, thinks he has lied to her, that both his parents are against her. She is determined to show him he's not to be afraid of happiness.

The first scene of act three is set back at the tavern, about seven that evening. Sara is cleaning up, with an attitude of disdain and disgust. Her father and his friends are at one of the tables, having finished their dinner. They are drinking claret and are boisterously drunk. Melody apologizes for the bad cooking and the poor quality of the wine, but says it's the best he can get in the United States. He apologizes also for the service, but explains that he'd be ashamed if the service were good because his daughter is after all a lady and not a waitress. Sara interrupts, accusing him of giving them the blarney about her: anyone can tell she's not a lady at all but the daughter of the cook. Melody, stung, ignores her; his friends exchange glances. He contrasts the tavern with Melody Castle in Ireland. Sara goes into the kitchen, slams the door.

The guests go into the bar and Sara reenters. Melody informs her that Simon Harford came to see him while she and her mother were out marketing. He and Simon went together for an afternoon drive with his thoroughbred mare. Simon asked for Sara's hand in marriage, but Melody put him off; he wants time to reflect. Now he has just about decided to refuse. Sara replies that neither she nor Simon cares what he thinks. Her father explains that it's because she's really not a lady: Harford needs to be saved from himself. Besides Melody has already selected a more fitting husband for her—Mickey Maloy, the barkeep. The two of them should be congenial: they can talk the brogue together, have a raft of children, squealing and fighting on the mud floor of their hut along with the pigs. Sara comments disdainfully that he is recalling well scenes in his father's first house. Melody ignores this, repeats that her marriage to Harford would be too unthinkably presumptuous for him to consider seriously, that is, unless— He wonders why Simon is so eager for them to be married at once; if the reason is to make Sara an honest woman, then he might reconsider. She reacts angrily, is about to strike him, but Norah comes in, scolds her.

Calls for Melody come from the bar and he excuses himself. Sara apologizes to her mother for bringing her more trouble, but won't tell her the cause of the quarrel. Norah doubles over with pain, but refuses to let Sara send for the doctor, says it's only a twinge of rheumatism; besides, doctors bring death. She'd get more comfort from a priest. Sara ridicules priests' fairy tales. Her mother, angry, again scolds Sara, then blames herself for bringing her child up a heathen; but she did it out of love for her husband. Sara admits she'd do the same: let anyone try to take Simon from her and see!

While they talk, Gadsby, the Harford lawyer, comes in. Norah goes into the kitchen; Sara calls her father, then leaves. Melody assumes the lawyer has come about the arrangements for Sara's dowry and says he'll even sign a note. The lawyer is flabbergasted. He explains that he is here because Mr. Harford is unalterably opposed to any further relationship between his son and Sara. Simon will be cast off without a penny unless he breaks off. Mr. Harford is prepared to offer five thousand dollars in cash if Melody and Sara sign an agreement relinquishing all claim and promising to leave and settle in Western lands. Melody is outraged. Sara, who has been listening, enters and tells her father not to dirty his hands with such scum. Melody calls his friends, who rush in from the bar and escort Gadsby from the inn, kicking him on his way. Melody vows to go to Mr. Harford, demand that he apologize, or challenge him to a duel. Sara warns him that he's not in Ireland now: Mr. Harford won't fight; he'll only think him a crazy Mick and have the servants throw him out. But Melody insists he'll *make* him fight; he'll take a horsewhip and use it. Cronin, one of the friends, agrees with Sara, but Melody won't be argued with. Sara pleads that he may ruin her happiness. Let alone, she and Simon will beat Mr. Harford. But her father, angry, asks how she can talk about still loving Simon. She replies quietly, "I do so—and I'm going to marry him, Father, in the end, no matter what anyone can do to stop it." Melody curses her, calls her a whore, and tells her to go to her lover. She begs him not to curse her, apologizes. But he goes with Cronin into the bar for a stirrup cup before proceeding against Mr. Harford.

Sara and Norah are left alone, Norah despondent. Sara makes up her mind to go to Simon, resolved to do all in her power to bind him to her. Her mother tries to dissuade her, but she is resolute. She tells her mother not to worry about the duel: there'll be none—only a fine for assault and battery. She goes. Norah is sunk, dejected; if she could only go to the priest and be comforted. She starts to blame Melody, but stops. Her turning on him would break his heart. But she can't go to the priest because of her oath; it's the price she's paid for her husband's love. She has her pride and it's as high as Melody's: she'll not betray him, no matter what he does.

The second scene of act three takes place later that night at the boat-shed. Simon again sits outside, dreaming, in a poetical mood of love and longing for Sara. He no longer doubts, is determined to marry her at once. It was cowardly to retreat into solitude, a flight from duty. It's his duty to love his fellow human beings, have a good life among them. Sara arrives and their interview begins with stammering embarrassment. She feels ashamed, but he reassures her. She confesses her determination not to let anyone take him from her. Simon laughs at her tale of the row at the tavern, imagining his father's outrage and his mother's amusement. *She* won't mind; her sense of humor will be grateful to Melody for the rest of her life. He talks to Sara about his parents' marriage, then changes the subject back to the duel, which he says will end in farce. Sara confesses she at first set her cap for him, but has now come to love him. He loves her all the more for her frankness, is determined to get a job, start at the bottom—although he's not very practical. Sara says she'll be practical for them both: she has a good mind for business, has had experience at the tavern. Simon confesses to a moment of uncertainty after his mother's visit: he wanted to keep her and Sara too, realized that he had to choose. Sara understands and prom-ises to be to him all that his mother has been. She admits that she came resolved to offer herself to him so he'd be bound in honor to marry her. They declare their mutual desire for each other and embrace passionately.

Act four opens back at the tavern, several hours later that night. Norah is sitting up waiting for Melody. She remembers her love for and seduction by him, and her happiness. But she should have let him go, not put him to the shame of marrying her (she had gone secretly to the priest and told him, and it was he who roused public opinion and Melody's creditors against him). Her thoughts return to the present. Her husband has been gone five hours; perhaps he's been murdered.

Sara returns from the boatshed, her face transfigured with happiness, confesses to her mother what has happened. Her mother laments the sin: God will punish Sara as He has punished her. But Sara is defiant: she's not afraid; she and Simon are to be married the next day. He wants it, and there's no question of his being forced. Norah is resigned to Sara's leaving her. She feels she hasn't long, but prays she'll outlive Melody—he'd be so lost and helpless without her. Her thoughts turn again to him and she expresses her concern. Sara tries to reassure her: the only hurt to Melody will be his pride. He's probably stopped at several saloons on the way home.

Cronin appears, bringing Melody, his clothes dirty, torn, and disheveled, a blood-stained handkerchief around his forehead, his eyes staring, glazed and stupid, looking past his wife and daughter as if unaware of them. Norah breaks into renewed lamentation. Sara assumes that her father is drunk, but Cronin explains that the police gave him a knock on the head. Melody refuses a drink, and Cronin is astonished.

Cronin tells them he and Melody went to Harford's house, but the servants refused to let them in. Melody announced that he'd come to give Harford a thrashing. The servants replied that Mr. Harford is a gentleman who doesn't permit any drunken Mick to come disturbing his peace: they only see his kind at the servants' entrance. They gave Melody a push; he struck back with his whip; a fight ensued; the police were called, and it was they who gave Melody the blow on the head and took both him and Cronin to the station and a jail cell. But Mr. Harford refused to press charges and asked that they be released. He did this so that the affair wouldn't get into the papers and put shame on his pride. Melody protests violently: "Shame on *his* pride! Good God!" He laughs wildly, then exits.

They listen, hear him going upstairs. Sara says he's gone to sleep it off, but Norah is frightened. She has seen the look on his face. She goes after him, then returns to report she heard him behind the locked door opening the old closet where he keeps his duelling pistols. He came out, passed her on the stair without seeming to see her, and left by the back way. She concludes that he's going to kill Harford and urges Cronin to run after him. Cronin goes, and Norah follows. Sara is left alone. Then comes a shot. Norah returns, thinks Melody may have killed himself; but Cronin comes back, carrying the pistol. Melody follows him, his face pale, his eyes glazed. Cronin reports that he's shot the mare, and goes into the bar for a drink.

Melody, in a hoarse brogue, tells Sara and Norah that he's dead. There's no use in any more lying and pretending; from this day out he'll be a walking corpse waiting for burial. Sara asks why he killed the mare. He explains that he loved her too much to let anyone else have her. He had become unworthy, had meant to kill himself with her, but once the mare was dead he knew his last shred of pride had died with her; without pride, how could he kill himself without being a coward? Watching her die was like seeing himself dying. Norah tries to comfort him: she loves him and always will. Melody for a moment is deeply moved, asks her forgiveness. He goes to the bar "to celebrate his glorious victory in being pulled in for drunk and disorderly on the public streets." Sara protests, but her mother sighs resignedly. He'll drink, forget his sorrows, and sleep sound. Sara laughs hysterically, then sinks on a chair and bursts into tears. Her mother stares at her uncomprehendingly, soothingly, says: "There, there. Don't be crying now. It's all over, Sara. It's all over and done." But Sara continues to sob.

An epilogue to the play is completely sketched in the scenario and contains little that was salvaged for either *A Touch of the Poet* or *More Stately Mansions* as published (O'Neill later changed Gadsby's first name to Nicholas and Roger Harford's to Henry):

Epilogue

SCENE *Private office of Gadsby, offices Gadsby & Lathrop, several weeks later.* GADSBY *discovered just welcoming* ABIGAIL.

GADSBY

Obeying your instructions, I had a private interview with the—er—lady and,

Grudgingly.

in spite of myself, I was impressed. She seems to have sound commonsense—for an Irishwoman—doesn't drown you in the floods of irrelevant verbiage of her race—has even a certain quiet dignity of her own. In fact, she rather overworked this dignity. It was amusing to see her trying so hard to speak correct English and lose her brogue, but it kept cropping out.— But these details are probably painful to you.

ABIGAIL
Laughs.
Not at all. I'm only thinking she must have impressed you overwhelmingly
for you to be so enthusiastic, Henry. But then I hear she is very pretty.

GADSBY
Indignantly protesting.
No, no.

ABIGAIL
Smiles provokingly.
You can't fool me, Henry. You always did have an eye for a pretty face.

GADSBY
Gallantly.
I would be the last to deny it to you—that is, as your remark concerns one
pretty face I remember. It is why I have always remained a bachelor.

ABIGAIL
Pleased. Laughs.
That is very gallant of you, Henry. But you can thank your stars. I would
have made you as miserable as I have Roger.
They get down to business.
Simon has not got a job yet?

GADSBY
No, they are still living in the boatshed. She still works as a waitress, takes
food out.

ABIGAIL
And she realizes Simon's father has arranged it so it will be impossible for
him to get a job?

GADSBY
Yes.

ABIGAIL
I encouraged Roger in that; in fact, I egged him on. It would not be good
for their happiness to settle around here.

GADSBY
And have you egged him on to the other?

ABIGAIL
Yes. I stormed and wept, about the scandal and the disgrace. Roger
seemed pleased that I'd at last been moved by social responsibilities. I said
I could not endure to live in the same part of the country with such a creature. I was very bitter about Simon—and Roger, like him, who has always

felt a secret jealousy there, was rather gratified by that. So he's given me the money to give her. It's funny that I have to pretend to be their bitterest enemy in order to befriend them. She has agreed to take the money?

GADSBY

Yes. No nonsense about her there—but then, what could you expect from a woman of her class? It's like a fortune falling from heaven. And although I must confess I think she sincerely cares for Simon, still I imagine that she has had her eye on other chances, too.

ABIGAIL

Her father didn't.

GADSBY

That scoundrel!

ABIGAIL

Poor Henry! Did they kick you very hard?

GADSBY

His dignity is ruffled. He quickly changes the subject to the matter in hand.

Sara ought to arrive at any moment. I do not approve your desire to see her personally; I could have arranged everything for you. I dread to think of what Roger would say to me for conspiring secretly with you, if he knew.

ABIGAIL

But he will never know.

GADSBY

But I can't, for the life of me, understand why you should want to have any direct dealings with her and so compromise yourself with Roger if he ever found out.

ABIGAIL

I want to face her in the flesh. So far she remains only an abstraction to me and I cannot feel her living. I rely much upon my intuition, Henry. It serves me in place of brains. When I can feel her inner quality I shall know if Simon is to be happy or not.

GADSBY

I should think, for that purpose, you would have wanted to see them together.

ABIGAIL

No, no. Then I would have felt nothing but Simon's love for her. Like to see them together, indeed! You must think me a most unnatural mother! And besides, you forget that it is imperative that Simon know nothing of this.

GADSBY

You trust her to keep him in ignorance, do you?

ABIGAIL

By the time I have finished talking to her, I think she will appreciate the necessity, yes.

> *Word is brought that SARA has come. Abigail becomes greatly agitated, feels courage oozing away.*

GADSBY

Do you want me to remain, Abigail? Perhaps it would be wise to have a witness present.

ABIGAIL

No, no; that is just what I don't want. Go, Henry, and let her come in.

> *Gadsby goes.*
>
> *Alone, Abigail is again agitated and frightened but regains partial control and forces a smile as SARA enters. She flutters forward and takes Sara's hand gingerly. Sara is as shy and embarrassed as she is; also her manner is tinged underneath with suspicious and guarded defiance. Abigail flutters.*

I'm so glad you could come—so happy to meet you at last. Do sit down.

SARA

> *Stammers instinctively.*

Thank you, ma'am.

> *Then, immediately furious with herself, stiltedly.*

I am happy to make your acquaintance, Mrs. Harford.

> *They get seated, facing each other, and there is a pause of dreadfully strained silence.*

ABIGAIL

> *Finally blurts out.*

You are very pretty—but then I knew you would be from Simon's description.

SARA

> *Embarrassed and pleased, forces a laugh.*

Oh, what Simon says that way don't count. Sure, love is blind, as the saying is.

ABIGAIL

> *Shrinks back into herself. A bit dryly.*

Yes, I know he loves you.

SARA

With quick defiance.

No more than I love him, Mrs. Harford.

Again an awkward pause.

ABIGAIL

Begins stiltedly.

I— I think it would be as well if we went over the details of the proposed arrangement, to get that definitely settled before— I want to be sure Mr. Gadsby has made clear to you exactly what— not that I've any head for money matters, but—

SARA

Breaks in a bit grimly and defiantly but also with confidence, sure of herself on this ground.

Then *I* have a head for them. I've had to have—helping my mother run the Tavern. Perhaps it would be easiest for you if I ran over everything that's happened for you and you can see if it's all clear and right in my mind?

ABIGAIL

Yes, that is really the simplest way. Thank you.

SARA

Well then, right after we were married, Simon's father sent Mr. Gadsby to Simon with an offer to give him five thousand dollars—but only provided he'd move away with me to other parts and not be around here where I'd be disgracing the Harfords.

ABIGAIL

Breaks in.

Please—oh, please don't be bitter. I know you have cause, but you're talking to me now, not to Simon's father, and I—I'm on Simon's side.

SARA

Reserved.

I hope so, ma'am—Mrs. Harford.

ABIGAIL

Almost pleadingly.

But you must *know* so. Simon knows. He must. I always have been—since the day he was born.

SARA

Answers meaningly.

Oh, I know you're on Simon's side.

Then abruptly going back to the subject.

Of course, Simon got in a rage. He refused to take a cent from his father. He disowned him. It was an insult to me, he felt.

She pauses.

ABIGAIL

And you? What did you feel?

SARA

Defiantly.

I felt Simon was acting foolish, though I didn't tell him so, of course, or let him guess for a minute I didn't agree with him. At the same time, if you can understand me, I knew he was acting the only way he could act, being Simon, and I was proud of him and his respect for me.

ABIGAIL

I understand.

SARA

But all the same I felt I was facing the facts of life—I've had to face them—and the future of our marriage and his happiness—and there's no comfort in poverty, whatever poets say who don't know it. It's only another enemy—the worst—that happiness has to fight against. And that's why I've accepted your offer.

She seems to read some sneer in Abigail's mind for she goes on resentfully.

I suppose you're after thinking I'm a creature with no pride.

ABIGAIL

No, no.

SARA

But there's many kinds of pride. I've lived with one kind—my father's, God pity him—and the end of it's coming soon, a dead man walking alive to a drunkard's grave!

Abigail shudders.

Sara goes on.

And there's other kinds, but mine is that I love Simon and I've sworn I'd make him happy and I will! But I'll not go on blathering about myself. You're not interested in what's in my mind.

ABIGAIL

Oh, but I am! That's just what I am interested in. This is the only chance I'll ever get to know you.

SARA
Takes up her story as if she hadn't heard.
All that was three weeks ago. Then a few days ago you had Mr. Gadsby see me and he said you'd arranged it so the five thousand would be given me and I could hide it from Simon until I could make up some lie about how I'd inherited it some way. But the condition still was that I must get Simon to move away.

ABIGAIL
Yes, I'll confess I insisted on that condition—because I know it's imperative for Simon's happiness that he go somewhere where he can start his life with you away from all old associations with a clean slate.
Then she adds slowly.
It's especially important for his happiness that he should get away from me.

SARA
Stares at her. Then, with admiration.
You're a brave woman, ma'am, and an honest woman. I know what it took you to say that.

ABIGAIL
Flushes.
Simply.
Thank you. And it's a great relief to me to see you know Simon. It gives you a chance to be happy. One so often falls in love with a stranger—but for marriage to last, one of the pair, at least, must know the other—and still be able to love them.

SARA
Smiles.
Yes, but I'm thinking it's better Simon should never know me or he'd lose his love, for he's a touch of the poet in him and he's made a great dream out of the common girl I am, who is greedy to eat well and sleep soundly and be successful and have money and rise in the world—everything he thinks beneath him, though I know he'd miss them, too, if he hadn't got them.

ABIGAIL
But—are you willing to go without all those things—for his sake? You may have to. I can't imagine Simon ever succeeding in a worldly sense.

SARA
Oh, I've hopes of converting him when I get him away—as he grows older. He has the brains to do anything he wants.

ABIGAIL

But—

SARA

But I love him and I don't care what he does or doesn't. If he doesn't, I'll do it for him but make him think he did it.

With pride.

I can do it! I—

Then, embarrassed at boasting, she changes the subject abruptly.

But I'll come back to the business as I know you want me to do. I'll accept the money, as I told Mr. Gadsby, and I'll carry out the conditions. I've already made up the lie I'll tell him when we get away about how the money came to me. I'll get Dan Cronin to have one of his friends come to us when we're settled and tell me he's just over from Ireland to find me and an uncle of mine has died in India and left me this money. Sure, Simon will swallow that, without any thinking. He's listened to my father's great fairy tales about the days that's gone in Ireland and his estates and castles and hunts and horses, and he's got a romantic notion that Ireland is a queer place where anything crazy is likely to happen.

With a tender smile.

Sure, Simon is a great innocent baby in some ways—you know it—and he's anxious to believe anything that's romantic!

ABIGAIL

Thoughtfully.

Yes, I know he wants to be romantic but—

She smiles a bit sadly.

can he ever let himself be, I wonder? I hope so—for your sake. Because, from what you've said, I see you are at his mercy. You must try not to think of him as a little boy. I know it's difficult but—you must push him out of the nest too—and make him learn to fly and be free.

SARA

For a moment, fiercely.

I don't want him free. I want him mine.

She smiles.

But that's only talking. I am at his mercy, as you say. I love him. I'm his— and proud of it.

Ruefully.

And that's just what, with the lesson my mother's marriage taught me, I swore I'd never be—be any man's slave. But what do the oaths of your mind count with you when love takes hold of your heart?

ABIGAIL

Smiles sadly.

I know. What, indeed?

A silence.

SARA

Stares at her, then suddenly blurts out impulsively.

I like you, ma'am, when I thought I'd hate you—and I feel I know you and you know me.

ABIGAIL

Yes. And I like you when I was so sure I couldn't help hate.

SARA

Then that's a reason the more why I've got to be frank with you now and tell you the truth.

ABIGAIL

A bit uneasily.

The truth?

SARA

I didn't want to fall in love with Simon. I wanted him to fall in love with me. I wanted power over him. I'd my own ambition to rise in the world. I'd no stomach for remaining a waitress and a slave to my father. I knew I was pretty. I knew the first step was to marry away from him and his kind. So the minute I met Simon and knew who he was and saw he was attracted, I set my cap for him. I made up my mind I'd marry him and use him to rise. Oh, it wasn't money I was after. I felt I could always make that myself once I was free of old things—and I'm not such a fool I didn't guess his father'd cut him off if he married me. But he was a gentleman and educated and I knew he'd teach me to be a lady, and so forth—a step up for me.

She smiles self-consciously.

Oh, I was all you suspected I must be at the start of it, a calculating, scheming hussy, and I fooled myself into thinking I still was that, long after I stopped being it; but finally I woke up too late to save myself and found I loved him, and nothing counted but that, and I was more his than he was mine.

She laughs.

It was a good joke on me, ma'am, and that's the reason I can tell it to you
now because it was all a fake.

ABIGAIL

And have you confessed this to Simon?

SARA

I did, surely, ma'am. I'm an honest woman. I was afraid he'd hate me but I
made myself tell him—and he only laughed.

ABIGAIL

And loved you all the more, I hope.

SARA

He said so, ma'am.

A pause.

ABIGAIL

And I like you all the more for telling me. And confession calls for confession. I thought I'd find you pretty, but vulgar and stupid. I hoped you'd
be vulgar and stupid. A common fool would soon disgust him, especially if
he was married to her. You understand that especially. It explains why I
was willing to help. I thought, of all cures for his infatuation, marriage
would be the only lasting one. And I didn't want you to be poor—at the
start. Simon would feel bound to you by poverty and privation—in loyalty.
Hence, my insistence about getting you money. Perhaps I had in mind even
the sneaking trick of letting him know afterwards that you had accepted
this money.

SARA

Indignantly.

You wouldn't!

ABIGAIL

Jealousy is not concerned with honor.—Oh, I wouldn't now—never. Now
I can wish you happiness with all my heart—resignedly, you know, for
knowing you, I think now he will be happy with you his whole life long, as
far as his lonely soul permits him to be happy.

SARA

Yes, he's lonely. He don't belong here with me. He's like you.

ABIGAIL

Yes—like me. But I know you will forgive him for that.

SARA

I love him.

ABIGAIL

But you—I like you enough now to wonder about you. Will you be happy?

SARA

If he is.

ABIGAIL

A whole soul for part of one is sometimes a bargain hard to pay for happiness.

SARA

I'll pay it gladly. I love him.

ABIGAIL

You must have children—many of them, so that one at least will help your bargain to be less one-sided. I know. I have had Simon.

With a smile.

You don't hate me after my confession?

SARA

Laughs.

Devil a bit—that's as we say—I mean, not at all, Mrs. Harford. I admire you—and I'm sure we can be good friends for the rest of our lives—if we don't see each other when he's around. For he was yours—and now he's mine.

ABIGAIL

Yes, I'm glad you see I can't forgive that in the flesh—only in the mind. And to think I hoped you would be stupid!

She gives a little bitter laugh, then flutters to her feet.

And that's all we have to say to each other, isn't it? And here's the money. And, as a great favor to me, you'll get Simon away at the first possible moment, won't you?

SARA

Yes.

ABIGAIL

Goes with her to the door, fluttering.

So good of you to come. It's been so nice meeting you, Miss Melody.

They get to the door, Abigail's hand is on the knob. Sara looks at her queerly.

SARA

Miss Melody? I'm Simon's wife Sara now.

They stare at each other.

ABIGAIL

Flutters.

Forgive me. I've such a poor memory for names. I want to forget—I mean,
I do forget—

SARA

Holds out her hand. Gently.

I'm sorry I reminded you. It was mean of me. Goodbye—and thank you.

She makes a move to go.

ABIGAIL

*Still keeping the door shut—a great struggle within her.
Suddenly she leans forward and brushes Sara's lips with a
fluttering kiss.*

Goodbye, Sara. May you be happy!

*She flings the door open before Sara can reply and bursts
forth volubly.*

So good of you to come. Watch out for the stairs in the hall. It's so dark
there unless you know the way. Goodbye.

*She hustles her out and almost slams the door on her. Then
she breaks into sobs—miserably.*

Oh, why couldn't I hate her! I'd so love to hate her!

Curtain

In subsequent notes for the revision of this scene, O'Neill contemplated
changing the setting to Abigail's garden:

Abigail has sent Sara a key by Gadsby. She enters by the door in the
wall. The atmosphere in the garden depresses Sara, who finds it lifeless,
enervating, stifling. She reacts against it, fights it with her vitality, primitive,
alive. There is an attraction-repulsion between the two women: Sara is
repelled by the frail, strange, sickly invalidism of Abigail, but is attracted by
her manners, her ease, her "great-lady" charm; Abigail is snobbishly re-
pulsed by Sara's peasant qualities, but attracted by her animal energy,
health, and passion. When Abigail warns of Simon's detached lonely self
which can never give itself, Sara muses: "I thought that too until the other
night. Little she knows of Simon's love—but she's only his mother!"

O'Neill also considered using throughout the scene soliloquies and asides, as
he had done in *Strange Interlude,* those by Sara to be spoken in brogue.[3]

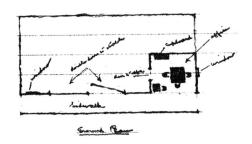

chapter three

February to April 1935

On 25 and 26 February 1935, O'Neill read for and made notes on the new second play and the next day got a working title, "Oh, Sour-Apple Tree." He finished a "very tentative skeleton" outline on the twenty-eighth but was not satisfied with it.[1] He wrote on 1 March to his friend Robert Sisk, formerly with the Theatre Guild and now a Hollywood screenwriter, about the whole six-play Cycle: "Well, I'm wildly enthusiastic just now on the new Work I'm on. I've been at plans and preliminaries for the past two months— switched from what I had started on to this. It's honestly the most ambitious conception I've ever had. There's years of the devil's own work to it—but it is really without precedent and has the possibilities of greatness in modern drama. I'll write you the outline later on and you'll see for yourself I'm not exaggerating."[2]

O'Neill interrupted work to enjoy a two-day visit from Russel Crouse of the Theatre Guild. He then made further notes on the second play and sketched in detail the last scene of *The Calms of Capricorn*, now the third play of the Cycle:

> The night is spent anchored off the Golden Gate, waiting for the pilot at dawn.
>
> Ethan has a guilty conscience over the captain's murder, which was inspired, on the one hand, by Goldie's immoral unscrupulousness and, on the other, by his mother's ambitious scheming for him, she hoping that if only the captain would die, Ethan could make a record with the ship and, incidentally, capture the owner's daughter for his wife. He justifies the murder to himself (the captain would have died anyway from his fall) so long as he can believe he did it for the sake of a record. He finally convinces himself that it was his duty. His passion to

make a record is part of his hate-love for the sea, his desire to defy her, to dominate her, to make her do his will, but never to let her possess him. When he realizes that he has failed, the murder becomes murder to him and he punishes himself.

He is impatient with his mother's practical standpoint—to possess the position of captain, to marry the owner's daughter in order to own the ship. This he cannot see: to hell with the ship; he'll smash her to pieces in order to get there in record time. Thus he is attracted to Goldie's unscrupulous recklessness. He thinks she understands, but she doesn't. She wants men to do everything to possess her. When she offers herself to Ethan as a reward for the murder, he spurns her: it's an insult to his idealism. She then becomes uncertain of her own value, needs reassurance. It is this that drives her to attract Wolfe—to make him stake his value on her, double or quits. She taunts the banker, Graber: "I care nothing for you; you're an old fool. Stake me, you'll lose me anyway." She taunts Wolfe to put a high value on her, restore her value in her own eyes. He does, but here again she fools herself, for it is only as an exciting stake in the game that Wolfe wants her.

Ethan at the end of the voyage confesses the murder to his mother, but only as the result of having failed. If he had been successful, the murder would have been justified. He wants her to judge and sentence him. She thinks of what Simon would have said. Ethan knows that: it would be to give himself up to the law. Her practical side immediately speaks: that would put hardship on the family from the start. Then she upbraids herself for this thought: it's the damn peasant in her lusting for position and power and wealth. Ethan says, ironically: "The touch of the poet in you, too, Mother?" She denies this, and, as the horror of his crime grips her, alternately bawls him out (the son of his father to do that!) and tries to excuse him ("Say nothing, forget it."), but he refuses this: "I can't do that, Mother; you know it." She: "Then why can't you be silent, why come to me?" He: "You know I had to, Mother." She (wildly): "What can I say to you? How can I reach you? You've always been outside me, even when you were in my womb, I think." (She crushes him in her arms.) "Come to me for once! Be me, so I'll not be able to judge you!" He: "I can't. I love you, Mother." But this is from the outside, she sees. He stands alone, like his father. Even her love could never reach his father in his loneliness. She can't tell him what to do. He must stand alone.

Then he makes her listen to his own judgment on himself: "I'll drop overboard; I'll go into the sea; in defeat, I'll give myself up at last—be hers, be possessed, swim out and out toward the horizon. In the quiet darkness, I will finally give up and go down, be one with the man I've murdered, the captain, who, in his way, also loved the sea."

The last scene is on deck at dawn. Sara keeps all their eyes turned on the land. Ethan commits suicide as the ship enters the Golden Gate.

Jonathan has proposed to the owner's daughter and been accepted by her father, after convincing him of his ability and the practical worth of his ambitions. (He is aided in this by his mother.)

Honey, an unusually handsome, curly-haired, blue-eyed type of *Screen-Romance* Irish good-for-nothing, is a shrewd, greedy scamp and his mother always sees through him. He has played the drunken Tom-Moore troubadour, a whiskey John-McCormack tenor, throughout. He has a sly, frank animal lust for Goldie, who treats him as an amusing pal whom she understands.[3]

O'Neill made further notes for *The Calms of Capricorn* later in March 1935 and continued to work on the second play, commenting in his *Work Diary* that it "seems to be working out as built around Abigail [Deborah], new conception [of] her character" (p. 212). He began a detailed scenario, worked on it steadily, deciding on the final title, *More Stately Mansions,* on 22 March, and finished the play on 26 April (pp. 213, 217).

Act one opens at Melody's Inn around 8:30 of a night in the summer of 1835. Dan Cronin and Mickey Maloy come in from the bar as the wake for Melody goes on upstairs. They agree that his death was not from drink but from a broken heart at Sara's marriage to Simon Harford and at her failure to come to see him or write, even when Cronin sent word that her father was dying. They wonder whether she'll come to the funeral. Mickey sneers at Sara's giving herself airs and believing her father's lies about his high position in Ireland. Cronin reminds him that Melody's corpse is lying upstairs and it's bad luck to speak ill of the dead. Mickey hastily remarks that Con was a fine man in spite of his faults, and they drink to him.

Mickey tells Cronin he plans to find another job: all the inn's creditors will be coming down on Norah for the thousands of dollars that her husband owed. He's sure that Sara won't want to help, even though she's written her mother that Simon is making good money in Connecticut, after having been cut off by his family without a nickel. Cronin, drunk, implies that this isn't true, but then refuses to tell Mickey anything. He says that he'll have a talk with Sara, and she will help her mother or he'll know the reason why.

Norah enters, overcome with grief. She has aged greatly, but there's a certain satisfaction and peace underlying her sorrow. She tells Mickey to go to see what they're wanting upstairs and give her a chance to rest; her legs are breaking under her. Mickey comments that it's a great shame her daughter wouldn't be here to help her, but Norah defends Sara, says she *is* coming. Mickey goes, and Norah and Cronin talk. He asks her if she is sure Sara will come, and Norah confesses she doesn't really know: "There was such pride between her and her father; maybe even death won't soften her. But she's *my* daughter, too—and she'll make herself come; I know she will!" Cronin says that if Simon is indeed making money, Sara will be able to help pay off her father's debts. But Norah says no, she'd never ask it: Sara has four young children and the old who are near death shouldn't be putting burdens on the young just starting life. But she admits it'll take a long time to make the inn prosper again as it did before Melody started wasting all the profits by trusting everyone. Cronin advises her to let the place go bankrupt and start anew, free of debt, but Norah won't hear of it. "I'm a poor ignorant woman, but I've my pride and honor, too, just as much as he had his. I'll pay every dollar my husband owed, and then I'll go into a convent, make up for my sin, and find peace at last." Cronin says savagely, "By God, and you'll have your peace—and you won't wait longer for it, either!"

Sara and Simon come in, each carrying one of the two younger sons. Norah, forgetting her sorrow for the moment, welcomes Sara with a cry of joy and pride. Sara, deeply moved, warns her mother not to wake the baby. Norah gushes over him, asks the children's names. Simon tells her, and Norah, seeming to notice him for the first time, is tearfully grateful at his addressing her as "Mother." They both greet Cronin, and then Sara asks her mother to help her put the children to bed. Norah is brought back to herself by a wail from the wake overhead, and apologizes to Sara. They go out.

Simon and Cronin, left alone, drink, Cronin defiantly toasting Ireland and the Irish, "and to hell with all that would keep them down!" Simon replies gravely, "And may they have here what they have longed and fought for for so long—freedom from oppression, and liberty!" Cronin stares at him and expresses his admiration: "Sara's right to be proud of you!" Simon laughs embarrassedly, "Oh, no, it's I who have a right to be proud of her—and am proud."

Sara returns, surprised at seeing Simon so chummy with Cronin. But she is superstitiously upset from having seen her father's corpse, with what she takes to be a sneer on his face. When Cronin observes bitterly that she gave him little time, she explains that she couldn't stay: she can't stand the sight of death, "and him with the sneer on his lips—like death sneering at the living." She shudders. Cronin gets rid of Simon by saying that all the guests at the wake, knowing he's down here, will take it bad if he doesn't go up and pay his respects. Sara protests that most of them, drunk, would never miss him; but Simon says he wants to go. He exits.

Cronin tells Sara that she's made herself into a fine Yankee lady, and accuses her of being like her father. She tells him he's unfair: she still feels friendly to him even if he doesn't to her. Confused and mollified, he asks her abruptly if she's going to help her mother. She answers that she will, of course, and Cronin asks if that means she'll pay off the debts. She protests angrily at the idea that she should ask Simon to give up the money they've spent years trying to save to enable him to buy out his partner. She and Cronin argue, and he warns her that she'll do the decent thing by her mother or, "By God—". His threat is broken off by Norah's return. He leaves.

Norah asks what's come over Cronin, and Sara answers that he's drunk. Norah has been much impressed by Simon. She has confided to him her intention to give up the world as soon as she can, enter a convent, and thus find peace for her soul. He admitted that he had tried that once: for him Nature was God; but it turned out she didn't want him, nor he her. Sara says it's coming back here that has led him to think such thoughts again; she had hoped marriage had cured him. Her mother tells her not to worry: Simon *is* cured. He explained to her that he had found his union with God through human love.

Sara protests at her mother's idea of going into a convent, but Norah insists that that's what she wants to do. When Sara comments harshly that it'll be a good joke on her father, her mother tells her that he came back to the faith at the very last, when he was dying. Sara can't believe it, but her mother insists. She had pleaded with him to do this if he's ever felt one bit of love for her. He didn't answer for a while, then opened his eyes, and there was a queer smile in them. He admitted he owed her this last bit of pride, and he's a gentleman about debts of honor. So he told her to bring in Father Ryan, if it'd bring her peace, and he died with the last rites of the church for his soul. He never spoke again or even looked at her. Sara knows now why he died with that sneer on his lips—that last sneer at himself and his pride. But Norah insists it was a smile of his soul at peace— a smile of love for her. She tells Sara not to take that from her and Sara, ashamed, agrees.

She asks her mother more about her plans, why she feels she has to pay off the debts. Norah explains that she wants to go into the convent with a clear conscience; it'll only mean a few more years of hard work for her. Sara, after a visible struggle, says she can ask Simon, but her mother forbids this: he and Sara are just starting to rise in the world, and they have four children to raise. She wants them to have wealth and power so that Melody, looking down from heaven, will be proud that Sara Harford is his daughter. Sara replies that she *will* have all that, but it's her mother she wants to make proud, not him. Norah rebukes her, then asks about the business. Sara outlines their success and their plans for the future. There's only one flaw: Simon keeps dreaming of retiring. She feels it's those old thoughts that hold him back in business. She has to argue him out of his scruples about whether this or that is honorable, but she's gradually getting him away from that foolishness.

They are interrupted by Simon's return. He tells Norah that the folks upstairs are asking for her. Her unconsciously comic comment is that they must have drunk up all the whiskey. She goes out. Simon talks with Sara about her father's debts, says Cronin told him she had said they couldn't afford to help her mother, but surely she didn't? She is miserably defiant, asks how they can help—with four children and not enough saved to buy out his partner? Simon says he doesn't have to do that right now. They *can* help, and they *will*. He can't believe she could be so bitter. She protests that she *had* suggested helping, but her mother refused. Simon is sure he can get Norah to agree: he can say he's suddenly come into some money from the death of a relative. Just leave it to him to persuade her. Sara, sunk and bitter, says she's no doubt he will. He feels it's a point of honor for them to do this. She replies that she's afraid she's all mixed up about honor, what it is or isn't; her only honor is her love for him, and that he should gain power and wealth and happiness. When he warns her that those things don't mean happiness, she comments that he's never known poverty and the hurt of it that kills pride and self-respect. But she comes 'round to agreeing with him that they must help, even if it takes their last cent. They'll work all the harder to make it up. He suggests she ought to be with the people upstairs. She expresses scorn for them, but says she'll go up to please him, for she does love him. He is moved, and kisses her. She goes.

Cronin sidles in from the bar, greets Simon enthusiastically. He admits he couldn't help hearing some of their talk. He knows it'll be all right for Norah now. They'll be rewarded, "for won't she wear out her old bones in the convent, praying for you to the Mother of God!" He drinks to their healths. Simon regards him with a look that is pained but at the same time amused.

There is a knock at the street door and Simon's brother Joel comes in. He has been sent by their mother. Simon introduces him to Cronin, who leaves them. Joel comments disparagingly on the "infernal noise" from the wake, forgets himself, and expresses his outrage at the sight of Simon, a Harford, in this "ignorant savagery." Simon comments coldly that last fall a mob of ignorant bigoted New England Yanks cowardly attacked defence-less nuns in Charlestown, burning and sacking the Ursuline convent there while the authorities stood by and did nothing. And our best families, including he is sure his father and brother, gloated approvingly when they heard the glorious news of this New England victory. So he'd not speak of "ignorant savagery," if he were Joel—unless in a mood of self-examination. His voice becomes sharp, and he asks Joel to come to the point: what does their mother want? Joel explains that she had read of Melody's death, thought Simon might come to the funeral, and asks him to meet her the next afternoon at his old shack. Simon agrees, and promptly breaks off the interview.

Joel is about to go when Sara enters. She and he stare at each other. He is impressed by her beauty, bearing, and tasteful clothes, is attracted to her—and furious at himself. Simon is obliged to introduce them. Sara is gracious, but Joel abruptly turns his back and goes. She is hurt, and Simon, seeing this, is enraged, offers to bring Joel back to apologize; but Sara refuses to allow it.

She asks him why Joel came, and is visibly apprehensive about Simon's going to meet his mother. He points out to her that he couldn't very well refuse: he hasn't seen her for six years. He wonders at her having made a confidant of Joel, whom she had always despised. Sara tells him that, when he left, his mother naturally turned to Joel, but Simon refuses to admit this. When Sara urges him not to go, he says she can't mean it: it would be infamous of him. She explains that it's only that she loves him and can't believe her luck, that he loves her. "Swear you wouldn't let even her come between us." He swears, but protests at the idea. When she learns that the meeting is to be at the old shack, she is again strangely apprehensive. Maybe it's seeing her father dead with that sneer on his lips that has made her feel not sure of anything. Simon blames himself for not realizing how unstrung she must be. She seems to set aside her worries, tells him to go to bed; she wants him to look well the next day so his mother will know that she takes good care of him. She will sit up with her mother. Simon offers to sit up too, but she won't hear of it. Besides, she wants him to be near the children in case they wake up. He goes. Alone, she sinks into somber brooding, addresses Abigail in her thoughts: "All the same, I wonder why—for don't I know that in your heart you hate me?"

The second scene of act one is laid at the boatshed the following afternoon. Sara enters furtively, and can be heard prying off a board at the back, getting in, then opening a window behind the boards on the front side. She speaks her thoughts aloud, showing a mingled defiant desperation and a remorseful guilt. Simon would despise her if he knew—but she doesn't trust Abigail. He has told her about his mother's letters, but has never given any of them to her to read. And after each letter's arrival, he's fallen into one of his moody silent fits, withdrawn in his old loneliness. And now this meeting here. She hates the place, even if it is the scene of their love. She has to find out. She sees Simon coming, has a last-moment impulse not to play this dishonorable trick on him, but then catches sight of Abigail in the distance. It's too late: fate has decided the matter for her. She goes and hides in the shack.

Simon comes in, expresses his thoughts, memories of this place when he lived here alone. He wonders at his mother's reasons for asking him to meet her here at the old cabin. Was Sara right? Then he blames her for putting such unworthy thoughts into his mind. Of course she did it out of love for him. He recalls the night she gave herself to him here. He should have brought her with him, not sneaked off to meet his mother alone. He sees her coming, goes to meet her.

Abigail enters. They embrace. She says he hasn't told her how she looks. He replies that she's more beautiful than ever, but she has changed. For one thing she is now intimate with Joel, whom she used to think so like their father. She explains that she's had fun in betraying Joel into a shameless display of warmth and affection that she could never tease from her husband. She's discovered that she has a genius for intrigue. She hopes Simon *is* jealous, for that will prove that he's not entirely lost to her. Besides he can't blame her for consoling herself for his loss. She agrees that she *has* changed: it's as if there were a strange someone in her whom she has never met. She has odd waking dreams in which she is suddenly transported to another life where she is someone else, very old and wise and what men call wicked. She tells him with a strange pride that in her dream she is a great courtesan, with a genius for secret plotting and intrigue, for playing one person against another for her own ends. There's no desire on her part, only men's desire for her—sin without sinning—so much more subtle. Simon stares at her, laughs. She is insulted; her face freezes: "You will please not laugh!" Then as she sees from his reaction that she has given herself away, she hastily hides her feeling, admits that he's right to laugh: the whole thing is very silly. It was childish to think it important enough to talk about, especially when they have so little time. For she must go before his father misses her, and Simon himself will be wanting to get back to Sara.

She asks about the children. And is Sara as pretty as ever after all those childbirths? What about the business? Is he still determined to retire as soon as he has enough? Does he read as much as he used to? He knows what she's driving at, admits that business doesn't leave him much time for reading. He hates himself for it, but it has to be, and he'll be out of it and free before too long. Then she'll see that the means were justified by the end. She says evasively that she was not condemning him. And even if he had to pay his soul, Sara would have been worth it, wouldn't she? He agrees, but insists that it's hardly a question of paying his soul: his love for her *is* his soul. She asks, "Well, then?" He answers, "Well, what? I don't understand you, Mother." She replies that she simply means that he is happy; he has love, and so there is nothing more to say, except God bless him and preserve his happiness and Sara's.

And now they must part. She asks him to go and let her follow him with her eyes. She gives him a push and he walks off. She stares after him, thinking. Her assertion that she is happy in his happiness is a white lie: as a dutiful mother she is resigned to her lot of virtuous resignation. But some-day she will have done with the cowardice of goodness and she'll be free—as she is in her dream.

Sara appears, at once humble, ashamed, and defiant. When Abigail speaks disparagingly of her idea of honor, Sara answers proudly, "I love him. That is the only idea of honor I care about." Abigail asks her why she felt it necessary to spy on them. Sara confesses to having been afraid of her. But now that she has heard Abigail tell Simon that she is happy in their happiness she feels she must confess her shame. Abigail in turn explains why she wanted the interview with Simon—to be certain that he *was* happy. They agree that he has something neither of them can possess: it's the curse of the poet laid on him. They must learn to be reconciled. But then Abigail changes her tone. Sara is talking nonsense; she doesn't have to be reconciled at all. She must for the sake of Simon's happiness do her best to kill his dream. If she keeps his nose to the grindstone, he will soon forget all such childishness. It's natural for her to think of herself and the chil-dren. The two women must unite in a conspiracy to drive all remaining poetic nonsense out of Simon's head.

And now Sara must go: if Simon doesn't find her at the inn, he'll wonder. She starts off, then asks Abigail if she does indeed forgive her for spying. Abigail answers, "Of course," and explains that she's grateful to Sara for having set her an example, for having corrupted her to freedom. Sara doesn't understand, but Abigail assures her that she will some day. Sara says she's afraid of her when she talks like that. Abigail, changing her tone, asks if Sara is taking her seriously: she has a fantastic mind, as everyone knows. Sara stares a moment, then goes off. Abigail shudders at herself, asks what she is trying to do; she herself doesn't seem to know. It's as if she were pregnant again. With a strange, proud, exultant laugh, she addresses the ocean: "O Sea, I am afraid I am becoming a very wicked woman—at last, thank God!" And she again laughs exultantly.

Act two opens in the sitting room of Simon and Sara's house in a Connecticut coast city on an evening in the spring of 1837. Simon is reading the paper, Sara sewing, Ethan dreaming, and Wolfe playing solitaire. Simon bursts out exasperatedly, having read about dissentions in the antislavery ranks: it's a crime they can't stay united. Sara tries to soothe him: what can he do about it? He says that at least his firm could stop all dealing with the South. When Sara, alarmed, points out that that would mean a big loss, he asks her why they must always consider profit above everything else. Sara lets this pass, but points out that there's plenty of slavery of whites in the New England mills. He agrees that he is not one to talk of freedom since he deals in goods produced by the factory workers. Sara says she didn't mean to reproach him, only to show him there's no use worrying about such things; they will always be. All one can do is ignore them, live one's own life with those one loves—the family, a first duty.

Sara draws Simon's attention to Ethan, "lost in his dreams," and asks their son what he is dreaming about. He talks of his feeling for the sea: "You have to learn to swim and beat her—and then she likes you for beating her, and she lets you belong to her, like a fish does." Sara says this is a queer thing to be dreaming; there's a touch of the poet in him—like his father. Simon says bitterly, "God forbid!" But Ethan agrees, asks his father if he feels like that about the sea. Simon admits that he did once—at times—but not any more. Now he feels more like a fish out of water—no, like a crab—a crab crawling sideways through the mud. Sara protests, and Ethan asks, "You mean on the sand, don't you?" But his father insists that sand is too clean: "Sand is of the sea. I mean, mud."

Sara changes the subject by asking Wolfe about his game. When he reports that he has made it twice, she teases him, says that sounds like cheating. He denies this, and his father says that Wolfe wouldn't cheat: he hasn't been corrupted by business yet; he still has his honor. Sara flushes: she was only joking; gentlemen don't cheat at cards. Simon queries her, "At cards—but otherwise you think it's quite all right?" Sara protests, but Wolfe comments that it might be all right to cheat someone who was trying to cheat you, and his mother agrees. But, he points out, it would be silly to cheat yourself, and his father adds, worse than a crime, it'd be a blunder.

Sara then turns the subject back to swimming, and all four discuss again their attitudes toward the sea. Ethan says he wants to be a sailor when he grows up. Wolfe guesses he wants to be nothing—but a gentleman. Sara tells the boys it's their bedtime. They kiss their parents and go to their room.

There's a pause, during which Simon stares before him and Sara continues to sew but keeps looking worriedly up at her husband. She finally asks him what's the matter, he's been so bitter and discontented lately. He answers evasively: only nerves, the strain of the panic they've been through. But Sara says they've weathered the storm and made money while others went bankrupt. Simon foresaw what was going to happen and took measures to profit by it. He admits that he did display "a low cunning." Sara asks if it would have helped anyone if he had gone bankrupt too. Besides, he's working not just to pile up money but to be able to retire and take up writing again. Simon disparages that dream: "I'll never have enough to do that, will I?" She points out that he already has a comfortable house, a loving wife, and fine handsome children. Isn't he being ungrateful? He apologizes and expresses his gratitude to her. His father's recent death has upset him, made him realize the futility of a life devoted to piling up money. She insists that if he does indeed want to retire, she'll agree: they'd have enough if they sold everything. But he says they can't now: he has too many irons in the fire. It'll be only a little while longer at the rate he's going.

Testing her, he begins to talk of his new schemes. She is at once eager, full of dreams of future opulence for him and the children. He seeks her admiration, like a child, and she, in praising him, reports that his mother has told her how proud she is of his success. He asks angrily: "She did?" Sara expands on Abigail's fears that Joel will not make much of carrying on their father's business now that the senior Harford is dead. They talk about Joel: Sara's feeling toward him has changed for the better. Simon asks if she's been flirting with him, and she denies it; but she is flattered that he'd be jealous.

Simon comments that his mother has changed lately, has become strange. When Sara says it's odd they haven't heard from her, Simon points out that they came back from his father's funeral only a week ago. Sara explains that she thought he'd hear about his father's will. He frowns and asks what that could have to do with him: his father wouldn't have changed his mind, and even if he had, he, Simon, would never change his, would never touch a penny of his. Sara points out that his father is now dead and Simon ought to forgive him—she has.

The front doorbell rings and Simon goes to answer it. Sara hears

Abigail's voice, frowns, and wonders why she has come, with no warning. Abigail, all in white, comes in with Joel, she talking volubly with a strange secret excitement. She explains that they arrived at six, are staying at a hotel—wouldn't impose on Sara and Simon—have had dinner there, and now here they are. Most incredible things have come up. She never understood her husband: behind his remote façade he had capacities she never dreamed he had of romantic recklessness and daring. It seems she ruined him. She leaves it to Joel to explain to Simon while she and Sara go to see the children. As they go she reminds Joel that whatever is done must be decided from the highest standards of unselfish duty and the honor of the family. Joel answers that it is unnecessary to remind him: if he hadn't agreed he'd not be here.

He takes papers from his pocket and tells Simon that they will explain better than he can. Their father's will has left the business equally to the two sons, who are to be responsible for the house and their mother, but Simon is to be in charge—to right the wrong done him, and because Joel hasn't the executive ability born of experience. But there is no money: the firm is on the brink of ruin, had been losing money for years, and their father had become desperate at the end and had gambled in Western lands. The panic finished him. Simon can't believe it, but Joel has had a statement drawn up showing that unless $40,000 in cash is forthcoming within ten days, the firm will have to file for bankruptcy. They are about to go into Simon's study to discuss details when Abigail comes back in. Sara has remained upstairs to get the youngest boy back to sleep.

Abigail sends Joel into the study; she wants a word with Simon. She insists again that she was the cause of his father's ruin. She has been evil, *wanted* to ruin him, is no better than a courtesan. She weeps. Simon ridicules this. His mother's face hardens; her tone changes to sensible matter-of-factness; and she agrees that it is of course ridiculous for an old woman like her, a grandmother, to have such dreams. She sends him in to talk with Joel, tells him to remember that Sara and the children must come first. He mustn't feel bound; she's sure that she and Joel will manage somehow. Simon is jealous, and she confesses she really hasn't much confidence in Joel. She has felt glad at the catastrophe because it may mean that he, Sara, and the children will come home to her, be all together. She thought Joel would refuse to accept this arrangement, but he seems to be pleased at the prospect, perhaps because Sara's charm has fascinated him. Simon frowns. Abigail is satisfied, and he goes into the study.

Alone, she at first stares after him malignantly, "You should not laugh at my dream, Simon. It will be the worse for you." Then, back to her normal self, she rejects such thoughts; she must stop: she must refuse to let Simon come home; she doesn't know what she might do there. Then she changes again: this is the chance she has waited for—to win back his love, even though she no longer loves him, only herself. Her husband died for her long ago; she is now free to be herself, the self of the dark garden. She will be the great intriguing courtesan, with life a game she plays, using other lives as chessmen. She goes and listens at the keyhole, saying that the end justifies every means; but she can't hear anything except Sara upstairs. She expresses her resentment at Sara's trying to make her into a grandmother. She lapses into her dream: the King is dead and she is free. Then there comes another change, a shudder. No, she will not cross the barrier! She will not! She is here!

Sara enters, and Abigail embraces her tenderly, expresses great love for her and a great envy, a great need: Sara is so sane and healthy, her feet grow from the earth; while she, Abigail, is so cut off, so alone and frightened. Sara is touched. Abigail, changing the subject, speaks of some of the reasons for the visit. Joining the two firms will be a great opportunity, fine for Sara and the children, and will give Simon an impetus toward success. Sara is fascinated by the prospect, but uneasy; she refuses to influence Simon in any way.

He comes in, sends his mother to Joel, says the decision is up to Sara. He explains that it will mean starting over, will take everything they've saved. Sara rebels, resentful at Abigail for having said nothing of the cost. It's always the dead laying burdens on them—like a trap. Since Simon's left it up to her, she says then they won't. But he reminds her that she must think of his mother, the family honor. He knows he can make it up. There's no other way out, with honor, although he admits it's a trap—for him too. Sara laughs bitterly; if it's down to a point of honor, sure her father was more full of honor than a hundred Harfords, and she's his daughter. "So bad cess to it, we'll do it! At any rate, it means I won't have to listen to any more talk of your retiring for a while—and that's a blessing!"

The second scene of act two is laid in the garden of the Harford mansion in Boston on a summer evening, two months later. Abigail is alone, brooding. She has never lived, as her flowers have. She rouses from this: the change in her is to spring, a new life. Joel comes out of the house, reports that all is in readiness for the arrival of Simon, Sara, and the children. His mother's feelings are mixed. When he reports that things at the office are in order for Simon to take over, she professes not to be interested "in trade." Joel adds that he has applied for a job in New York and will leave as soon as Simon assumes charge, making over his half of the business to her. Without Simon's money there'd be no business, and he has no right to share that money. Besides, he has seen the change in his mother, knows he has been only a poor substitute for his brother. She accepts his decision, agrees it's the wisest course.

But then her attitude changes, and she asks his forgiveness, professes her love for him. He hopes she will not have to spend much time alone in her garden from now on. He has felt a change in her: at times she has seemed to be a stranger to him. He has heard her talking to herself here in the garden. She flies into a passion, accuses him of eavesdropping. Then she laughs gaily: "Do I sound angry? It is all playacting. Don't you know that I have always been considered a little crazy? Dear Joel, where is your sense of humor?" He explains that it's because he's felt that she was sinking deeper into her dream—that there was danger for her in giving way to it so deeply. She stammers, "Deeply? What do you mean? Are you trying to frighten me?" Angrily, she accuses him of trying to poison for her the mood of Simon's homecoming. Then she laughs again, tells him not to worry. As long as her dark garden remains outside, "That is a good sign, don't you think?" A servant comes out of the house to announce that Simon and Sara are arriving. Joel hurries in.

Alone, Abigail gives way to a vindictive rage against Joel. It's only his jealousy of Simon. She watches the lights go on in Sara's room, feels a thrill of triumph. She will gradually draw Simon away from his wife and children, back to her in her garden where he belongs. She becomes conscious of her dark self, waiting to possess her—the longing to step over the barrier and give herself to it. She becomes terrified, then defies it, pushes it back.

Simon comes out and he and his mother embrace. She recalls the old days. He asks about Joel's decision to leave, feels Sara will be hurt. Abigail says she's glad Joel's going: he's no longer needed, would have been a disturbing influence. Simon vows to show her he has more ability than his brother: he'll make them all rich. She mocks his boasting—and in her garden!—says she's rich already having him with her. "There will be just you and me from now on." He reminds her of Sara and the children. She explains that for the moment she can only remember the old days; she recalls incidents, and they laugh together.

Sara enters from the house, stares at them, suspicious. She conquers this, comes forward and embraces Abigail, who is effusive in her welcome, wants Sara to be happy. But then, turning to Simon, his mother suggests that they go in: "It is not the same in the garden now. I mean it has suddenly grown chilly, don't you think?" Simon hasn't noticed. Abigail guesses she's getting old, can't stand the night air. Sara says she'll love this garden, asks if she can come here often. Abigail answers, "Yes, of course— but never without asking me. There are certain hours when I wish to be here alone." Sara is hurt, but promises not to intrude. Simon laughs this off, explains that his father never dared come here. His mother reminds Simon that *he* was always welcome. She tells Sara to put her feeling down to something childish in her that has never grown up. As they go in, she repeats that she wants her to be very happy here. Sara replies that she knows she will be, but there's just one thing: Abigail has given her and Simon separate rooms. They don't need them; they always sleep together. Simon confirms this. His mother forces a frozen smile, says, "Of course—I did not stop to think, was merely turning over to you the same rooms I and your father occupied during all of our married life. I wanted you to have the best, you understand." They go in.

Act three opens at the office of Simon Harford & Brother on a spring morning in 1842. Simon is shown as the efficient, driving executive. Joel has remained with the company after all, but there is tenseness between him and Simon. Sara enters, and Simon is boastful with her, like a child showing off before his mother. He owes his success to her, the inspiration of her presence and their daily conferences. She says she's just listened to his ideas and agreed with them, but he insists he needed her to give him confidence. He could retire right now, but he won't: he has become tremendously interested in the business, is more contented with life. Sara asks if he really means that, and he answers, "Of course. Isn't it obvious?"

She says yes, she feels it here at the office, but at home he's seemed so changed lately, so tortured. He laughs this off, of course he's been worn out and a bit grumpy.

But Sara insists something queer is happening to all of them, even to herself. She wishes they were back in their own home. He asks what specific things have happened. She mentions his suddenly taking up writing his book again. He explains that it's only amusement, a harmless hobby to take his mind off the business. But she wonders why he did it without ever talking it over with her, was it his mother who suggested it? He admits that she and he did perhaps refer to it when they were reminiscing about the old days, but what difference does it make? "And now we've blown that ghost away, what's the next?" She asks him why he's taken to sleeping alone lately. He blames this on his insomnia: he didn't want to disturb her. Sara: "You are sure your mother didn't suggest that to you, too?" Simon: "Mother? Of course not. Why she would think it grossly indelicate to speak— I don't think she could ever bring herself to admit— Mother is an unworldly innocent—a creature of pure spirit, innocent as a newborn babe, to whom the passion of the flesh is unknown." Sara: "She was a wife. She had two children." Simon: "No." Sara: "No?" Simon: "I mean you can't feel about her somehow that she ever was a wife—only as a mother, my mother—"

Then, with a laugh, he accuses her of having taken a peculiar tone about his mother lately, of dark suspicion, as if she were an enemy engaged in some devious dark intrigue. It's ridiculous and makes him unhappy. Sara says that she's sorry, but she can't help it. There *has* been a change, and she blames his mother for it. Simon defends her, "She's nothing but a whimsical, poetic child who has never grown up, who has her real being in a fantastic, far-off world of dreams and make-believe." He doesn't take her seriously and Sara mustn't. He promises to come to her tonight, tells her to forget his mother. She finds it hard to be specific, because there are no facts, it's only her feeling that Abigail hates her in spite of a surface smiling agreement. He protests that his mother is as incapable of hate as a butterfly. But Sara says she seems even to be trying to turn the children against her— to take them away, and not because of love but of hate. Simon dismisses this as nonsense. But Sara wishes he wouldn't go straight from the office to his mother in her garden every evening. It changes him: he comes in afterward so strange; he seems to hate her. He insists that this is crazy. She knows he loves her more than anything else in the world, doesn't she? She answers, yes, here, now—but out there? He says that such fantastic suspicions are wicked and insane: to suspect his mother, of all people! Sara sees that now, here with him, but out there he seems so far away from her. He attributes it all to her imagination. His visits to his mother relax him. The garden is just a whim of hers. He goes there to talk with her, humor her. That's the least he can do. After all, she is his mother. He's all she has. She's getting old, lives in her dreams; her only happiness is in the past with him. He makes Sara promise to try again to see his mother as she really is.

And now he has a surprise for her—a wedding anniversary gift: the old shack with the farm in back, the Knox estate. Simon has pushed Knox to the wall, will ruin him and make him sell the estate. Won't that please her? She is delighted and they make plans—but they will require lots of money. He says he'll make it, given time. He's going to reduce the wages of the workers; Sara agrees (in brogue). He's beginning to love this game for its own sake. He has to laugh at his old silly childish scruples—no place for honor here. Sara was right, life belongs to him who has power over it, who fights for it and takes it and makes it his. He embraces her passionately. She is exultant: "You are mine, aren't you—mine?" He agrees, but not here— later tonight. "I adore every inch of your body—I always will." Sara answers, "Then I'm not afraid any more—not of anything—or anyone."

There's a knock at the door and Abigail enters. Simon is rude to her at first: she's interrupting a serious discussion, in the realm of facts—not dreams. He and Sara are agreed that life belongs to the man of action. His mother smiles, agrees. He is astonished. Can he believe his ears? She credits Sara with having converted her, long ago. But it will take lots of money, and she's come at a bad time—to ask a contribution for the cause of the Abolitionists. She remembered he used to be so interested in freedom from slavery, liberty. He laughs: that was long ago. He can't afford to give anything right now and, anyway, it's bad for business; the Negroes are better off in slavery. Sara agrees. Simon laughs at his mother as he would at a child, shows her out. She submits, tells him he's so like his father. But she'll expect him in her garden. He says he's sorry he won't be able to be there this evening: he's been wasting too much time in the garden with her. And he's going to give up work on his book: it's ridiculous to try to reconcile opposites—only the real exists. He's going to spend his nights

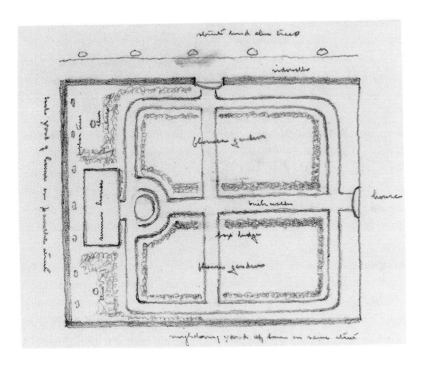

Deborah Harford's Garden and Summerhouse. O'Neill's design for the set in *More Stately Mansions*, Play Four of the nine-play Cycle. (YCAL, Size of original: 11.6 × 20.2 cm.) Manuscript notes: (*at top*) "street lined [with] elm trees/sidewalk"; (*at right*) "house"; (*at bottom*) "neighboring yard of house on same street"; (*at left*) "back yard of house on parallel street"; (*in center*) "flower garden/brick walls/box hedge/flower garden"; (*at center left*) "poplar trees/elm summer house elm/hedge[?]".

with Sara after this, "Aren't I, Sara?" He kisses her and she answers that she hopes so. Abigail smiles gaily, "Well, I will be there, as always, in case you change your mind." She goes.

The second scene of act three shows the sidewalk, the wall-door, and the interior of Abigail's garden that evening. She is alone there and in her thoughts expresses satisfaction at the way her intrigue is going. But she must proceed warily: Simon must not realize where she's leading him. She is enjoying her struggle with Sara for possession of him. It is a duel without honor.

Joel enters. He complains of Simon's unethical deeds. After he has gone, Abigail continues her intriguing thoughts, with plans to make use of the rivalry between her two sons.

Simon comes down the street, hesitates, passes the garden door, then comes back, argues with himself about his feeling for Sara as opposed to that for his mother, who has given him the only key to the door. He opens it and goes in. Abigail welcomes him in her old, whimsical way. He is at first amused, then laughs and says that she never grows up. She joins in his laughter, but resents it. She mentions Joel's visit, and he reacts with jealousy; then she makes fun of his brother and he is placated. He sits down and begins to relax, feels ten years younger. She encourages him to forget the sordidness of business, its unscrupulous methods. Of course he's only doing it for love of Sara, who can't help being greedy. Simon agrees that he does humor her, and Abigail supposes that so long as he does not lose his soul, there's no use worrying. Simon insists that Sara can never possess his soul, he leaves that in his mother's safe-keeping, here in her garden.

They discuss Sara and the children, and Abigail warns him that he must fight for his own—as much in love and marriage as in business. But he doesn't want to fight: he wants peace. He finds it here; but in the house he feels he's being torn apart. She urges him to forget all that, reminds him of his childhood, tells him of her latest dream. She is the wicked Queen and he the Prince, in the Enchanted Garden with the Magic Door, the entrance to the country where all dreams are true. But at the last moment the Voice of the Genii of the Door warns that she must not open it because he, the Prince, still too earthbound, would at the last moment not dare to follow her. Simon says he thinks he would follow her anywhere. But she confesses to being afraid—of what awaits her beyond the door. He is shaken, says broodingly that she makes it very real. If the final answer is there, he'd like to go and find out. It would help him with his book, wouldn't it? She asks intensely, "Then—sometime—you will go with me, if I dare to open—?"

Sara comes in from the house. She knows she's not wanted—only a greedy peasant who can't appreciate beauty. She talks and talks, while Abigail and Simon only stare at her in silence. Finally she asks Simon if he's not coming in: it's only the insane who sit staring at nothing in the dark. He doesn't answer, and Abigail says gently that she'll bring him in in a moment. Sara goes. Simon protests that he'll order her never to intrude again, but Abigail tells him not to take her so seriously: she's only an ignorant peasant child, with only her primitive animal instincts to guide her. They speak again of the gate and she asks him to promise. But Sara calls from the house, and he starts to his feet angrily, "God damn her!" His mother says he mustn't blame Sara for crying aloud when she is hurt. She has broken the mood successfully: he will want to go in to work now. He agrees, and she says, "Poor Simon, you will never be able to reconcile the opposites on this plane. It will drive you mad. Let us go in."

The third scene of act three is set in the Harford mansion later that same night. The sitting room is shown at the left and Abigail's drawing room at the right. In the sitting room Sara is sewing; Jonathan and Honey are playing checkers. Sara asks about Ethan and Wolfe, and Honey supposes they're in their grandmother's room as usual, with her reading poetry to Ethan, and Wolfe pretending to listen. He gives a comical and malicious imitation. Sara laughs, but then reproves him for making fun of his grandmother. The boys talk about her: she is getting crazier all the time, doesn't really like them. Why doesn't their mother make her leave their father alone, stop treating him like a kid? Sara scolds them. They talk of school, and then go up to finish their lessons.

In Abigail's room, she stares at her book, a volume of Byron, without reading, a smile of triumphant malice on her lips. She notices that Wolfe is looking at her, and her face changes. Using his full name, Wolfe Tone, she asks him why he stares at her. He protests that he's not Irish: he can't help his name; but Ethan tells him he ought to be proud of it: Wolfe Tone was a hero who died fighting for liberty against the English, just as Ethan [I, later Jonathan I] Harford, his namesake, died after he fought for liberty in the American Revolution. "Isn't that right, Grandmother?" Abigail frowns, then forces a smile, "Of course. There was only a difference—in kind."

The boys talk of their Irish grandfather; then Abigail comes back to her question about Wolfe's staring at her. He answers finally that he was wondering why she pretends to be doing something when she's really doing something else. She starts, her face freezes, and she replies that she was wondering if the maid Bridget wasn't probably breaking the china in washing up. Wolfe asks her why she suddenly fired all the old servants and got Irish ones. She answers that it was simply a matter of economy: the Irish are cheaper. Wolfe doesn't believe her, says he's going for a walk, asks Ethan if he wants to come. Ethan says he will stay with his book, *Two Years*

The Harford Mansion (with rooms). O'Neill's design for the set in *More Stately Mansions,* showing the façade cut away to reveal the rooms. (YCAL, 15.2 × 10.2 cm.)

before the Mast. Wolfe asks if he's still dreaming of running off to sea. Ethan tells his brother to mind his own business: he can go to Harvard if he wants to. Wolfe says he really doesn't care about it, but his mother wants him to go and anyway, a gentleman ought to have an education. But he'll do as little work as he can; it means nothing to him. Abigail stares at him strangely, believes he's more truthful than he knows. He's a queer boy; that's what she likes him for. She smiles strangely. He blurts out that he's going for his walk, and hurries out. Ethan calls him crazy, then asks his grandmother if any of the Harfords were ever that way. She denies this, wonders why he asks. He grins and says that he wants to know where Wolfe got his craziness from. Abigail admits that a lot of people have thought at times that *she* was a little crazy. But he says he didn't mean her, and he goes on about Wolfe. He asks Abigail to read from Byron's *Childe Harold's Pilgrimage* the stanza beginning, "Roll on, thou deep and dark blue ocean—roll!" and asks her if she really meant what she said last night that it would be all right for him to run away to sea, if his mother insists on his going to Harvard. Abigail replies that it's always right to be free, but warns him this is their secret: he mustn't let his mother know she's encouraging him. He says he'll never tell, and he knows his father wouldn't mind. Besides she could always get around *him:* he does anything she wants him to. Abigail is pleased, does he really think so? He says that he *knows* it— and so does his mother, and she doesn't like it either. Abigail professes to be sorry. Ethan says he wouldn't want to do anything to hurt his mother. Abigail points out that she has his father and the other boys; she'd have forgotten all about him in a month. Ethan conceals his hurt and supposes she would—he'd forget too. As he starts to go to his room to study, Abigail has a change of heart, tells him he mustn't pay attention to what she says: it isn't right to set him against his mother. He replies: "I know. But I'll decide for myself—when the time comes." He goes.

Left alone, Abigail is at first triumphant, then horrified, then justifies herself. Her advice to Ethan was for his own good and, as for Simon, she is only trying to save his soul. But she admits to herself that she has "set a ball rolling that now rolls of itself and in the end will—must—" She stops, again shocked at herself. She must go to Sara and confess, ask her forgiveness. But then she says coldly, "Sentimentalist! No, I *will* see her, but only to gloat and laugh." She goes out.

Sara, alone in the sitting room, drops her sewing, thinks aloud, alternating between blaming and excusing Simon. She feels Abigail always working against her, but can never catch her in it. Bad luck to the day they ever came to this house: she'd like to walk out of it now and take the children— but she loves Simon too much. There's no way out. If only Abigail would die!

Abigail appears silently in the doorway, laughs at the grim, sinister expression on Sara's face: "One would think that in your thoughts you were killing someone!" Sara starts, confused, says Abigail has frightened her, explains that she was thinking of the "thief of a butcher"—she'd like to murder him. Abigail thanks her for taking all the housekeeping off her hands, and compliments her on her efficiency. Sara dismisses it as a thankless job: any servant could do it, but it does wear her out. Abigail flatters her, is concerned that she has seemed worried of late. But Sara denies this: how could she help being happy when Abigail is so kind to her?

Simon comes in, turns upon his mother: he finds he can't work after listening in the garden to her nonsense, must she always live in crazy dreams—like an insane child? Abigail echoes pitifully, "Insane, Simon?" She tells him that he has grown to be like his father, saying the things she could always hear her husband thinking. She doesn't know, *won't* know, what Simon means by "insane." She weeps. Sara sympathizes with her: she mustn't take Simon seriously; he doesn't mean to be cruel; he's only a selfish, irresponsible child. He tells Sara to let his mother cry; he wants to talk with her alone.

They go to the far end of the room, where he upbraids her for being always with the children, having no time for him. He's nothing to her but a money-grubbing machine for her to run. Does she think he's a child that she can hoodwink? She kisses him tenderly and tells him he's her eldest and best beloved, doesn't he know that? He responds passionately and reminds her of her promise to let him sleep with her. She agrees and answers his suspicions of her motives by blaming his mother for having put them in his mind. Simon agrees that she is crazy and evil. But they'll soon be rid of her, have enough money, and return to their estate, where he'll be able to work. He can't here.

He goes to Abigail and reproves her: doesn't she know that all beyond the Magic Gate is insanity, and does she think he would ever—? She puts her arms around him tenderly, calls him her poor lonely boy. He admits that he is tired, complains that Sara puts absurd suspicions in his head. But she is driving him too far: he'll divorce her and live here alone with Abigail. But his mother tells him he mustn't be cruel to Sara: she is only a passionate primitive child.

Sara calls to Simon: "It's nearly bedtime." He agrees, and breaks away from his mother. She protests, says he's surely going to work on his book. But Sara tells him he's too tired, and he agrees: his head aches, he cannot see how opposites can be reconciled. But he *will* see! He turns on them both; both women seem to agree, and offer comfort. He eventually succumbs to Sara and they go. Abigail bursts into tears, then tells herself that this is not reality: she doesn't live here nor does he. She lapses once more into her dream.

Above, the lights go on in Sara and Simon's room. Sara begins to undress, but Simon rebels, feels he can't sleep with her here in the house. She weeps, and he suggests that they can make use of the spare room at the office. He'll have it fixed up as a bedroom. She can be his mistress. There he can give himself; here all is poisoned. He looks at her here and he doesn't know her: she's a common whore he's keeping. Down at the office she'll be the Sara he adores. It'll serve his mother right to play this trick on her. Sara agrees dully, but says she's tired and is going to bed. Simon, excited, says he's going to work on his book. If he cannot unite the opposites, he'll at least keep them separate, each in its place. He goes out, and Sara sits miserably on the side of the bed.

Below, Abigail hears Simon go to his study and is triumphant.

Act four opens back at the office in the morning of a day in Indian summer, 1847. It follows the pattern of the earlier office scene except that now everything is more hectic. Simon orders the old bookkeeper to doctor the books and, when he protests, fires him. Joel speaks of the scandal of Sara and Simon using the office as a bedroom. Simon sneers at him for a lifeless moralist. He objects to the over-expansion of the business and Simon accuses him of being a stick-in-the-mud like their father. Joel points out that a whisper would ruin them. Simon agrees, but says that Joel wouldn't do it since he would also be ruined. Joel argues that he's thinking of their mother's interests. Simon asks why he doesn't tell her, but is confident that she will take his word rather than Joel's on business matters. She knows nothing of life, lives in her crazy dreams, is going a bit insane. He says that Joel will never take a realistic attitude and orders him out.

Sara enters, and they discuss the latest gamble—to ruin their competitor, Knox. She agrees. He laughs and says he's beginning to love the game, and it's all for her. He wants to give her the earth: "I will be a King and you will be my Queen." She becomes alarmed at this and accuses him of spending more and more time with his mother in her garden. He says that she is getting older and more fantastically childish every day; he has to humor her more and more. Sara can't be jealous: doesn't he tell her all his secrets—just as he makes up dreams to please his mother? Sara tells him that Abigail has now forbidden her to enter the garden, and Simon counters that he has told his mother never to set foot in the office. Sara asks what they do in the garden: she has looked at them from a window and they often seem to sit in silence. He answers that he humors his mother by keeping silent and not bringing reality into her dream.

There is a pounding on the door and Abigail's voice pleads to be let in, but Simon tells her to go away: "You have had your life. You are dead. Please have the decency not to haunt the living." Sara thinks she hears her weeping, but Simon answers, "Nonsense. What difference does it make? Women her age always weep. But she has gone. My word is law with her." He embraces Sara passionately. She at first protests that she must look after the children, but then yields. She stops as they enter the bedroom, looks back at the outer door of the office, and addresses Abigail in brogue: "Let you snivel and listen then, you auld dead fool—and my curse on the dead that be like a blight on life!"

The second scene of act four is set again in Abigail's garden that evening, and follows the pattern of the previous garden scene. She, alone, is triumphant at her success in getting Simon farther and farther back, away from Sara. Soon she will open the gate; he will take her hand; and she will lead him over into beauty and peace, freedom and truth at last. She stops, frightened, but then vows not to be afraid of the face of beauty.

Simon enters and flings himself into his mother's arms, weeping, telling her his fears. She begins the game, getting him to remember back to the moment of his birth. She starts to open the door. Then Sara, calling him from a window in the house, breaks the spell. Abigail orders her to go away. But Sara asks if it's not her job to protect Simon from the wiles of an evil old witch. Abigail retorts that he no longer wants her. They exchange insults. Simon rouses, complains of the poisonous air in the garden, and goes into the house. Abigail thinks that if she'd gone a little farther, he could not have been called back. The next time she will be too strong. She half opens the door, but then is horrified and frightened. She's not sure what awaits her there—it may not be peace but madness.

The third scene of act four takes place in the house that night. It follows the same pattern as the preceding house scene, but with the strangeness intensified. Sara is alone. Simon enters, at first embraces her, then feeling this appeal gross, turns on her: if she thinks she can make him sell his soul, he will prove he can free himself. She weeps, and he is at once penitent: he's been working too hard. But then he tells her resentfully that it is her greed, never satisfied, that makes him overwork. She protests: she's quite willing he should retire—if he really wants to. He answers that if he did, she'd think him a weak fool. He'll show them he can beat them at their own game: he'll stuff her greedy belly with gold and land until she bursts! Sara weeps again.

Abigail appears in the doorway, defends Sara, who is grateful. Simon is contrite: he knows it's not Sara's fault. He turns on his mother, accuses her of destroying him with her fairy-tale nonsense. She weeps, and now Sara intervenes, scolds him for talking that way to his mother. What if she does like him to dream with her? It's little enough for him to do for her happiness. Abigail is grateful, and Simon again contrite: he doesn't mean what he says; his mind is all at sea. In the garden he is Abigail's self, in the office Sara's. Between them they've devoured him. He curses them both, sobbing hysterically. Why can't they love each other? They answer that they do, and come together before him. He gets up, puts his arms around both, makes them kiss each other, then kisses them, says now he can work. He goes into his study and begins to write. When, below, the two women separate, he at once flings his manuscript on the floor: "This is drivel. There is no union." He picks it up again: at least in this search he escapes them, and it is the quest for truth that has meaning for the soul. But, distracted, he cannot work. He goes to the children's room, where all four are studying or pretending to. He speaks to each one as a sage, a teacher, tells them they must comfort their mother, she has only them; he is *his* mother's son.

In the sitting room Abigail and Sara argue whether Simon's going to the children's room is a good sign. Abigail says she feels the end is near, wants to thank Sara for the honorable way in which she has fought.

The conversation between Simon and his sons continues in their room. They talk about playing games, cheating or abiding by the rules. He bids them good night and goes out.

Abigail reports that Simon has gone back into his study, says she will soon bring him peace. Sara responds, no, *she* will. Abigail points out that they both want the same thing for him, but one of them must lose—and it will not be she; Sara will have the children to fall back on. When Sara gets up to go, Abigail bids her goodnight, says she leaves her son entirely in her charge for this last night he'll be here. Sara asks her what she means. Abigail answers that she'll find out, and goes. Sara stares after her, then breaks down: "Glory be to God, it's mad she is, stark raving mad—and she'd drive him mad, too!"

The fourth scene of act four is back again at the office the following morning. Simon is alone, very hectic. His mother is right: his soul is being destroyed, but this evening she'll bring him peace, the Magic Door. What will he do with the business? He can't leave it to Sara: it would corrupt his children. His rival Knox is coming and a whisper to him will spread like wildfire: the banks will come down on the firm and smash it. Sara will be what she was when he found her—the Irish peasant waitress with an empty belly. Then he is contrite, aghast at having such thoughts: Sara is so sweet, so good—his wife whom he adores.

She bursts in, alarmed. He denies he's given orders that she not be admitted, embraces her passionately. He tells her they're all lies. She asks, what? He replies, his thoughts: he'd suspected she might have overheard them. She asks him what is the matter? He seems so strange. But he denies the charge. He'll make his dreams come true today. Knox is coming. Simon has ruined him. This evening he'll retire forever. Sara is worried: last night she had heard voices in the garden, had thought it was a dream. Was it he and his mother? Simon confesses that he hadn't been able to sleep, had heard his mother in the garden, and had gone to her there. Sara says he's never done that before; why has he changed so? He's not his natural self.

Simon, angry, asks if she thinks the money-grubbing cheat she sees here in the office is his natural self? She protests, and he apologizes, explains that he was teasing, talking as his mother would.

Here's something that will really interest her: the inventory of the Knox place, down to the last cabbage and pig—362 pigs, all hers. He wagers that her father never had that many in his castle in the old country. Sara again protests, and he again claims that he was only teasing. Where is her famous Irish sense of humor this morning? He suggests they go into the bedroom: "Come, if you love me." She yields miserably, "When you say that, Simon, I'd do anything." He suggests, if she really means that, "Let's set fire to all this, be free, and go back to Mother Nature where there is unity." She agrees. Then he changes, tells her she'd despise him as a silly child who'd never grown up to be a man among men. "No, Greedygut, you have called the tune and we must dance till we drop!"

Joel bursts in. He protests Simon's having given orders to pay all the workers double what anyone else will pay, says it's crazy. It means ruin, knuckling under like that right after he'd broken their strike. Sara joins in, tells him he can't. Simon seizes on this as the true Sara speaking. He agrees with Joel that they can't increase wages and thus reduce profits: he'll see them in hell first. Joel rushes out.

A Negro comes in to thank Simon for a check for the Abolitionist cause. Simon explains to Sara that the contribution was to ease his conscience, but she protests that if he makes such gifts they'll never be able to retire. He admits she's right, asks the Negro whether the check has been cashed. When he says no, Simon asks to have it back and tears it up. It was all a mistake: he has no sympathy for the cause whatsoever. "Who are the Negroes to be free while we are all slaves?" He tells the Negro to get out. The black man exclaims to Sara that her husband must be crazy, isn't he? No man could be that cruel—only the devil. He runs off, frightened.

Sara cries. Simon turns to her: now that he's proved the depth of his love for her, he wants her to go with him into the bedroom. She refuses, is frightened of him. He seizes upon this eagerly, saying that by her refusal she has freed him. He thanks her, tells her to go home to her children. He must set his affairs in order. She protests that this is the first time he ever sent her away from the office. He explains that today he must be strong: all his happiness is in the balance. In a last desperate effort to win him back she tries to get him to go to the bedroom. For a moment he yields; then the door recalls the Magic Door and his mother, and he changes his mind. He has no time for pleasure: there is important business to attend to.

She says she now realizes that the whole marriage was a mistake: he was never free to give himself. He is furious, denies it: he *was* free—free in his solitude. He had cast off the dross of the world, until she came, swinging her hips. She retorts that there was a visitor in his solitude—the owner of his soul. He forces a laugh, "You mean poor little mother? You *will* take her so seriously!" Furiously he forbids her ever to utter again such obscene charges. Sara starts to reply angrily, then becomes sadly resigned, admits that he no longer needs her. She'll take the children and go away. He agrees that's a good idea: they can live on the farm the old peasant life of the soil. Caught up in this, he appeals to her suddenly, asks her to take him with her. She refuses, but tells him he may come later—when he is free. She says goodbye to him and goes. He looks around, prepares to set fire to the office. Knox is due. He's a skinflint: he'll see that the well known merchant Simon Harford is smashed flat as a pancake. He laughs. A clerk comes to announce Knox. Simon says, "Send him in."

The final scene of act four is set in the garden that night. Abigail is alone there. Her thoughts follow the same pattern as in previous garden scenes, but with more tense expectancy, more vivid dream reality, and, at the same time, more dread, which she tries to dismiss, more fear of what lies beyond the door.

Sara forces her way in from the house. Abigail is furious, and Sara talks to her, in brogue, like a rebellious Irish servant, then begs her pardon: there's evil enchantment here; maybe she was talking to herself. At that Abigail welcomes her, says she needs her. It *is* a garden of enchantment. Does she see the Magic Door? Sara answers no, but she remembers hearing fairy tales as a child about such a door and an evil old witch who tempted people to go through, promising them Paradise. But when they opened the door they found the Land of Living Death instead. Abigail denies this, accuses Sara of lying. Sara insists: "And the rest of their lives they spent as mad fools, seeking for the door again that they might come back to light and life and sanity. But the curse was on them: they never found it." Abigail frantically repeats, "You lie!" But Sara continues to insist that it's ancient wisdom she's telling her. Abigail accuses her of resorting to sly peasant tricks to keep hold of Simon. "But it's too late. I've won. You know you're beaten."

Sara agrees that all is now in Abigail's hands. Sara knows she has lost— unless Abigail at the last beats herself—for Simon's sake. Abigail refuses to understand, tells Sara to pack up her things and leave with the children the first thing in the morning. Sara says she has already told Simon she's leaving, and he has given his blessing. Abigail rejoices in this: in a way she'll be sorry to see Sara go tomorrow morning, but she and Simon expect by then to be far away from here too. Sara says she's leaving right away and has come only to ask Abigail to have pity on Simon. Abigail says that Sara can't go now; she forbids it; she won't let her; she must wait. Sara asks, "So you'll have the satisfaction of throwing me out, is that it?" Abigail pleads, offers to pay Sara, make Simon give her money. But she refuses. Abigail confesses that she needs Sara's strength forcing her to ignore all her silly scruples. It is she who inspired her to be unscrupulous: she can't desert her now. Sara tells her she's mad—and that's the only hope she has for Simon: that he'll realize his mother is mad and wake up from the evil spell she's put upon him before he too goes mad. Abigail flies into a fury, tells Sara to get out; thanks her for making her hate her again—that gives her the strength she needs. She sees behind Sara's scheme: that by a pretence of self-sacrifice, of honor, of giving up, she may regain posses- sion. But her subtlety is too obvious. Sara turns to go, then stops and draws a circle, pronouncing an Irish curse: "May you pass through the Magic Gate, alone, and find it the Land of Living Death." Abigail, hor- rified, cringes, covers her ears. Sara goes. Abigail, alone, attempts to reas- sure herself, but is afraid. Then she sinks into her wish-fulfillment fantasy of the Kingdom—Simon will be so happy there.

Joel comes in, tells his mother the news of the fire. The office is burned to the ground; no one knows how it started. Abigail says exultantly, "*I* know." But when Joel questions her, she is evasive. He goes on to say that the firm is ruined; the banks have come down on them; a whisper got around, but who could have done it? Not he, and not Sara: it'd be against her interest. His mother laughs: "Oh, no, not Sara!" Joel protests that Simon is the only other one who knew. Abigail agrees, says it's a mystery, and Joel's soul was not made to harbor mysteries. He answers that he doesn't see what soul has to do with it, and she replies, "No, that's what I said." He is surprised that she doesn't seem to care, laughs when they are irretrievably ruined. Abigail tells him not to fret: this is his world; he'll manage to make good his claim to a slice of it. She asks him to go—she's expecting Simon. He replies gravely, "I'll be in the house, will be waiting to discuss what must be done to retrieve the firm's honor and property," then stalks into the house.

Abigail laughs. She'd like to take Joel with her and Simon into their Kingdom: he'd make such a quaint Court Jester. Her thoughts turn to the fire and the company's ruin: "Simon has laid waste Sara's passionate fields; he has burnt her clutching fingers from his heart. He'll come to me, pure from the sacrifice." She no longer fears or hesitates. She will open the gate right now and look in, will be able to tell Simon of the truth and peace and beauty there, so he'll want to hurry in with her. She does open the gate, averting her eyes at first, then turning determinedly to look in. She gasps, shrinks back in horror, staring with frozen eyes: "It isn't true! It can't be true!" Then, despairingly: "Oh, God, it is, it is!" She hears Simon approaching from the street. He must never see her like this. "I can never face him now, I must never see him again. I must run and hide forever— from everyone on earth. It will be taken into account, won't it, God, if I save him?" She hears his key in the lock. "Ah, Beloved, goodbye forever!" Just as he enters, she passes through the door and closes it silently behind her.

Rushing in exultantly, Simon stops as if he'd come up against an invisible wall: "Mother! Why are you running away? Give me your hand!" She sits down, no longer sees him, stares ahead with childlike, placid, insane eyes: "Life trickles in tears of blood from the burnt-out eyes of love." She smiles, childishly pleased: "I don't know what that means, but it's pretty. I will put it in a poem sometime." Simon asks her what's the matter, what has happened, doesn't she know him? She replies, "There is no you, there is no I. There is nothing here—no one. To be—that does not exist here. It is all long before that—and deep beneath it." He insists: "I am Simon, your son, Simon." She denies that she ever had a son, has ever been married. She's not even been born, and will never be because they tell her life is ugly. Because she knows she is beautiful, she does not wish to live. That is all she'll ever say, for words are useless: "One understands in silence."

Joel has come in, has listened to her and examined her critically. He asks if she knows him. She is silent. He observes, almost with satisfaction, that she's insane, hopelessly insane. "I knew it would come to this. In spite of her pretending to laugh, the news of the fire and ruin was a terrible shock to her." Simon begins to recover his sanity, recognizes that their mother is mad, gone forever. But *he* is alive and the garden is dead and poisonous. Suddenly he asks about Sara, and Joel replies that she has left, as he knew she would. She only married Simon for his money. Simon faints away. Joel examines him, says it's only a faint. "These neurotics are worse than women. I'll take over the business now. I can pull it out. I always land on my feet." He addresses his mother: "I'll look after you. I'll stick to you. Simon will go running back to his brats and that Irish slut—to live in poverty. They don't deserve to be rich. They'll never get a cent from me. I only help the worthy, those who can help themselves." He pats his mother's hand, "Don't worry. Don't be afraid. I'm here." She continues to stare.

The epilogue takes place in a potato field on the farm, in the late afternoon of an early spring day in the following year [1848?]. Sara is working barefoot. Honey, loafing, sings an old Irish ballad. His mother applauds. He does no work, but he does amuse his father. She saw him smile at Honey the other day, the first smile she's seen. Now his mother's death will set him back. But maybe it'll put her out of his mind. Honey says he's glad she's dead: he hated her because she hated his mother. Honey asks if that's not why she stayed away from the funeral. Sara denies this: she pitied his Grandmother Harford, knew that there was nothing she'd hate worse than to have her there, looking down at her, dead. Sara has her idea of honor to an enemy.

But she's through with putting on airs and graces and will be her mother's daughter from now on, the woman Simon loved and married. And hasn't she found herself again, here in this field with her bare feet in the earth? She has strength enough for anything. If it hadn't been for that strength she'd not have found the courage to get them through this past winter—a leaking roof, no money, and Simon sitting staring into the fire at nothing, while she knew he was seeing his mother in the flames, staring in her garden at nothing. Well, now it's spring, and their troubles are over. She'll beat life yet. She has great plans for her sons: Ethan will get rich in shipping; Wolfe, in the bank, will learn the value of the dollar; Jonathan is all set for the railroad, no fear *he* won't succeed; and Honey has the head if only his body weren't so lazy. Honey, in brogue, vows she'll find he does the best of them all, and he'll hang a weight of diamonds on her that'll make her drop. She laughs, but reproves him for the brogue. He asks what about his father? She hasn't mentioned plans for him. She answers that he's worked hard enough; he's a poet at heart and a philosopher and he can go back to his books and his dreaming. Honey comments that her plans to be rich don't exactly jibe with her newfound contentment with her bare feet in the earth. She says it's what his father's always loved and she's kept him from—make what he can out of it with his questions.

Simon arrives. Sara sends Honey on an errand, mothers Simon, makes him sit down. He keeps silent, and she begins to work again, as he watches her. She begins to sing, then stops in confusion, apologizes. He gets up, comes to her and explains that it's over, his mother's gone. The strangest feeling of relief came upon him when her coffin disappeared in the grave. Does that sound inhuman? He's trying to face the truth. He felt suddenly free—free to live—to become a man. As he watched her now, Sara seemed to grow from the soil, the strength of Mother Earth flowing through her out to him. When she sang he suddenly felt spring singing in his heart. The past is dead. They've passed through fire; the dross of greed has been burnt off. He has done with all barren thoughts and scribbling. There are no opposites any more, only Mother Nature. He'll work beside her.

He takes Honey's hoe, starts to weed but suddenly grows weak and dizzy. She sees this and puts her arm around him. He smiles feebly, is afraid he's not strong enough yet. As soon as he is he'll do the rough work. She humors him. But for the present she'll be strong enough for them both. He asks her to sing again. As she does, he falls asleep. She smiles tenderly, vows never to let life hurt him again; he's her poet, her gentleman. But she must get back to weeding if she's to finish before dark. She gets up, takes the hoe, stands leaning on it, looks around with her eyes shining with exultant pride, breathes in the air, her bosom swelling: "I feel young with a thousand lives, singing with youth that can never grow old. Beauty, truth— now *there* are words for fools who need talking to tell themselves why they're alive. But I've known the real thing they mean ages ago!" She laughs merrily at herself: "God forgive me, am I going crazy with a touch of the poet, too? It's hoeing weeds'll cure that!" She sets to work and resumes her singing. Simon sleeps.[4]

In the process of writing this scenario, O'Neill decided to reverse the order of the first and third scenes of act three. He wrote a note to himself that "what has gone before in this Scene [three is] to be revised to fit in with [the] end of Scene II" and then added a new conclusion to the act.[5] Apparently much later, in October 1941, O'Neill considered a prologue set in Abigail's garden. He wrote its scenario, but eventually decided not to use it.[6]

chapter four

April to July 1935

On 25 April, the day before he completed the scenario for *More Stately Mansions*, O'Neill jotted in his *Work Diary*, "New possible title for [the] Cycle[:] 'Threnody For Possessors Dispossessed'(?)" (p. 216). On the twenty-seventh, he made notes for revising the scenarios of the first two plays. He spent a day on general notes and reading and then began work on the third play, *The Calms of Capricorn*, featuring Ethan, the oldest of the four Harford sons, as its principal character. Despite a toothache and a visit from Carlotta's daughter Cynthia and her husband, O'Neill sketched plans for the scenes on shipboard and made other notes. He began the detailed scenario on 6 May and, working almost every day, shifting occasionally to general notes for the entire Cycle, finished it on 9 June. Ideas for possible changes, some of them incorporated, others not, were set down later that month. The scenario, exactly as O'Neill wrote it, with notes of some of the changes not incorporated, appears as part of *The Calms of Capricorn* as published in 1981 and 1982. It follows, generally, the outline O'Neill had made for it in January, except that the first mate no longer dies from natural causes but is struck by Ethan, falls, hits his head, and is killed. A separate character is introduced to serve the minister's role. Nancy, not Ethan, murders the captain, although Ethan does assist her. The final scene differs little from O'Neill's earlier plan for it, except that Nancy joins Ethan in suicide.

In mid-June, O'Neill turned his attention to the fourth play, "The Earth Is the Limit," the story of the second Harford son, Wolfe. By the end of the month he had completed a rough outline, changing the names he had given to several of the characters in the summary made in January. The development of the play had obviously not been established clearly in his mind at this stage, and it is difficult sometimes to be certain of his intentions, but the action seems to be as follows:

A prologue [i.e., act one?] takes place at a hotel in San Francisco two months after the Harfords have landed. Jonathan, who, in this plan, has not been with the family on shipboard, arrives and hears from his brothers the story of the voyage. They tell him that their mother is still in a condition of apathy brought on by the death of Ethan. Honey introduces Elizabeth [formerly Irma] to his brother and, after Jonathan leaves, denies to her that, in spite of their shipboard affair, he has any feeling but friendship left for her. She urges him to go to the mines: she doesn't want him hanging around; the past is over and done with.

Warren [formerly Hull] has proposed marriage to Sara, who doesn't love him but is apathetically willing. Jonathan gives practical reasons why it would be a good idea, but Wolfe is opposed. Sara says that she can keep Warren on the hook for a while; he will be useful in providing capital for her plans—a hotel, a hardware store. Wolfe offers to give his mother twenty thousand dollars from his winnings as a gambler. Jonathan is queerly resentful.

Wolfe and his mother discuss his relationship with Leda [formerly Goldie], who is still in love with him, although he professes to be indifferent to her. He plans to be going around the mines anyway and that will put an end to their affair. Sara says that that may be the best way to get rid of her, but Wolfe denies this as his motive. He says good-bye to Leda, whom he has handed back to Graber. She knows he has given Graber money, and accuses him of doing it to provide for her support. He denies this, but she will not believe him, says that she will find him wherever he goes. [She subsequently gets Sara to tell her his plans.]

Honey promotes a marriage between Jonathan and Elizabeth: "He's as cold and calculating as she; it would be a great match."

The play's first [i.e., second?] act opens two years later, in the winter of 1860, at the same hotel. Sara, rejuvenated, is now absorbed in running the hostelry, which, under her efficient management, has become prosperous. She is now dominated by Jonathan and his idea of life but, underneath, rebels against his rigid morality and willingness to sacrifice everything to success. He and Warren have become partners in a hardware business and have just opened a branch in Sacramento. But Warren is too conservative, is content to stick to his trans-Pacific line of sailing ships. Jonathan has a small share in that and also owns an interest in a freighting line to the Comstock Lode. But he is up to his ears in debt and appeals to his mother for a loan. He asks her if she has sounded Warren out on his marrying Elizabeth. Sara reports that Warren is willing to leave the decision to her; she thinks Jonathan is clever and will go far. He says that is all he wants: he knows he can convince her and doesn't require that she love him.

In a following scene with Graber, Wolfe denies that he is giving him money for Leda: he is giving it as a gambler who has won all Graber had; it is nothing to him what Graber does with it. Graber insists that Wolfe has some responsibility for Leda and, whether or not he acknowledges it, is beginning to fall in love with her. Wolfe denies this, saying that he hates her. Graber replies that he had the same experience of hating loving her; he could never buy her love. When he lost her to Wolfe, he felt free; he still loves her, but without desire now, as a father might. He refuses to take her back.

Wolfe continues to be lucky in his gambling, and Jonathan plans to use the money to add to his capital—but through his mother, because Wolfe's denial of the worth of money humiliates him. He, needing capital so badly and disapproving of gambling, is furious at tales of how Wolfe throws money away. Honey reminds him that this is California—not New England, and suggests that they get their mother to influence Wolfe to set up games in the hotel. Wolfe, approached, is surprised, and asks his mother what their father would say.

The first scene of act three takes place in Sara's hotel, the set showing the hall, the billiard room, and the bar, with a balcony above. Wolfe is dealing to a crowd of players, who have come to take money from a sucker; but he wins. At first they suspect him of cheating, but they gradually become convinced that the game is honest. In spite of themselves, they are at first awed, then admiring, and end by cheering him.

Honey is in and out of the bar, keeps telling funny stories, sings, is very popular, and shows he's no fool when he talks politics.

The following scene is between Jonathan and Leda. She awakens desire in him, which he resents. He offers her money, but she refuses: "I am Wolfe's."

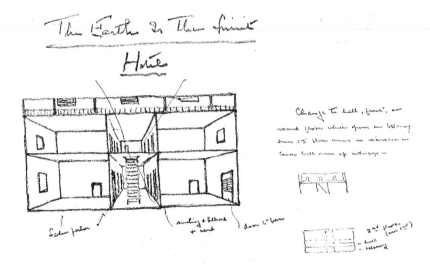

Sara Harford's Hotel, San Francisco, California. O'Neill's design for the set in "The Earth Is the Limit," Play Six of the nine-play Cycle. (YCAL, Size of original: 11.6 × 20.2 cm.) O'Neill has cancelled the center section and has written at right: "Change to hall, front, on/second floor which opens on balcony/over 1st floor rooms—staircase in/lower hall runs up sideways—"; (*sketch at bottom right*) "2nd floor/(over 1st)/-hall/-balcony"; (*at bottom*) "Ladies parlor smoking & billiard/& card door to bar". (Notes in upper right corner do not relate to the set and have not been transcribed here.)

Next, Jonathan appears with Elizabeth on the balcony. They discuss marriage in cold-blooded, business-like terms [as in the scene on shipboard in *The Calms of Capricorn* as published]. Elizabeth, hoping that Leda will get Wolfe—whom she sees as a symbol of all the Harfords—bets Jonathan that Leda will win: "If she fails, I'll marry you at once." He accepts her wager, although he feels that Wolfe cares as little for love as he does for anything else: "He'll soon get tired of Leda's nonsense and see a way to get rid of her."

A scene follows between Jonathan and Sara, who advises him not to marry without love. He argues that Elizabeth doesn't want love, but his mother is not convinced. They speak of Wolfe, and Sara asks Jonathan to do something about him: "Wolfe is becoming a public laughing-stock. We can't afford that."

Next, downstairs, Graber and Leda are at one table, the three Harford brothers at another. Honey, drunk, teases Wolfe about Leda: "Can't you give her her bit of fun?" But he's joking; he understands the real trouble: "If *I* had crazy ideas of life like yours, *I'd* be afraid to put them to the test. She's too beautiful. Once she had you, she'd turn you into her slave." Wolfe protests. Jonathan warns Honey, but agrees with him on one thing, that Wolfe is too much the Puritan Harford, making this into a struggle of Good and Evil. Wolfe answers: "Nonsense! You don't understand. I will not compromise the integrity of my own soul. I will not possess and be possessed." Jonathan replies, dryly: "Then why don't you get rid of her?" Wolfe says he has tried but can't. Jonathan then suggests Wolfe go to Leda, offer her money to sleep with him all night: "Bring this nonsense out of dreams into reality. Make it real to yourself. In the morning you will have bought something, paid for it; she'll be a whore in your eyes and in her own. You will have made the whole thing into something common, of no value." Wolfe is convinced, vows to do it: "Anything to be free again!" Honey tries to dissuade him: "You can't insult the poor woman like that—not if you've a heart in you at all." Jonathan tells Honey to be quiet, accuses him of being a sentimentalist: "Of course, she'll accept—any means to her end."

In the subsequent scene, Wolfe does make the proposition to Leda in the presence of Jonathan and Graber, who also tries to dissuade him. Leda answers that he can't buy her because she already belongs to him; she loves him. He denies this and she starts to go. He asks where, and she replies: "To the dance hall. You've sent me about my business." Wolfe shrugs: "Do as you like. It doesn't concern me. Your life is your own." She replies: "Yes—to throw away." She and Graber go out. Jonathan says: "Well, it wasn't what I expected, but it's just as good. You're rid of her now." As Wolfe stares before him, Jonathan repeats: "I said, you're free now."

In the first scene of act four, at dawn of the following day, Sara tells Honey that Jonathan may marry Elizabeth. Honey supposes he's honorbound to tell Jonathan of their brief affair, although it won't make any difference to him: "He's out to own the world and he'll take any means to that end." Sara wonders if Jonathan's not afraid his means will ever make him theirs. [She makes Honey promise that he won't tell Jonathan.] Honey confides to her: "The only woman I'd be happy married to would be Leda. She knows me for what I am and we'd give each other fair value of what we wanted from each other and, beyond that, she'd let me be free as I'd let her." When Sara remonstrates, Honey accuses her of being jealous. She retorts: "And what if I am? Ethan is dead. I'm done with Wolfe and Jonathan. You're all I've got left." Honey answers: "And you can't lose me, for I wouldn't give your little finger for all the women in the world." Sara replies: "It's you who've kissed the blarney stone."

In the following scene, Graber has finally refused to take any more money from Wolfe, because it keeps him tied to Leda and he wants to be finally free of her. He suggests that Wolfe, in spite of his denials, has taken their game seriously, has been gambling with life, not him, and advises him to try to lose Leda, get someone to bet with him as a symbol. But Wolfe refuses. Graber goes. Elizabeth comes in and taunts Wolfe, gloats over his suffering. He pretends indifference. Then her attitude changes suddenly. She sits down beside him and admits that she knows what he is going through: "The horrible humiliation of feeling one's own spiritual pride dragged in the gutter of desire and of realizing that it is oneself, in spite of oneself, who drags it there." Wolfe denies this, but she insists: "If one could only be without pride—content to love one's love of baseness!" He replies that he loves nothing; he doesn't know what she means. But then he understands: "You mean Honey?" Elizabeth responds: "You know?" and he answers: "I observe." Then she, contradicting what has gone before, says: "Don't let Leda get you. I hate her. It is the love in me which gave itself to Honey, which still desires, which—" Wolfe once more insists that he doesn't know what she's talking about: "Leda is gone. I sent her away. It is finished." Elizabeth answers: "Oh, no, she will never give you up. She will be back." Unguarded, he asks eagerly: "You think so?" She seizes on this: "Ah, you are glad!" Then she triumphs with Leda again, jeers at him: "You are among them but not of them, eh? You will soon be of her." He receives this coldly and says: "You think so? You will see."

Next, Honey comes in with Elizabeth. She would like to resume their relationship, having engaged herself to Jonathan in order to revenge herself on Honey and make him jealous. He cannot see that he would do any injury to Jonathan in sleeping with her. "It means nothing. He'll have all of you. Of course, after you're married, I'd never dream of it." Elizabeth comments: "The Harford honor, eh?" Honey replies: "And anyway he's not in love with you; he wouldn't care: it's not *that* he wants you for but as a business partner." All this drives Elizabeth to make a bet with Honey that

Leda will win. Elizabeth says that she's afraid she's bound to lose, but at the same time she longs for Leda to triumph over Wolfe.

The following scene is between Wolfe and Sara, who tries to comfort him. At his cold denial, she turns against him and his pride. She hopes Leda will come back and conquer.

Leda and Graber enter, and Graber announces that he has brought her back to Wolfe. His own duty is now over for ever. He throws gold on to the floor and shouts: "Sweep this out into the gutter, where it belongs!" Wolfe replies: "Oh, no. I'll not be mocked again—although I'll be glad to pick the money out of the gutter." Leda weeps. Wolfe, distracted, proposes a game: "Who'll play me for her?"

Sara and Elizabeth are indignantly angry at him for betting Leda, reducing womanhood to nothingness. They hope he'll lose, then he'll see—with all his independence. But Elizabeth wants someone else to do the betting—not Honey. He says: "Why not? What do you care about me?" She answers: "Nothing."

Honey *does* bet and wins Leda. Sara objects to her taking him upstairs: "You whore, you! Would you take my baby from me?" And, to Honey: "Would you do this in your own mother's presence? For shame!" Elizabeth joins in: "And in my presence? For shame!" Honey replies: "It's all right, Mother. I'll marry her"; and he and Leda go. Sara and Elizabeth turn on Wolfe with scorn: "You weren't man enough to hold her. You've lost her for ever." But after Wolfe has shot himself they turn on Leda with equal scorn: "You couldn't hold your man."[1]

Probably because he had failed to resolve many points in the development of the plot, O'Neill decided not to write the scenario for "The Earth Is the Limit" but to take up similar rough outlines of the remaining plays. His continuing enthusiasm for the project is reflected in a letter written at about this time to Lee Simonson of the Theatre Guild:

> I've been hard at work practically ever since I came down here—on reading, notes, outlines, scenarios for several new subjects. It's only a short while ago that I finally made up my mind which I'd concentrate on as the next opus. But it's still in the pre-dialogue outline stage and many angles have to be worked out before I'll want to divulge the astounding details. Suffice it that the possibilities are Gigantic, Epic, Colossal, Enormous—as the Hollywood half of the Guild Committee would probably phrase it now,

lightly, in passing—and that this Work has the chance latent within it of making "Electra" & "Strange I[nterlude]." look like variety skits— provided its author can release said latent. In short, it's a challenge to carry on farther than I've carried before, and that's about the only thing that can still rouse my enthusiasm in writing for the theatre.[2]

And now the "astounding details" were again expanded. O'Neill would add a final, seventh play, tentatively titled "Twilight of Possessors Self-Dispossessed," to the series, bringing the action up to the present. For this play he would use a plot that he had been trying to develop, off and on, for almost eight years.

On 12 August 1927, O'Neill had first set down in his notebook an outline, then titled "It Cannot Be Mad":

Billionaire—vast symbolic play of the effect upon man's soul of industrialism—a man, risen from a mechanic, becomes a billionaire—from a man with simple ambitions for success for the sake of wife and family & his standing in community, after his lucky investment with fellow mechanic, money suddenly pours in and bewilders, swamps & corrupts him & his family. It fascinates him by its power. He soon discovers that money is really beyond good & evil, that it can do no wrong. He experiments—even crime can be bought off—the laws whether of man or of God through his ministers are for sale. Money is really God—a billionaire is really God's envoy on earth, to a billionaire all would be possible—he directs his ambitions to become a billionaire—he buys many banks—he concentrates on making money with cash—his final ideal is to possess a billion in gold which will give him control of credit, etc. etc.—In the meantime, this wealth has corrupted his six children, each in a different way they become haunted, neurotic—He has thrown over his first wife, it pleases him to flout the laws, he lives with a harem of kept women, he gives each as an annual present the cost of the exact weight in gold her body represents— he wants their bodies to be gold to him—he is pleased with the illusion that everything he touches turns into gold, that he has the gift of Midas— and in the rear of his immense house he builds a temple, the exact replica of the Taj Mahal, a photo of which he has seen, and in it he puts an enormous solid gold figure of [Dionysus] (God who gave Midas gift). He finally comes to the erratic point where everything he owns that can be made into gold, he has it done—But he finds it necessary to send for his old wife from time to time to tell her about his achievements. She insists on living still in their old cottage, she saves money as she used, in spite of the enormous income he allows her, she is a simple placid soul who thinks everything he does is right, even casting her off. She lives in the faith he will sometime come to visit her and settle down. He is obscurely irritated that he can never make her suffer, he finally dresses her in heavy cloth of gold, he loads her with gold jewelry and a massive crown, her heart gives out and she dies. His illusion is shattered, his is the tragedy of Minos [i.e., Midas], he sees himself and his children, he sees the gold as something that possesses him, he makes up his mind to get rid of it, in a panic he starts to throw it away, give it away, it is hard even to throw away his income. He becomes like [the Emperor] Jones in the forest, his accumulating gold possessing him, he throws it away on everything, he goes in for mad schemes, he gets the idea that to revenge himself on money, to insult it and kill it, he must spend it in absolute stupidity, do nothing useful. He has a mountain removed and builds it up again. His children take alarm—a lunacy commission is appointed. The father with a mad sagacity sets up the defense that a billion in gold cannot be mad, that if he is mad so is all industrial society—the decision becomes a symbol to the world—airplanes wait to take verdict to all countries—masked multitudes before gates chanting "Billion in gold cannot be mad." And this is finally the doctors' verdict and the world rejoices—and the man going into his temple and addressing the statue: "You win," shoots himself.[3]

It was not until October 1928 that O'Neill got around to making a more detailed outline of the play and to beginning work on its scenario (*Work Diary*, p. 59). As he envisioned it,

> There would be two parts, each of two acts, the central characters Howard and Bessie Camp, and Tom Braddock. The action would begin at the farmhouse of Bessie's father, Ed Wilks, in Indiana in 1894, with Bessie a young girl of twelve. Money would be made primarily through Bessie and Braddock's capitalizing on Howard Camp's inventive genius. By 1928 Bessie would have become the moving power in Camp Motors, Inc., of New York, while Camp busied himself with research on rockets. The second act of part two would be laid in the Temple of Midas in Detroit, and the catastrophe would come with a rocket explosion in which Camp would be blinded and [some of?] his and Bessie's four children would be killed.[4]

This seems to have been O'Neill's rough plan for the play, but other matters took precedence, and it was not until February 1929 that he found time to resume work on the project. He began to write dialogue but soon stopped out of boredom; in early March he altered his scheme, working on the first scene according to this new plan. He changed the title to "On to Betelgeuse" and finished act one. He had made revisions in that act and had begun act two when proofs for *Dynamo* arrived from his publisher, Horace Liveright. That play had been unsuccessfully produced in New York by the Theatre Guild while he was living in France. He now had the opportunity to make the changes that he might have made had he been present during rehearsals. The consequent extensive cutting, revising, and rewriting took him the better part of a month. In April, when he was at last free to return to "On to Betelgeuse," he read over what he had already done and, in his *Work Diary*, set down his reaction succinctly as "don't like". Admitting that he had grown stale on the play, he decided to abandon it for the time being (pp. 68, 69). From then until April 1931, with only a few interruptions, *Mourning Becomes Electra* took all of his creative energy.

Although O'Neill made a few more notes for "On to Betelgeuse" in July 1931, other projects again occupied him to its exclusion: production and publication of *Mourning Becomes Electra*, the building of Casa Genotta and consequent move to Sea Island, Georgia, and the writing of *Days Without End* and *Ah, Wilderness!* At the end of September 1932, although he had gone over all he had done of "On to Betelgeuse" and had found a new title, "The Life of Bessie Bowen," he finally came to the conclusion that "inspiration [was] lacking . . . for any urge toward it" (p. 141). He did more work on it in the final months of 1932, but in the first days of the new year he rethought the play, made notes of new ideas, and spent nine hours on a new outline. Preliminary work continued during most of January, in February, and again in April, though with little progress.

The revision, production, and publication of *Ah, Wilderness!* and *Days Without End* took most of O'Neill's attention during the remainder of 1933 and early 1934. Then came a rest cure prescribed by his doctor. Relaxing at Big Wolf Lake in the Adirondacks, he was able for the first time in nine months to entertain at least the idea of writing. He went over his notebook and, during a period of eleven days in August, actually worked a little on a new, third outline for "The Life of Bessie Bowen": "The play was now to open in Bessie's office at the Bowen Automobile Company in Carthage,

Michigan, in 1928, and was to be told in a series of flashbacks: first, scenes of Bessie's childhood in Nazareth, Indiana, in 1891; then scenes from her youth in the same town in 1902; then her young womanhood in 1904, and her marriage to Ernie Wade (formerly Howard Camp). Scenes of success—1915 (?) . . . alternate between Office and Home, each growing larger, more pretentious at every reappearance—noise of factory louder—Wade more & more lonely, lost & pathetic, swamped in his enormous surroundings."[5] The third outline stops in the middle of act three, which like the first two acts, was apparently to contain five scenes. O'Neill reported in his *Work Diary* on 7 September that he was giving up the idea of trying to write while at Big Wolf Lake, feeling "no impulse" for it (p. 196).

Back at Sea Island in November and December 1934, he set down a fresh slant for the play, now called the "Career of Bessie Bowlan," discarding a "combination Talkie scheme" that he had briefly contemplated (p. 203):

The play was still to be in two parts, each now of four acts. The first act would take place in Bowlan's livery stable on a side street just off Main Street in a small town in the Middle West—late afternoon in the spring of 1897 [later changed to 1900]. Act two was to be set in Ernest Wade's bicycle shop, next door to the livery stable, on an afternoon in summer 1901 [later 1903]. Act three would be in Bowlan's garage (the old stable and bicycle shop combined) in the fall of 1907, and act four in the plant of the Bowlan Motor Company in 1908. Act one of part two was to be at the plant in 1928, act two in 1930, act three in 1932, and act four back at the garage in 1933.

The carriage plant goes broke in the panic of 1907. The garage becomes agent for the plant's at first two- and then four-cylinder car. At the outset, the Bowlan Automobile Company cannot afford machinery: everything is made to Wade's designs by outside manufacturers, and only assembled at the plant. By the fall of 1907, Bessie Bowlan has taken complete charge of the company and renovated it.[6] [She] . . . has learned about motors from Wade, reduces him to an assistant mechanic . . . to keep him out of spotlight, encourages him to play with his inventions, his car, which she dismisses as harmless toy—Loft of old livery stable now transformed into a sort of workshop nursery—[She] delivers children [Tom and Bessie] to his care—puts him more & more into state of irresponsible child-like dependence, while at same time [she] consciously feels contempt for him for this—[7]

O'Neill worked on the play all through December (now spelling the name "Bolan"), actually writing part of act one, but on the last day of the year he found himself "Fed up on 'Bessie' for [the] moment".[8] Taking up the play again in January 1935, he found that it was still not right and sketched a "new slant on this—combination of old & new schemes":[9]

> In the new outline (a combination of the third and fourth) part one consists of five scenes of Bessie's childhood (in which some of the principals are masked), revealing her unhappy home life. She becomes engaged to Tom Bradford [formerly Braddock], who is after her for her money. Her father goes bankrupt, murders his mistress because she won't lend him the funds that would tide him over, and then commits suicide. He leaves only the house and the heavily mortgaged garage. Bessie makes plans to run the garage with Bradford. He breaks their engagement, but wants to go on with the business association. Bessie is determined to show that she is a better man than any man in town. She agrees, as a business proposition, to marry Wade, a mechanic in her father's garage, who has given her a plan for a cooling (or lubricating) system, which she has had patented for him. Bradford sees the plan and is impressed by it. He suggests that he and Bessie form a company to market the patent, which becomes the keystone of their commercial success.[10]

Part two was then apparently to follow the earlier plan for it.

Later that month, O'Neill worked out a new fifth outline for the play:

> The opening scene is the office of Bessie Bowen, president and general manager of the Bowen Motor Company, in early spring, 1929. Bessie is being interviewed for radio:
>
> Announcer— . . . the Universal Broadcasting Company is bringing you tonight the first of a series of interviews with the great industrial leaders of America today in which they will tell you their true life histories and, as far as is possible, impart the secret of their success. . . . how rung by rung they climbed the ladder to leadership and preëminence in their chosen fields, . . . how they built up character in themselves, self-discipline, the will to succeed.
>
> The story of Bessie's childhood and youth is told in part one. Part two, opening in 1900, shows Bessie and Wade happy with their children. Bessie has worked with Wade in the shop until the first child was born,

then become mother and housekeeper. But Wade has gotten into financial hot water. By 1906–07, Bessie has taken over. Wade is in the background as a third child. He invents mechanical toys for children. He has secretly worked on a car as a Christmas present for Bessie, to surprise her; has no idea of any commercial value. Bradford's wife flirts with Wade in order to steal the patent. Bessie is jealous. She mortgages Wade's garage to the hilt. The children are neglected, are sent away to school; only Bradford is let in—to take him from his wife and keep him bound to her by greed.

The radio interview reappears in part two, set in the spring of 1928, the last of the series of talks with Bessie. She is in menopause, hints that her husband is insane. The noise of the plant seems to madden her. Bradford comes with an offer of fifty million dollars for the company, but she refuses it. His wife, Louise, gloats to Bessie about her lovers. What does the plant amount to if one is not desired and loved? Wade is putting the finishing touches on a rocket. Bessie has encouraged him but has kept him in the background, a freak inventor, she refusing, through jealousy, to exploit his airplane, talking of him as an impractical dreamer; but he is quite content. Bessie dreams of her old ideal, her two fierce cravings: (1) home, husband, no ambitions; (2) money and power, instilled in her by her upbringing and her inferiority as a woman. The last scene takes place at her old home. Bradford and Wade are playing cards. Bradford and his wife, reconciled, conspire with Bessie's children to take the business away from her. Bessie herself realizes that she is "mad as hell." Wade's rocket explodes, and her love for him is reawakened as she visits him smashed up in hospital.[11]

O'Neill began to write dialogue for the play on 16 January 1935, but only four days later he commented in his *Work Diary:* "this damned play won't come right—not big enough opportunity to interest me—should be part of something, not itself". On the twenty-first, when new ideas for other plays had come to him, he made a firm resolve to "chuck 'B⟨essie⟩. B⟨owen⟩.' out of further present consideration" (p. 208). The play refused to be dismissed, however, and O'Neill told Carlotta at luncheon on the twenty-fifth that he thought he could work it "into the last of his Cycle of "A Touch of the Poet"— (the 5th)".[12] The decision seems not to have become definite until August, when "Bessie Bowen" indeed finds its place as part of the final unit of the seven-play Cycle, then titled "Twilight of Possessors Self-Dispossessed."[13]

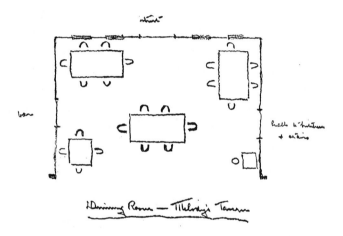

1 Dining Room — Milady's Terrace

chapter five

July 1935

On 3 July 1935, after the Theatre Guild had released a publicity statement about the Cycle, O'Neill made a more extensive report to Robert Sisk:

As to the new project, I'll sketch it briefly for you. (To go into detail would take a book!) It's a cycle of seven plays portraying the history of the interrelationships of a family over a period of approximately a century. The first play [then "The Hair of the Dog," finally *A Touch of the Poet*] begins in 1829, the last [formerly "The Career of Bessie Bowen," then "Twilight of Possessors Self-dispossessed," and finally "The Hair of the Dog"] ends in 1932. Five generations of this family appear in the cycle. Two of the plays take place in New England ["The Hair of the Dog" and *More Stately Mansions*], one [*The Calms of Capricorn*] almost entirely on a clipper ship, one ["The Earth Is the Limit"] on the Coast, one ["Nothing Is Lost but Honor"] around Washington principally, one ["The Man on Iron Horseback"] in New York, one ["Twilight of Possessors Self-Dispossessed"] in the Middle West. As to titles, the [*Mourning Becomes*] *Electra* pattern will be followed—a general title [then "A Touch of the Poet," finally "A Tale of Possessors Self-Dispossessed"] for the Cycle, and one for each play. Each play will be, as far as it is possible, complete in itself while at the same time an indispensable link in the whole (a difficult technical problem, this, but I think I can solve it successfully). There will, of course, be much less hang-over of immediate suspense from one play to another than in *Electra*. Each play will be concentrated around the final fate of one member of the family but will also carry on the story of the family as a whole. In short, it is a broadening of the *Electra* idea—but, of course, not based on any classical theme. It will be less realistic than *Electra* in method, probably,—more poetical in general, I hope—more of *Great God Brown* over and under tones, more symbolical and complicated (in that it will have to deal with more intermingling relationships)—and deeper probing. There is a general spiritual undertheme for the whole cycle and the separate plays make this manifest in different aspects.

And so on. I won't give you any more of that nature because prophecies on that score at this stage are subject to contradiction when actual writing comes. I'm only telling you from the way it shapes up in scenario. I've written detailed scenarios running to 25,000 words each of the first three plays, finished the outline but not the scenario of the fourth, and am now working on the outline of the fifth. I won't start actual dialogue on the first play until I've completed the scenarios of all—that means, late next Fall at the rate so far.

No religion to any of the plays except very incidentally as minor realistic detail.

The family is half Irish, half New England in its beginnings. But the New Englanders are a bit different from any I've tackled before—and so are the Irish. . . .

And that's about all the dope up to date. . . .

I probably won't let the first play be produced until I've got three plays finished and a first draft written of the remaining four. The Guild expect to do the first [play] two seasons after next but it's doubtful if I'll be far enough along by then.

Some of the above information appeared in the statement [Russel] Crouse sent out. But a lot did not. So please keep it under your hat. I sent out that statement to contradict a damn fool rumour in the papers that I was writing a nine-play autobiography! That would be enough to set everyone agin me—and I'd [not] be the last to blame them![1]

O'Neill worked steadily on the outline for the fifth play, "Nothing Is Lost but Honor," the story of Honey Harford, the politician, finishing it on 28 July 1935. It is summarized as follows:

A prologue opens at Sara's hotel in San Francisco in 1860, the night before Wolfe's funeral. His body is laid out on the pool table. Sara, Leda,

Elizabeth, and Honey are seated near the table, all silent, staring before them. Jonathan arrives and Elizabeth, away from the others, tells him that, since she lost their bet on the outcome of the Leda-Wolfe affair, she considers that he and she are engaged. He is exultant, and promises her that she will never regret marrying him. She suggests to Leda that they both leave: she feels that the Harfords would like to confer with their dead, and she and Leda don't really belong in the family yet. Leda addresses the dead man, says that he and she were both beaten, it was a draw. But Elizabeth protests that Wolfe won, proving he'd rather die than go to bed with her. Leda ignores this, says she realizes Wolfe wants her to forget, but is grateful for having known him. Jonathan accuses her of sentimentality, and she and Elizabeth go.

The Harfords, left alone, talk about Wolfe and the reasons for his suicide. Sara has an incongruous burst of pride in him: maybe this was his honor—the honor of a gentleman; he was his father's son and her father's, different from other men; he gave his life for his dream, a high dream you couldn't buy with gold or land—or touch with the love of woman. There was a touch of the poet in him, a poet who couldn't sing and had to live his poem in silence and darkness. She turns on Honey and tells him that he must marry Leda, the family owes her that. They can't see her go into the gutter and be smeared. He agrees. Jonathan is about to protest, but their mother warns him to keep out of this. It may not fit in with his schemes, but, on the other hand, Wolfe had $30,000 and left it all to Leda. Jonathan wouldn't like to see that get out of the family, would he? Leda will give it to Honey, who will let Jonathan use it in his scheming. Sara leaves them and goes up to bed.

The next day, in the presence of them all, Elizabeth tells Jonathan about her shipboard affair with Honey. Honey tries to stop her, but she insists that a business partnership should be founded on an absolutely frank basis. Jonathan asks if she still loves Honey. She replies that she's indifferent to him: love never came into it. Jonathan says, well, then, they can forget it; but he'll expect fidelity. Each agrees that that is part of their bargain: infidelity leads to scandal, and scandal gets in one's way, is bad for business.

Sara and Leda go. Elizabeth points out that it will be desirable that the two families have as little as possible to do with each other; she feels they have nothing at all in common. She leaves. Honey, abjectly contrite, calls Elizabeth a bitch for telling Jonathan about the affair. Jonathan reminds Honey that he's referring to the lady who is to be his [Jonathan's] wife, then shows his real hurt that his brother would have let him marry Elizabeth without knowing. Honey explains that it was their mother who made him promise not to tell. Jonathan says that it doesn't really matter, and tells his brother of his plans. He doesn't care about Wolfe's money, and Honey must think carefully before he marries Leda: her unsavory reputation may endanger his career as a politician. Honey answers that he doesn't care: he doesn't want to own her, nor she him. A shifting population means that the whole thing will soon be forgotten. Besides, he'll have an organization that'll make anyone who does remember sorry that he did. Jonathan concurs in this and tells Honey he can come in on his scheme as a partner. His brother leaves, and Jonathan communes with Wolfe's corpse, justifying himself, explaining his dreams.

Act one opens at the hotel in the summer of 1862(?). Jonathan and Elizabeth have just returned from Washington. The clerk tells them that Sara and Honey are out at a political meeting, and Leda is upstairs with the baby. Shall he call her? Elizabeth says that she wants to tidy up first, and Jonathan accuses her of not having forgiven Leda for marrying Honey. She insists she doesn't care and, if she did, would that bother Jonathan? He admits that it wouldn't. (Both keep up the pose to each other of absolute indifference to the past.) Elizabeth doesn't see why they had to come here, asks him when they are going to have their own home. Jonathan says that that will be as soon as he can spare the money; their savings now have to go to pay for a charter for his Railroad Company. They have one child, Johnnie, who is sickly, and Elizabeth is pregnant again—she says for the last time. Fatherhood means nothing to Jonathan; he hardly knows Johnnie is alive. They argue about responsibility for the child's poor health. He suggests they not blame each other. He has no time to waste on stupid personal matters. He needs her cooperation in keeping her father [Warren] in hand. She agrees on condition they can have their own home in Sacramento, away from here. Jonathan accuses her of wanting to be away from Honey, to whom she had said she was indifferent. She answers that she cares nothing for him, but would think that, for practical reasons, Jonathan would not want Honey associated with his company. He's cheap, vulgar, a liar. Jonathan points out that she has described the ideal politician, and that is just why they need him. They'll use him and when the time comes will drop him, as ruthlessly as if he were a complete stranger. She asks, with eager hatred, if he promises that, and he agrees, but wonders why she is so intense: he thought she'd said she was indifferent.

Leda comes in. Jonathan is struck by the change in her: her beauty has become maternal. Elizabeth is antagonistic. Leda, strangely frightened, comments that Jonathan reminds her of Wolfe. He asks how?—he certainly doesn't *look* like him. Leda merely laughs this off.

Honey and Sara return from their meeting, and the brothers greet each other boisterously. Honey boasts that Jonathan was right in thinking him a natural-born political crook—as crooked as a statesman! But he thinks he'll give it all up in order to enlist: he's greatly stirred up over the Trent affair. Elizabeth encourages him, but Jonathan says merely that they'll discuss it later. The men go. Leda accuses Elizabeth of still hating Honey so much that she wants him to go to war and get killed. She denies this, insists on her indifference. Leda says that, in any case, she wouldn't let Honey enlist; she could laugh the war out of him in five minutes. And if he went to war he'd always talk someone else into getting killed in his place—not that he's a coward, but he'd feel someone was playing him for a sucker if he died for anything as remote as the Union or free Negroes or the stuff he talks about in his speeches to get votes. Elizabeth asks her if she doesn't see how low she makes Honey. Leda answers that she gave up long ago guessing which is high and which low. Honey loves living and that's what she knows about. He loves the joke of life, loves to laugh even at himself. All she wants for the rest of her life is to be a mother and laugh at life—to laugh even at being a mother.

The second scene of act one is set, again at the hotel, later that same year. The Transcontinental Company is meeting to hear Jonathan's report. He's just back from Washington with the charter for his railroad, having spent all the available capital on bribes. Warren is alarmed at this. Honey is cynically amused: there's more money in politics than he had thought; perhaps he'll have to reconsider his decision not to run for office. Jonathan agrees, points out that that's a contribution he can make to the company's success. When Honey still talks passionately about the Trent affair and enlisting, Jonathan remarks dryly that his patriotism is an asset: there are lots of Irish voters. Jonathan silences Warren, outlines plans for a construction company. They are all ecstatic at the prospects. When a lawyer member warns that they must be careful about the laws, Jonathan smiles and comments that he has just bought one law although it cost all their available capital; state laws will come cheaper. They must get the railroad started at once in order to begin collecting money from the government.

The third scene of act one, set in the hotel parlor, actually occurs simultaneously with the first scene: dialogue from one, then the other, the women's scene on the ground floor, the men's in the room directly over it. [A similar technique had been used in some of the scenes on shipboard in *The Calms of Capricorn*.] Elizabeth and Leda, both visibly pregnant with their second children, discuss childbirth with Sara. Elizabeth dreads the idea of bearing her second child, is having it only because she had heard that Leda was pregnant and to prove she is as much a woman as her sister-in-law. Searching for love in a loveless marriage, she also thought she might love her children, especially if she had a daughter. For Leda childbirth is nature. She wanted a boy, and got one—Cornelius (named for Sara's father), healthy and husky, like Honey. She looks forward to her second child, wants another boy. Honey himself is her eldest: she has good natured, maternal affection for him and doesn't mind his infidelities. Sara joins in with reminiscences. She's glad she's beyond the age for all this and is at peace, and yet at the same time she is envious. But she asserts proudly that all four of her children were born of love. Leda says hers was born of natural physical desire and nothing more. Elizabeth asks, was she dreaming of Wolfe when—? She answers that she's forgotten him; he wouldn't want her memory chasing him. She turns on Elizabeth: was *she* thinking of Honey when—? Elizabeth fiercely denies this: Honey was never anything to her. They talk of the men's meeting, and Elizabeth and Sara express pride in Jonathan's ability. Elizabeth says that her husband consults her in everything he does, considers her advice invaluable. Sara is stung at this: Jonathan has said the same thing to her.

The fourth scene of act one is back at the men's meeting as it breaks up. Jonathan has been authorized to proceed with his plans. The engineer congratulates him as a fellow dreamer, saying that he wouldn't care if they never made a nickel. Jonathan at first gives way to this, then repudiates it: he wants every cent he can get; money is power to do things.

Warren and Honey join the ladies, both loud in praising Jonathan: Sara and Elizabeth ought to be proud of him. They answer together that they are, then stare at each other resentfully. But Warren is uneasy about Jonathan's recklessness: he's as big a gambler in his way as— He stops, embarrassed, and Sara says: "As poor Wolfe was, you mean?" Warren needn't mind bringing Wolfe up on her account: she's forgotten him, who never remembered her. And Warren is mistaken: there's nothing of Wolfe in Jonathan—none of his crazy dream. Elizabeth agrees; but Leda speaks up suddenly: "I'd never thought of it before, but Jonathan *is* like Wolfe."

Jonathan comes in, asks Leda who is like Wolfe? She answers that *he* is. He stares at her, asks in what way? Warren says that he's a gambler. Jonathan replies, "Oh, that. But I take risks to show how much I care; Wolfe took them to show how little he cared." Sara tells him that they had said he was a dreamer like Wolfe and she had denied it. Jonathan agrees; facts are his dream. Warren is about to go, and asks if Elizabeth and Jonathan are coming with him. Jonathan starts to join them, but his mother says she wants to talk with him.

In the first scene of act two, the rooms in the hall of the hotel are seen from the side street, the balcony and main street at the right. It is election night, 1864, and they are celebrating Honey's winning the contest for mayor. He makes a speech from the balcony expressing his jovial, cynical contentment—confidence that he can continue as long as he likes.

The next scenes are in two rooms, run concurrently, and finally join. In one, Elizabeth and afterwards Honey, Sara, and Leda, are just back from a triumphal speech-making tour of the town; in the other, there is another Transcontinental Company meeting. The scene shifts from Elizabeth in the room below, to the meeting above, then back to Elizabeth and Leda, then to the uproar outside in the street. The band plays "Hail the Conquering Hero." Below, Honey and Sara join Leda and Elizabeth. Above, the meeting breaks up. Below, Jonathan joins the others, tells Honey to make a speech to the crowd, get them to disperse. He goes out and *à propos* of nothing at all, boasts that he'll deal with Queen Victoria if she should ever come to San Francisco. He ends on the slogan: "Honey for all." Returning, he explains his speech cynically: they are just the same as we are—want all they can get for nothing, and want to believe they're going to get it. If he could even become President, wouldn't that be the grandest joke ever was known on earth? He roars with laughter.

Elizabeth asks Jonathan why he is insisting that his brother go into politics. He explains that he needs to have someone in Washington whom he can trust absolutely. Besides, he likes Honey, wants him to succeed. When she suggests that he may be over-proving to himself that he bears his brother no grudge, Jonathan denies it, but she insists that the thought is still alive in his mind, that he has some plan. When he sketches the career he proposes, Honey at first refuses, and the women back him up. Jonathan silences Elizabeth by asking her if she doesn't want Honey to rise: surely she doesn't still bear him a grudge for her weakness on shipboard? Honey, embarrassed, asks Jonathan if he hasn't forgotten that, and Elizabeth warns Honey that he hasn't. Jonathan's explanation that his brother is the only one he can trust wins Honey over, although Leda still holds out: they don't need the money. Jonathan, scornful, asks who's talking of money? It's dreams. She, frightened, accuses him of being like Wolfe—not human; but Honey agrees that his brother is right: there's no such thing as too much money. Finally, Leda and Elizabeth are left alone. Leda asks her sister-in-law what Jonathan is trying to do. Elizabeth confesses she doesn't know, but offers to join forces with Leda against him.

The first scene of act three is set on the plains of Utah, in May 1869. The ceremony of the Golden Spike is to take place the next morning. At a meeting of the Holding and Finance Company in a private car the night before, it has been decided to burn the books and wind up the company's affairs after the sale of a final issue of bonds. Warren has used up all his profits in buying a monopoly on coast shipping. He is outraged at the revelations about the company, but Jonathan silences him. He plans to go to Washington with Honey and do his best to stave off an investigation by distributing bribes of stock: the people in Congress will look out for their own property. He points out that it would be bad for the railroad if the Holding Company scandal broke while he was still head of the railroad, and proposes that the others buy him out. Of course Elizabeth and Honey will stay on and be able to claim that they forced Jonathan to sell.

After the meeting breaks up, he tells Honey the truth: the records must be destroyed. He advises his brother to sell out. Honey is eager to build San Francisco the finest hotel in the United States. Jonathan points out that it will never make money, but Honey doesn't care; besides, it will be a good advertisement for him politically. Jonathan argues that the time is not yet. He wants Honey to turn his money over to him. Honey is mystified: he thought the railroad was the darling of his brother's heart. Jonathan replies that it *will* be when it's his. This is the only way to get Warren out. He's getting old and too cautious—no vision; he would make the railroad subservient to sailing ships. As the scene ends, Honey explains that he has promised the ladies they can see the laborers working at night by the light of the bonfires. He persuades Jonathan to go with them; it'll do him good to forget his dream of owning America for a while.

The following scene is on top of a butte (or hill). Honey, Sara, Leda, and Jonathan stand together, Honey and Sara excited and enthusiastic. Honey reproves his brother for his coldness: this is a great moment, a tremendous achievement. The harder part—east over the Sierras—was Jonathan's; the road from the Missouri west was just over the plains. Honey brings in Irish patriotism, rationalizing his enthusiasm cynically. He'll have to put all that in a speech for his Irish districts, for in every Irishman is a vote. But he admits he'll have hard work explaining why Jonathan needed so many Chinamen, and why Honey, whom they regard as the power behind the throne, allowed his brother to employ them. Jonathan tells him to say that there weren't enough Irish and he had to hire ten Chinamen to do one Irishman's work. Honey accepts this enthusiastically. Sara scolds him for his cynicism, but is proud of both of her sons. She dreams of money pouring in: she will be able to have her estate, and Honey will have his hotel.

He tries out the climax of the speech he plans to deliver at the next day's ceremonies. He's worried about the rate of progress from the east, will go and speak to the workmen. He asks his mother to go with him, tells her the laborers like to be reminded that their statesmen were born of woman; otherwise they'd soon believe them monsters. As he goes, he has the wonderful idea of taking off his coat, grabbing a pick, and helping. He asks Jonathan if he's coming, but his brother refuses: "No. They stink of sweat. It nauseates me. I can't help it." Honey grins, says that if Jonathan read his speeches he'd know that "the sweat of honest labor is America's perfume of Araby."

Leda starts to go with Honey and Sara, but Jonathan grabs her arm, motions her to stay behind. She, almost frightened, asks him what he wants of her. He pretends at first that he wants to tell her she's being a bad influence on his mother, is encouraging Sara's easy indulgence. She retorts that Sara should be allowed to live for herself, have some fun. He agrees, but says this isn't the time for it: he still needs her. Leda asks if there's not something else he wanted to talk about, and he confesses: it's himself. He talks about his plans, and says that only she can understand his motives, his feeling that the end justifies the means. She becomes enthusiastic, asks him if he wants her to tell him he's justified. He insists that he *is* justified, feeling her life beside him justifies him. He kisses her. She is America for him tonight—a symbol in the darkness. But she is frightened: she doesn't want to be a symbol. She *was* that for Wolfe, who couldn't see her even though she loved him; and when he finally did see her and loved her, he ran away into death. Jonathan comments that *he* won't run away from her into death. When she protests that he's certainly not trying to tell her that he loves her, he agrees, asks her what they have to do with love? or desire? He wants power. Life is the reward of power. Perhaps when he has the power he will claim his reward of her. They go to join Honey and the others.

In act four, the scene shifts to the New York home of Jonathan and Elizabeth. He is meeting with a fellow businessman, Goddard. They have sold the railroad stock short to the hilt; an upward flurry of the market would ruin them. Jonathan has decided to throw Honey overboard, to give information, through Goddard's agents, to the newspapers—the list of those whom Honey has bribed, and full details. Warren, Elizabeth's father, has come to the rescue of the railroad stock. He has strained his credit to the limit and is on the verge of ruin, with his Shipping Company mortgaged. He comes to New York to try to raise more money, appealing to Jonathan for help, which Jonathan cannot give. When Warren, in desperation, asks him to accept control, Jonathan again refuses.

The next scene is between Jonathan and Elizabeth. Her father has asked her to plead with Jonathan, but she is too proud. He points out that it is too late: a false move now would ruin *him*. She says that the blow to her father's pride will kill him; besides, it's in Jonathan's interest, since she is her father's heir. He answers ironically that he's already indebted enough to her, promises to give her all the money she wants. She says then he'll think he owns her at last; he has great confidence in his star. He answers, no—in his dream. She asks about his brother's money. Jonathan tells her that it is safe, and she comments: "So Honey isn't to be punished—or Leda, whose fault everything was?" Jonathan insists he doesn't know what she means, but she accuses him of never having forgiven her. If she knew he was doing this to punish her, because he was jealous, she could accept it. He has never believed that she has grown to love him. He says there's no place for love: this is a business proposition. As for Honey, if he suffers, it will be only politically. She seizes on this, "So you *are* punishing him." He asks if she'd care, and she insists she despises Honey and hates Leda. He says, then it's settled: Honey will get a chance to ruin himself. And now he, Jonathan, must go to Washington. He leaves, and she rushes to go there herself—to warn Honey, who is the father of her first child. It's her duty for the child's sake—and in memory of the only joy of self-surrender she's ever known.

The second scene is at Honey and Leda's home in Washington. It is night, a few days later. Leda and the children appear. She has become indifferent to them, has exhausted motherhood as an emotion. Sara arrives (Jonathan is at his apartment). They discuss Elizabeth, Jonathan, and Honey. Honey comes in, drunk, gives a laughable account of the day's proceedings in the Senate. He grows serious. He has become disillusioned: most of the senators are cowardly crooks. He thinks he'll get out at the end of his term, is bored hearing himself talk the same old bunk. Sara is scornful, says he'll fool 'em into making him President yet. She asks him why he is blue, has anything happened? He admits that he feels something hanging over his head—not a hang-over either. They laugh, relax, and drink together.

They talk again of Jonathan. Honey wonders what he is up to. Sara advises letting him alone: he's promised her he'll make them all rich. Honey says he'd like to get their projects started, and talks about their plans. Sara, tired from her trip, goes to bed. Honey and Leda continue the conversation. He tells her she's not been herself lately, asks what's the matter? She says she wishes she could feel alive, would like to set fire to the house and watch it burn, and dance naked and scream with joy. Honey agrees: he likes bonfires; they remind him of elections. She can dance and he'll make a speech to the crowd on the sacred rights of property and the sanctity of the American home. But she must give him time to raise the insurance first. She laughs, and calls him a nut; but she forgives him everything because he can always laugh, even at himself.

He goes to meet Jonathan at his apartment. But just then Elizabeth arrives, warns Honey that his brother plans to betray him. Honey denies that Jonathan would do such a thing; they've been chums from childhood. He goes, promising not to tell Jonathan that his wife is in Washington. Leda comes in, and she and Elizabeth talk, with the hate-love, repulsion-attraction between them very much in evidence, along with jealousy in relation to Jonathan. Elizabeth tells Leda of Jonathan's scheme to ruin Honey, but asks her not to tell Honey that she told her. Leda sees at once where Honey will be really hurt—his brother's double-cross. In the end the two women acknowledge their mutual attraction. Their lives are two parts of one life, and Elizabeth says she is betting on Leda again. Leda professes not to understand what she means.

The third scene of act four is laid in Jonathan's Washington apartment. He is alone, indulging in self-examination, remembering Elizabeth's accusations. Honey won't mind being ruined, and the ruin will make him rich. But he can't keep the personal aspect from his thoughts: he and his brother have always been so close. He gradually silences his conscience. As for his mother, she must never know.

Honey comes in, at first jokingly admiring and affectionate, then uneasy at Jonathan's manner, asks: "What's up?" He is genuinely concerned, but his concern is for Jonathan. His brother explains, in the most cold, matter-of-fact way, that Honey's political ruin is necessary to his plans, that Honey's own fortune is involved. Honey says: "To hell with that—we're thinking of you now." Jonathan explains his position, how he can get control, through panic, of various railroads and shipping lines to the Orient. Honey: "And what do you want me to do?" Jonathan: "Confess, resign, read list of bribes." Honey: "What? Squeal? No, I could never do that. Most of the people we bribed were members of our party. I must be loyal to the party." Jonathan: "How about being loyal to the country?" Honey (grins): "As everyone knows, it's for the good of the country to leave our party in. You must find some other way." Jonathan: "There is no other way. If you don't, *I*'ll give lists to the paper, etc." Honey (really stricken, bewildered): "You wouldn't do that to me, after our life-long friendship, for money, for a damned railroad?" Here Jonathan justifies himself—his dream; but Honey waves this aside, cynically: "Keep that bunk for the interviews!" Jonathan (angry): "You don't believe?" Honey: "No! And neither do you!" Jonathan: "You lie! I do! But, of course, you can't understand: you have no dream beyond your belly, gold, a woman's body! By God, that's what I can't forgive, why I hate you!" Honey: "Hate me? Don't say that. You're the only person I love, except Mother." Jonathan: "I mean I hate that in you." Honey: "I know you didn't mean it. (Then, miserably): Hate me! And you'll double-cross me, you'll ruin me. I don't understand. If you'd only some human reason—to get your own back from me—some wrong I did you—then I'd be only too glad, if this would make it square between us. But I never did you any wrong, I'd have cut my heart out first." Jonathan: "You lie! You're forgetting—Elizabeth." Honey: "Ah! A woman's body, you said. So that's it." Jonathan: "Shut up!" Honey (overjoyed): "Ah, now I see why. She told you—before you married—so as to be honorable, the fool!" Jonathan: "Shut up!" Honey: "I understand now—even if I think you're foolish, for what did it amount to between us but a little fun? There was plenty left for you." Jonathan: "Shut up!" Honey: "Well, I understand anyway, and now I'll take my medicine graceful, and it'll all be square and we can start all over. Sure, I might have guessed, only I never dreamed that you loved her." Jonathan: "I don't. I *might* have loved her, and she me." Honey is grief-stricken: "I'll pay." As he speaks, he sees how he can dramatize the situation, make a martyr of himself, for the party's good, etc., his speech, he'll make 'em cry. He'll justify himself for giving the list. Then he becomes greedy: he'll have lots of gold—his hotel. Jonathan is contemptuous: his belly. Honey is indignant: his dream. Jonathan then asserts coldly that he was lying: there is no question of Elizabeth; his brother was simply in the way. But Honey waves this aside: Jonathan is human at the bottom, like them all—as Wolfe was. He offers to shake hands. His brother insists it's all a matter of business. He'll promise to make five millions for Honey, who can retire and drink himself to death in his damned hotel.

Honey feels that Jonathan still has it in for him. He has noticed that

Leda has been making eyes at him, is tired of her husband. Jonathan is shocked, but Honey insists that he'd like his wife no less if she slept with Jonathan. He wants her to have all the fun she can from life. He goes, a bit pathetic at the end about forgiving. At bottom, there are only his mother, he, and Jonathan in the world. Jonathan, left alone, is violently agitated, furious at his brother. And yet Honey is right: "What are all those things we make a fuss over? We're pigs fighting to win our sows and a place in the trough, to keep other swine away."

Leda arrives. She hasn't seen Honey. She comes straight to the point: why is Jonathan planning to ruin his brother? Jonathan asks her how she knew, but she refuses to tell him; she won't stand for it, that's all. He becomes cold, driving, begins to seduce her with utter unscrupulousness. What is Honey to her? She is horrified, calls him a monster, but is all the time fascinated by him. He reminds her of the night of the Golden Spike, tells her he is going to take possession of the railroads—of the country. And she is his, too; he wants her. She agrees that she wants to be possessed, and he takes her into the bedroom, she alternately resisting and surrendering.

The next morning, when he tries to offer his utopian excuses, Leda, in a rage, bawls him out as a hypocrite. He insists what he says is true, and he'll prove it in the end; but he's got to win control first, that is necessary for his dream. Leda now pretends that she surrendered to him in order to save her husband. He professes moral guilt toward Honey and Elizabeth; then when Leda tells him he's lying, he feels triumph instead of guilt: love was too strong for him. Leda laughs at his making love his moral excuse; he means love for his wife. He denies this, but she insists. And she'll make him pay for last night through Elizabeth, and through his mother: she (Leda) will tell her. Jonathan forbids it; she's his property now. When she again insists that it was to save Honey that she let him take her, he accuses her of lying and she admits it: she wanted possession. Jonathan says that he wanted possession of his own desires, by taking her he possesses them again. She's nothing to him now. He gives her back to Honey, this time without reservation.

Leda asks if that means he won't ruin his brother. He agrees that it does, but adds that he can't help it if Honey ruins himself—and refuses to explain his meaning. He bids her goodbye, advises her to tell Elizabeth about their sleeping together and say she can divorce him whenever she wishes. He no longer needs a wife; thanks to Leda, he has passed through that desire and come out in freedom on the other side. But there's no need for a divorce: Elizabeth can have her freedom—and all the lovers she wishes. As his wife she'll get more money, for divorce is a trade and he'd naturally drive the hardest bargain he could. When Leda says that Elizabeth has her own money, her father's, Jonathan assures her that by tonight he thinks that that will be money she had once but has no longer.

The fourth scene of act four takes place the following evening at the home of Honey and Leda. Leda is alone. A servant brings in the paper and she reads that the scandal has broken. As Sara enters, Leda hides the paper. She pleads with Sara to go with her, Honey, and the kids back to 'Frisco. But Sara feels she must stay with Jonathan, who needs her. Leda comments that he needs no one, but Sara insists that he has to be helped at times to believe in his great dream. Leda asks about Sara's own dream—her estate. She replies that that's no dream: she'll soon have enough through Jonathan—and that's another reason for staying with him. But as soon as she's in society, she'll tell 'em all to kiss her arse and will live alone. She goes.

Leda resumes reading the paper, grows puzzled. Elizabeth arrives, in a rage at the news, but satisfied too. She tells Leda that she has lost again. Leda agrees. Then Elizabeth expresses her sympathy. Leda tells her Jonathan really loves her, though he'll never let himself know it. She answers that she does love him, but will never tell him so because he'd never believe it. So that's over. Leda agrees that there's nothing to do but pray he gets his dream, help him to it, then she'll have her revenge, for he'll be alone, with hands and heart and soul empty of everything but guilt. She gives his message to Elizabeth, who agrees that she will have lots of lovers, suggests that they have them together. But Leda says she's finished. Elizabeth then offers herself: she's always wanted to love Leda, to be loved by her. The Harfords have driven her to the wall.

They talk of the panic. Elizabeth's father is ruined, and she is penniless, has only Jonathan's millions. But what of Honey? Elizabeth will make Jonathan pay. Leda says that's what she thought at first, but now she's not sure that Honey hasn't had the biggest day of his life. When Elizabeth protests that Jonathan has betrayed him, Leda explains she's sure he has told Honey it was revenge for the affair with her. Honey would forgive for that. Elizabeth says, "Oh, those Harfords. They cheapen life to dirt." When Leda admits she hasn't told Sara, Elizabeth rushes out to tell her in spite of Leda's trying to keep her from it.

Elizabeth soon returns with Sara, who is furious at the lies reported to her about Honey. When Leda confirms the report as true, Sara justifies him: "That's all a part of politics. There's never been honor in politics— but still he shouldn't have done it." Elizabeth says that Jonathan made him do it.

The scene shifts to Honey and Jonathan. Honey, half drunk, says he'll tell their mother that someone had the list and he, Honey, only beat him to the punch. Jonathan, deeply moved, says he'll never forget this. Honey says aren't we the best brothers in the world and all old scores forgotten?

They join Leda and Sara, who attacks them as soon as they enter. Honey appears broken by this: isn't it bad enough without his own mother joining in? Jonathan tells her the list was given out, and Elizabeth adds, "Yes, you gave it!" Honey roars, "Who says that about Jonathan, that he'd double-cross me?" He explains to their mother that he had to beat the others to it. He made the greatest speech of his life. He has resigned and they can't kick him out. And the reaction on Wall Street has been just what Jonathan wanted: the panic is on; he can pick up his railroad for a song. He'll make millions for them; Sara will have her fine estate and he'll have his hotel. There's nothing lost but a bit of honor and he never had it anyway and they think him more honorable now than ever before. Sara stares at him, mumbling that she doesn't know, she doesn't know. Suddenly Honey bursts into tears, tells her not to look at him like that. It's not like herself she is now but like his father's ghost. She addresses the ghost: "Go away now, Simon. Will you never stay dead? It's not Honey's fault at all, and don't you blame him, for he's my son." She too begins to sob.

Jonathan speaks coldly, tells her not to be sentimental. All of this will be forgotten tomorrow; it's part of his plan, part of his dream. She believes this, doesn't she? She replies, "Of course, I believe," and Honey, re-covered, joins in. Jonathan turns to Elizabeth, who answers, "Of course, Jonathan. I am your wife." And then he addresses Leda, who replies, "How could I *not* believe, Jonathan? I'm your—" The three women all burst into tears.

Jonathan, himself once more, tells them brusquely to stop it: he can't stand sentimentality. They are all going to New York. He has to be in the office in the morning. There's nothing more to do here. He suggests that Honey and Leda take a trip abroad, let things blow over. Then he comes back to his triumph: "By the end of the week I'll have control of—!"[2]

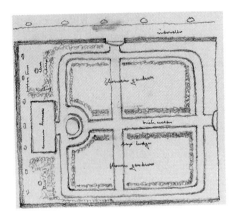

chapter six

July to September 1935

On 29 July 1935, O'Neill made further general notes for the entire Cycle and prepared a Melody-Harford family tree. The next day he went fishing with neighbors and on the thirty-first began the detailed outline for the sixth play, of Jonathan Harford, "The Man on Iron Horseback." On 8 August he came down with sore throat and worked on notes on the psychological and hereditary pattern of the whole Cycle until he felt better, resuming work on the sixth play on the thirteenth, finishing the outline on the twenty-seventh. It is doubtful that, in his plans for this play, O'Neill got any further than rough notes of scenes, in haphazard order, feeling that much of the action would depend on how the preceding plays in the Cycle evolved. The following summary indicates merely how, at about this stage, he seems to have conceived of the play. The order of the scenes is based primarily on a later outline:

> The first scene of a prologue is laid in the New York home of Jonathan and Elizabeth, in 1874 or 1875. All four children— Jonathan and Elizabeth's Johnnie and Beth, and Honey and Leda's Con and Sara—have been left with their grandmother, who is acting as Jonathan's housekeeper and hostess. She and they play together the games her sons used to play. The children leave, and the maid comes in. To her Sara expresses her weariness and boredom: she longs for Honey to make her laugh, for Leda's companionship, and shows resentment against Elizabeth for having saddled her with most of the responsibility for the children. She drinks, gradually becomes drunk, and sings Honey's song. The maid cautions as to what Mr. Harford will say, but Sara dismisses this: "He'll never notice, never see, and, thank God, I'm my father's daughter; I can hold my liquor like a lady."

Jonathan returns, triumphant. He has control of the Western and Trans-Missouri Railroad, has beaten Goddard to it. Goddard will never forgive him: there'll be a fight from now on. Jonathan has cabled Honey, Leda, and Elizabeth to come home, indicating to Sara that he feels they all belong to him now. She is caught up in his triumph, and boasts of her own success socially: they thought she'd be an ignorant monster, but she's proved she can play the lady with the best of them. She wishes, almost vindictively, that her father could have lived. Jonathan, startled, asks why she brings him up. It's as if a ghost had entered the room. They fall silent.

Then Sara asks him for her money: she wants to be able to retire. He grows uneasy: he can't give it to her right now; he needs it to make his control more secure. Sara is bitter. He becomes suspicious, frightened: can it be that she doesn't believe in the worth of his dream—to be a benefactor of humanity? He hasn't said much about it of late, but that's only because there was no time for it during the depression, and now he has consolidated his gains.

Sara has finally to reassure him. He brightens, tells her that she won't feel so lonely when the others get back. He asks her what news she's had from Honey. She says that he's homesick. He's been to every café, restaurant, and hotel in Europe, is full of ideas. She tells Jonathan, emphatically, that he must give Honey *his* money—for the hotel: she'll have no nonsense about that. When he explains that he can arrange it with first-mortgage bonds, she asks if he means that the hotel is to be built of paper. He answers: "Paper is more powerful than gold: it creates something from nothing. I'll take up the controlling interest in the bonds myself." But his mother insists there be no mortgage: the money must be Honey's and free or she'll leave. Jonathan protests, but finally gives in.

He asks what else Honey writes. She replies that the girls are having a fine time. Jonathan has heard all about that from Elizabeth, who writes every week, addressing him at the office, thinking it mocks his work. She tells him in detail about her lovers, saying that she knows his passion for facts. Sara is outraged: "You ought to divorce her!" He answers: "That would be to give up my property. I can't do that—and Elizabeth will never divorce me. I'm sure that Leda is behind all this—it's her revenge. But I have reports that Elizabeth's men get tired of her in spite of my money, with which she tries to hold them. They turn to Leda, but *she* has remained faithful. And you'd think Elizabeth would hate Leda, but they've grown to be inseparable friends. We'll know all about it when the travellers get home."

His mother says that it'll be grand to hear Honey laugh and sing again. Jonathan frowns, grimly reproving: "My report is that Honey has stopped laughing and singing, has become unhappy; otherwise I couldn't consent to bringing him home; it would be too indecent, too shameless. What would our father have thought of Honey laughing and singing after having made the Harford honor a byword for corruption?" Sara, momentarily crushed, bursts into drunken brogue: "It's a cub like you to be waking your father out of his grave. Shut your mouth or, old as you are, I'll put you across my knee and whack your behind for you!" Jonathan accuses her of being drunk, remarking dryly that he doesn't think his father would have liked to see her in that state. She insists she's not drunk—and anyway Simon understands her.

The second scene of the prologue shifts to Paris, to Honey and Leda's hotel suite. He is miserable, homesick, and lonely, resentful against Jonathan. The women come in. Elizabeth, in order to look more like Leda, has dyed her hair blond, with startling effect. The two join in mothering Honey, bossing him, scolding him. They suggest that he go for a walk. He tries to be cheerful, but breaks down pathetically. Since Jonathan has double-crossed him the world has become untrustworthy and he is morbidly suspicious. They finally succeed in persuading him to go out.

In the following scene between the two women, Elizabeth is shown to have come completely under Leda's domination. She loves it, but is at the same time deeply humiliated and resentful. The strange alliance of love-hatred between the two is unconsciously Lesbian on Elizabeth's part. Both have the sense of belonging to Jonathan and hating him for it, desiring revenge. They rationalize their feeling as hate for what he did to Honey, for whom both show exaggerated maternal care. It is Leda who encourages Elizabeth's affairs as revenge. They make her a whore, while at the same time Leda remains faithful—faithful, as she rationalizes it, to Honey, with remorse because she has been unfaithful to him, but really to Jonathan. She has become the moralist, Elizabeth the immoralist.

Elizabeth confesses to Leda that she loves Jonathan—or hates him, she doesn't know which. In any case she feels she belongs to him, body and soul, and can't free herself. Her reasons for hating him are not reasons at all: he didn't ruin her father, who would have died anyway, and who was a dirty lecherous old man, as Leda well knows. Leda says that his having slept with her on the ship ought not be held against him: he was a poor, lonely old man using her to remind himself of his lost youth, to make a passionate face at death.

Jonathan's cable arrives, telling them to come home. They grow excited. Leda can prove she has been faithful to him. Elizabeth has proved she is as sexually attractive as Leda. They will go back to collect. Honey returns from his walk. When they tell him of the cable, he is at first overjoyed, then overcome by fear and guilt. They coddle him like a child.

The third scene of the prologue is set again in Jonathan's New York home, a few weeks later, shortly after the travellers' return. He has got control of the Central Pacific, and now has a scheme for getting possession of the Union Pacific. Elizabeth tells him she assumes he will want a divorce. But he denies this, says that her unfaithfulness in Europe means nothing to him. He forbids it here at home however—for the children's sakes. She ridicules this: "You don't know they're alive!" He says: "Well, then, for social reasons—for the sake of my mother: she has turned into quite a social climber while you've been away." Then, impatiently, he adds: "For the business's sake: scandal now would hurt my plans." He understands her resentment and her wanting revenge because she blames him for ruining her father and disgracing Honey. She denies this: "You weren't to blame for my father's ruin—and I care nothing about Honey." Jonathan agrees that Warren's ruin was his own fault—his blind greed. And Elizabeth is now worth more than if she had inherited all that money. She asks if she can have it, and he answers: "No, I need it just now." She laughs: "I don't want it anyway." Jonathan: "That's just as well since you can't have it!"

She proposes a reorganization of their bankrupt relationship. She made the mistake of getting emotional and falling in love, but that feeling is now dead. She admires his ruthless ambition and wants him to let her in on his plans. She'll prove to him that she can be a valuable partner. She goes. He is moved, starts after her, then forces himself to be rational: he was getting sentimental. After all, she is quite right, and this is exactly as he would wish it. Elizabeth has brains; she can appreciate what he is trying to do.

The first scene of act one is set in Jonathan's office in 1885. He has now gained control of both the Central Pacific and the Union Pacific and is scheming to get the Eastern. It has come down to a duel between him and his principal rival, Goddard. They meet as friendly enemies outside their offices. It is part of their pride to keep this up, never mentioning shop. In reality, when they meet in their offices, they just sit together, secretly scheming. After a desultory conversation in which they discuss with wary indifference the things they have bought and their supposed hobbies, there is a blackout in the middle of the scene. A clock registers the passage of two hours. Then the curtain rises again and the two resume their wary conversation. Again they become silent; then Goddard goes, saying that he has a hard day before him tomorrow; he wishes he could sleep.

In the second scene of act one, either Elizabeth or Sara has had a doctor come to examine Jonathan at his new house. The doctor cautions him against overwork, tells him to rest or he is liable to pop off. Jonathan's reaction is mixed: subconsciously he welcomes the news, but, consciously, he waves it aside brusquely: he's too busy, has no time to die yet. He'll go when his work is done.

The third scene of act one is set at Sara's estate. Jonathan has at last turned over to her the money with which to purchase the property, and she has made extensive investments in land. But she has come to feel that he is lost to her—more so than Simon ever was in his book. It has become an obsession with her that Jonathan will ruin himself as Simon did.

Jonathan comes to visit her, in the evening. He is caught up by the beauty and peace of the night, and speaks with longing and poetry. Sara is deeply moved, speaks of the song of a poet in him. At once he chills: he's sorry Honey isn't here to sing "The River Shannon." She unsuspectingly agrees. He tells her that he has arranged the first-mortgage bond issue that will enable Honey to build his hotel. Of course it will be a monument to his vanity, but this joke on him will be too subtle for him to see. Jonathan talks about his mother's own grand estate, but then realizes with disgust that she has been drinking again: no wonder she feels poetic! She sobs, asks him why will he always blame her for whatever it is he blames her for? He says that he blames her for her sentimental romantic nonsense and her cheap talk of ideals. But she doesn't think it's for that: she'd say he blamed her because he'd lost those ideals, and she was the cause. He dismisses this as nonsense, insists that he's grateful to her for that.

The second act opens in Omaha, in 1892. The first brief scene is between a confident Jonathan and an anxious banker, who is frightened to death over the chances being taken in the reorganization of the Union Pacific.

The second scene of act two takes place in Jonathan's study back in New York. He and Goddard are talking of painting. Jonathan begins by expressing genuine appreciation of Corot, but then interrupts himself: "I know nothing of painting. But it's the thing to collect, a good bargain, an excellent investment." Goddard admits that he too knows nothing about art, but he likes pictures that represent nature—a ranch or a farm; he loves nature. Jonathan says that for him nature is something to frame a railroad. He gets out a map and shows Goddard his railroad lines: the Central, Union, and Eastern Pacific, plus the Burlington, which he has just taken from under Goddard's nose. Goddard smiles: "Now I know why you brought me here, Harford—to gloat. Well, you caught me napping. No hard feelings, but you won't catch me napping again. Of course you know it means war. You've invaded my territory, and you must expect the consequences. Well, it was inevitable, I suppose. We'd gone as far as we could in our own territories. We had to go on or stagnate. If you hadn't invaded, I would have." Jonathan: "Of course. War is always inevitable, and we'll make it a good war." Goddard asks what lines, and Jonathan points on his map to Manchuria, across Russia, and steamer lines around the world. Goddard: "I see that they're already marked in red. You're pretty sure of yourself, Jonathan." Jonathan: "Yes, I'm going to the East now. With the Burlington rounding out my system here, there's nothing much to do—for a while."

Then he continues: "But that's not what I brought you here for. I'm going to let Elizabeth get a divorce, so she and you can regularize your relationship. I haven't wanted to before, for the children's sake; but I see now that it's best. I feel I owe it to you and to her to be fair—especially after the Burlington." Goddard: "I want none of your generosity! What I want of you, I take!" Jonathan: "Well, you've taken her, haven't you? And I'm admitting it. There's no generosity: at the beginning of war I don't want an enemy in my tent—I was about to say sharing my bed but that would be—" Goddard: "A lie!" Jonathan: "Yes, I suppose she's told you that that seemed better—long ago." Goddard: "I want none of your favors. I want her and she wants me." Jonathan: "I'm glad you don't go in for sentimental talk about her." Goddard: "I love her and she loves me. That's what I meant." Jonathan: "Did you?" Goddard: "Yes, I did. And don't put on the superior air of giving me something. She is already mine." Jonathan: "Yes, you keep saying that. And I agree. But surely you want to marry her, don't you?—so everyone will know you've taken her." Goddard: "Yes, I do. I love her, I tell you. But it's useless to try to make you understand that. I don't believe you ever loved anything in your life—or did you?" Jonathan smiles: "No. I can't give you that satisfaction. I was never hers. You're getting nothing of me."

After a pause, Goddard asks: "How did you know? I've been pretty careful—not that I wouldn't have come out before the world—" Jonathan: "I know." Goddard: "But for her sake. Did you have us spied on?" Jonathan: "Why no. She told me. Didn't she tell you she did?" Goddard: "She told you? Why?" Jonathan: "Every time she went to you, she told me. She is a very honorable woman." Goddard: "But—she didn't tell *me*." Jonathan: "She was too considerate, I suppose. She didn't want to spoil your gloating that I was being made a fool of." Goddard (bewilderedly): "But why? I don't see why she should tell you and keep it a secret from me." Jonathan: "Well, I wouldn't try to understand a woman's motives, if I were you. (Then briskly) So I have your promise to marry her?" Goddard: "Of course. Damn you, you don't think me capable of making her a kept whore in everyone's eyes, do you?" Jonathan: "She will continue to be whatever she is in her own eyes." Goddard: "What do you mean by that?" Jonathan: "My dear fellow, how should I know? I don't pretend to understand women—or even to any desire to understand them."

After another pause, while Goddard stares at him, Jonathan gets to his feet, says brusquely: "Well, that's all. Good night. We can still shake hands, eh? Here's to our good war—when I get back from the East!" Goddard: "You'll be gone long?" Jonathan: "Six months—a vacation, I've always wanted to go East, and I need a rest, the Burlington deal took a lot out of me." Goddard smiles wryly: "Out of *me*, you mean, don't you? You're a cold-blooded fish, Jonathan. I don't think there'll be much satisfaction in it for me now after I have smashed you." Jonathan: "Because you're a superficially selfish person, while I am deeply selfish. I mean, you ought to love your railroads as much as yourself." Goddard: "Do you?" Jonathan: "I do. I don't love myself at all." Goddard: "I confess that's all too paradoxical for me." Jonathan: "Yes, it is. That's why *I*'ll smash *you*. Good night, and don't say that I didn't warn you." Goddard: "We've both been warned, it seems to me. Good night."

The third scene of act two returns to Sara's estate. Jonathan has come to see Sara before he leaves on his trip. He has stifled her in wealth, encouraged her social climbing. Her life has become a round of exhausting duties. She is indignant at the attacks on him and the storms of criticism. But she is bothered by the stories in the press of what his triumphs have meant in terms of loss to poor investors, and feels guilt. She has begun to long for Honey: with him there would be no guilt. (Jonathan has encouraged Honey in building his hotel until it has become grotesquely magnificent and completely unprofitable; it now takes a huge income to support it.)

She brings up the subject of Elizabeth and her affair with Goddard. Jonathan admits that he knows his rival is crazy about her. Sara comments that he sounds glad. He says that he is: it fits in with his plans. She urges him to be fair—divorce Elizabeth; but he says she doesn't want a divorce: this is her revenge, she thinks. His mother points out that the affair will make him a laughing stock. Jonathan counters that they'll see who laughs last, then. Goddard is an ass, to let a woman involve him at a time when he needs all his brains. He's a voluptuary. It is immoral—bad for the country for such a man to have power.

Sara finally decides that she can't stand Jonathan's indifference to her real feelings: it's like living as a ghost; he doesn't seem to know she's alive. The big estate has become to her a jail. Jonathan reminds her that it was her dream. The pathetic part is that she is really pleading with him to show that he still needs her. She tries to make him jealous by telling him of Honey's letters, urging her to come to San Francisco, describing the grand suite he has for her in his hotel. He sounds unhappy, and she's afraid he's drinking himself to death. Jonathan says coldly that that might be the most honorable thing he could do. She is aghast, frightened, and rebukes him. He apologizes: he's sorry, but he can't be approving of Honey's sentimental self-pity. He's done everything for him that he could do with honor: he used his influence to get the bribery hushed up. His end was his duty to his brother, above all to his mother, to his father.

When Sara asks him if he'll never see the lies he tells himself, Jonathan is terribly agitated; but she repeats the charge, it has come out of her at last.

He protests: "You can't mean to tell me *that* now, when I'm just on the verge of my final success. You know my high aim." She asks: "Do you really believe that?" He replies: "Of course. Don't you believe I believe?" She answers desperately that she must believe because, God help her, she sees now it was she who made him what he is. This stings him, and he contradicts her, insists he is himself: he made himself. Then he adds, coldly, that if she thinks he is hers, it's time she went to Honey. She was quite right in what she said at first, although he denied it to spare her feelings: he *can* stand alone; he no longer needs her. Sara, in an Irish rage, lapses into brogue, curses him. Jonathan is superstitiously appalled. She falls into his arms, sobs that she didn't mean it. He says that any other time he'd laugh at it—but now— He goes out to the study. Sara calls after him that she's an old woman; this may be goodbye; but he doesn't hear her. She sobs and goes.

Act three is set later in 1892 or in 1893. Jonathan is in Shanghai for a conference. His patriotism has come to be that the United States must possess the world by possessing the East. He waits after the reporters have gone. An old eunuch says to him: "It is dangerous to wink at one's lies for one thereby conspires with them to make them into one's truth." Jonathan asks him: "What should one do then?" The eunuch replies: "One should look with quiet eyes of peace at everything and see that it is nothing." Jonathan: "Even at oneself?" The eunuch: "Above all at oneself." Jonathan says: "You must possess everything in order to be free of it. It is easy to give up things you have not, but I suspect the desire is still there. To possess desire, then you can be free of it."

He keeps on to Japan, and the second scene of Act Three is set there in a Buddhist temple. Jonathan is at first absorbed in his plans for possession, triumphant over the East. But the atmosphere takes hold of him: gradual panic, fear, which he defies. He makes arrangements for a special steamer to take him home. [In one plan, later abandoned, O'Neill had Jonathan boasting to the statue of Buddha in the temple, justifying himself. He has, in his will, left all his money to Christian missions for the purpose of converting the East. He finally blows out his brains—as the billionaire in the very first plan for "It Cannot Be Mad" had done—because his work is finished. He is not under the thumb of life: he dies when he chooses. But, of course, although he won't admit it, it is fear of his impending death that drives him to this.]

The third scene of act three has Jonathan back in New York. Goddard tries to get the Union Pacific, and thus provokes Jonathan to wreck the Southern to get that. The panic ensues, and Jonathan retains control. He has bought all as before secretly and runs the price up to the skies until Goddard's credit is exhausted—then he sells and smashes him, pounding his railroad at the same time.

A scene follows between Goddard and Elizabeth. He realizes that in her frenzied use of sex she is forcing it, trying to drown some memory, and for revenge; that she really loves her husband. She asks what she is to him except something of Jonathan's that he wants to possess. He admits that this was true at first, but insists he has come to love her. But Elizabeth cannot return his love. She says goodbye to him, warns him that she feels obliged to tell her husband his plans.

She goes to Jonathan's office to warn him. He has deliberately told her the wrong plans. At the last moment she could not bring herself to destroy him and actually told Goddard the opposite—which is the right plan. But Goddard is suspicious, thinks what Elizabeth has told him must be the opposite of what Jonathan actually plans to do, and acts accordingly. Jonathan is at first furious, then gives himself away. He has betrayed his betrayer—but only in the interest of his dream. Elizabeth accuses him of counting on using her betrayal. He explains that the point of honor, in a duel like his with Goddard, is that every means is justified—provided the prize is great enough. He ignores her and begins to make further plans. She pleads pitifully that she didn't betray him, she betrayed Goddard. But she cannot admit to him that it was for love: she insists it was a matter of honor.

The next scene takes place in Jonathan's office a few days later. Goddard comes to congratulate him, admits he's beaten. As Goddard is about to leave, Jonathan says that, in divorcing Elizabeth, he won't name Goddard as co-respondent: he doesn't kick his rivals when they are down. It's not honorable—and besides, during her stay in Europe Goddard was preceded by many others of whom he has evidence. Goddard: "It's a lie!" Jonathan: "Oh, you mustn't blame her—her marriage has always been one of convenience; I gave her complete freedom. I've said no time for love, but

I've realized to a woman it was important. So don't think you took anything that I wanted." Goddard: "I see. Well, I'm leaving for Europe. Will you say goodbye to Mrs. Harford for me? I won't be seeing her again." Jonathan: "Not ever again?" Goddard: "Not ever again." He starts to go, stops: "You were wrong if you thought she loved me." Jonathan: "Love, perhaps, isn't the word. But I know nothing of her—and care less." Goddard begins to laugh: "Jonathan, I was about to congratulate you on being the world's prize bastard, but I think now I'll change that and say that I feel damned sorry for you, for you can't congratulate the blind for being blind, can you?" Jonathan starts, then smiles coldly: "You have a good brain; don't spoil it. I can travel on my own line now from New York to Yokahoma. You can congratulate me on that, can't you?" Goddard: "No. I'm afraid I can't: for when you get to Yokahoma you will still be you. Goodbye, Jonathan. Here's to our next battle. This isn't the end, you know." He goes. Jonathan, left alone, begins to have doubts; his mind becomes confused.

The next scene has him at his house, alone, lost. He regrets that Sara has left him; but he can't go to California to see her now; he has to finish the job, then he'll be able to boast to her of his goal attained. Elizabeth comes in. He welcomes her, wants her to reassure him. She does so, dully. He offers again to allow her to divorce him in order to marry Goddard, but she says she doesn't want that; she doesn't love Goddard. He asks if she means that to the victor belong the spoils. She replies, no, and says that she loves him. He answers that they are primitive animals, and starts to take her. She resists, but finally gives in. Afterward, he tells her he has changed his mind again: *he* is going to divorce *her*.

Sara has returned East for a short visit, and the following scene is between her and Elizabeth. Sara is hostile, tends to blame Elizabeth for the cold monster Jonathan has become, although she feels that the fault is really her own. She finally breaks down, and the scene becomes like that between her and Leda in "The Earth Is the Limit." Elizabeth explains bitterly that Goddard really loved her; she had happiness in her grasp if she only could have loved him. She tried desperately, through sex; but Jonathan has drained her of all capacity to love, and so she comes back like a beaten cur bitch. She hates Jonathan and loves him: how *can* she love him? What is there about these Harfords? Sara says she doesn't know—

except it's something that drives life higher or lower, makes life more intense; it's the feeling they're not to blame, that they're the slaves of themselves, that only the impossible can make them happy, that they carry a fate in them and they're driven to make their lives a symbol and a lesson. It's the touch of the barren poet in them that can only create with the appearances of things and never gets beyond them. Elizabeth complains desperately: if Jonathan would only give her back some part of her life, make her living to herself. Sara says, without believing it, that maybe now he's got his ambitions he'll begin to live, to change. Elizabeth asks if Sara will get him to forgive her, take her back. But Sara thinks he'll say he never sent her away, that there's nothing to forgive. Elizabeth answers, "I know! Oh, God!"

The fourth scene of act three is set at Sara's old estate. Jonathan, alone, defiantly asserts his truth, having sent his mother back to Honey. He has denied himself in order to possess himself—to be responsible to no one but himself. In his loneliness the bitter revelation comes to him: "I am I. I am what? I am a railroad. My spine is the main trunk line, my ribs are feeding lines, my heart is steam, my brain the operating department—and my soul is the dead clinkers from the firebox, or a lonely whistle at night out on the rolling prairie. I am a monster. At some moment in our lives, life offers us the choice: to which one of the fates within us do we wish to be enslaved?"

In the fifth scene of act three, Elizabeth has shot herself, lies up in Jonathan's study. He comes, finds her, and is seized by an agony of remorse and regret: he *did* love her. Then cold-blooded denial. He reads her message to him: "From the dead to the dead." He wonders: did she know about the doctor? Is it a prophecy? He is terrified, but then regains control. He sneers that the message means that he is dead to love—woman's only living. She was a fool!

He rings, and the butler comes. Jonathan tells him that Mrs. Harford has shot herself. He'll phone for the police. "You take her out of here." But the butler protests, he doesn't think they ought to move her until the police come. Jonathan flies into a fury: "Can't you understand? I haven't time to think of death now." He shakes the butler by the lapels, goes out to phone. He gets the Police Commissioner, tells him the news, explains that the suicide was the result of temporary insanity, melancholia, her time of life.

Then he thinks bitterly that of course gossip will have it that he killed her on account of her affair with Goddard. Well, let them think what they please, the scum! Maybe he'd like to have them think that—he knows it would please Elizabeth to think that he murdered for love of her. Well, now that she is dead, he can admit that he wanted to; he wishes he had! He laughs, "Doesn't that make you happy over there? I can hear you laugh. Wait for me. We'll meet over there, and start again with life's idiot problems and stupid answers wiped off the slate. The maps of my railroad system trace the form of a grasping hand, grasping the lie of a dream." But then he is furious at himself: what he is saying now is an idiot's mumbling. Life is a fact, and power over life is the fact above the fact.

Then his loneliness returns; he yearns for his mother. He sent her away as no longer needed, but he didn't know: he must at least feel that someone possesses him, that he has given birth to himself. Loneliness overcomes him once more, a sense of futility, disbelief in his dream, a premonition of death. He phones to his secretary (he has given her the night off), asks that a special train be readied to make a record to the Coast. He hangs up: "Christ, what a silence in this house! What a piercing, shrieking silence! God, I want the quiet of locomotive wheels in the night of peace, of clanging bells, the sound of wheels clanking over rails. I want life to bear testimony that it lives." Finally the doorbell rings, and he thanks God for the sound. Life has come back. He hurries to the door, greets the Commissioner, apologizes for having had to rout him out at such an hour.

There follows a scene between Jonathan and a Catholic priest. Jonathan has made donations to charity, has established a home for fallen women, named in honor of Leda or Elizabeth. He rationalizes this as an honor, refusing to admit its revengeful irony even to himself. He has made additional gifts, in his mother's name, to a Catholic Church Seminary, underlining an impulse to square himself with God in case there is one, but he is rationally an atheist. He explains the gifts by his wish to bring comfort to believers: on a material plane, the Catholic Church will be a valuable ally in keeping labor satisfied. But his giving in his mother's name has, underneath, also a revenge motive, to give her a guilty conscience, fear, make her revert to her own mother's conflict. His father was a deist, therefore Jonathan is an atheist—freedom through facts and reasons. The priest to whom he has given the money for the Seminary tells him that he is at heart a Catholic, why doesn't he become one in fact? Jonathan denies this, explains why.

The final scene in the play has Jonathan on his death bed. He has doubts: was it all justified? Did he ever believe? Sara has gotten out of her own sick bed to console him. [This is a change from the original plan in which Sara was to die just before Jonathan.] Honey and Leda are there. He tells them that he planned to sell everything and give to Missions to convert the East. But he's beyond blasphemy now: money no longer makes him feel he has power. They were all pigs in the same sty and he the prize hog. He asks his mother, what was the use? She rallies him to his dream, although it takes all her strength. He tells her that she has been his genius. But she insists, no, she has destroyed him. He advises her to keep records, retrench. He foresees failure: if he could only live, he'd do it!—he'd—. He dreams again: then at last he'd be big enough to forgive Elizabeth, to ask her forgiveness, to forgive his mother, and ask her forgiveness, and Honey, and Leda. He would know he had done God's work in the world.

Just before he dies, the news comes of Dewey's visit to Manila. Jonathan exults that the West *is* conquering the East. Power, possession is truth! Then he warns them that fate's hand is upon the United States: they will possess everything until they possess nothing, pay the soul for the everything which is nothing! He asks his mother to live in order to look after the children. He warns of the coming panic: sell everything. The good citizen has *cash* in troubled times. He says to her: "I want my monument to crumble into dust—a heap of dust to mark my grave, a symbol of the person beneath—no heavy weight above to hold me prisoner, but dust dissolving into the all of air and earth—freedom! And freedom for you, too. I am sorry I punished you so long. What had I against you, Mother? I don't remember. Oh, yes, you wanted the earth for an estate."

Honey, after Jonathan's death, is aghast, says he was a great man—a great son of a bitch. "He really believed in that dream of his. By God, I think now he must have believed in it all along, and I thought it was all a fake!" Leda tells him to shut up, but then throws herself into his arms: "No, Honey, no! Please don't talk now or I'll hate you!"[1]

At the end of August 1935, O'Neill made notes for the seventh and final play, now called "Twilight of Possessors Self-Dispossessed" (eventually "The Hair of the Dog"), incorporating much of the old "Bessie Bowen" material. It is apparent that the names, sexes, and even the parentage of the children had not yet established themselves definitely in his mind. Here those of Jonathan and Elizabeth seem to be, at first, Johnnie and Josie (formerly Beth), and Honey and Leda's children are Ourni and Lollie—rather than Con and Sara, as in the outline for "The Man on Iron Horseback." O'Neill had apparently decided that the father of Elizabeth's Josie was Honey and that Leda's elder child was fathered not by Honey but by Wolfe—although the outline for "Nothing Is Lost but Honor" has Elizabeth saying to Leda that Wolfe "proved he'd rather die than go to bed with you!" and although, in the same play, O'Neill has described Leda as sure that her first child, there named Bette, was Honey's. A later plan changes the name of Leda's elder child to Sara II and gives her father as "probably Wolfe." Of course these changes would have required rewriting passages in the earlier plays. The action now planned for the seventh play seems to be as follows:

A prologue takes place in Honey's hotel in San Francisco at the time of the panic in 1893. After the enormous cash bequests to charity of Jonathan's will have been paid from the sale of his securities at post-panic prices (and Sara insists in honor on paying every dollar of them), there is nothing left except Sara's estate and the trust fund Jonathan had established to cover the expenses—but which doesn't allow her to sell it. (He, on his death bed, had, before witnesses—Honey and the others—repented this arrangement, and it would have been possible to break the will, but Sara insists on honoring it as punishment.)

It is Sara who is determined to overcome despair and start life again. Honey has lost the hotel. He gradually recovers his spirits, but his son Ourni is crushed by the shame of his father's losing all his money. Leda mourns the loss of luxurious comfort where she has never had to move. Sara makes the decision that they will all go East in a private car if it takes their last cent.

The first scene of act one is set on Sara's estate in 1898. The value of Jonathan's trust fund has shrunk and its income now produces very little over taxes. The grounds have grown wild. In the vast stables there is only one horse, in the dairy only one cow, etc. The old Irish coachman and his wife stick with Sara. (The estate has been willed to a Catholic Seminary when Sara dies.) It was Jonathan's ironic punishment to buy the estate which Sara and Con Melody had coveted, including the farm and Simon's old log cabin. In the town a livery stable now stands on the site of Melody's Inn and this Jonathan has purchased and bequeathed to Honey.

Sara has become a miser, practises every economy. Her reason for living now is to save enough to give a nest egg to Johnnie and Josie. Johnnie is her favorite, because he is like Simon. She doesn't like Josie (peasant re-minder), but pities her, and is bound to be fair to her because of her promise to Jonathan. She tries to bind Josie to Johnnie by emphasizing the fact that she might as well give up any idea of marriage, on account of her looks, devote her life to Johnnie: he has the touch of the poet; he's a great dreamer; he'll be a great author, poet, but impractical, must be protected. He's no money-grubber, thank God. This is her obsession. It's useless to point out to her that Johnnie is only interested in machines, never reads a book. As for Honey and Leda's children, Sara has no worries about Ourni, only a contemptuous affection. He'll get on. He's a likeable scamp like his father. She hates Lollie, who is not like her mother, but resembles her great-grandmother, Abigail [Deborah]. Sara excuses herself by saying that Lollie is pretty; she'll marry money.

Leda has grown enormously fat, a terrible glutton who lives only for eating. She hates Sara for cutting down on her food—on orders from the doctor. When her belly is full, she is content and affectionate to all; when she is hungry, she is venomously bitter.

Johnnie works in Simon's old shack on inventions, although Sara is told he is writing a book.

Josie has been told by Leda, who hates her because she manages the house for Sara, that Jonathan was not her father, but Josie won't admit this for she despises Honey. She had hero worship for Jonathan, who hardly noticed her, but she attributed that to her ugliness; she couldn't blame him. And Sara lies to her, saying that Jonathan *was* her father.

Honey has become a lecherous drunken old man, living in the past, talking of politics and his hotel. His treat is a visit to the local whorehouse every Saturday night. His old vanity about his looks gives him a resentful feeling of aversion toward Josie as his child. His paternal affection is centered on Ourni. He is the handsome romantic Irish type again, like his father when young, but less shrewdly intelligent, less honest, not a scamp who knows it and laughs at it. He is full of moral hypocrisy, has the gift of gab, is hail-fellow-well-met, is popular with men and attractive to women, but weak. He leans on women, is greedy and ambitious. He fools himself—which his father never did. Honey sees through him, feels an aversion and contempt for him, makes him a butt of his sarcasm. To Honey he seems a debased and degenerate version of himself. Honey is jealous of his mother's affection for Ourni, who flatters and kids her and wheedles money out of her—just as Honey himself once did. But Honey knows he had love for Sara whereas Ourni loves only himself. Ourni also kids and flatters Josie, says he would fall in love with her if they weren't first cousins—and more, if scandal is true. He laughs at her behind her back, is repelled by her physically. Josie, in spite of the fact that she sees through him and knows he is a liar, loves him, likes the idea that he is her half-brother, akin to her, belongs to her while at the same time she hates and denies that Honey *is* her father.

He spends most of his time with his cronies before the livery stable. He laments his come-down from owner of the biggest hotel in the country to keeping a boarding house for horses. But he always laughs at himself and is very popular with the town politicians, loafers, and sports. He boasts about his brothers. They were all supermen: Ethan the most daredevil of skippers; Wolfe a great gambler; Jonathan would have owned the world had he lived. But when they were moral, their worries wrecked them. (He blames Elizabeth's coldness for Jonathan's downfall.) He, Honey, is the only weakling of the family. But he was something himself. He bought Congressmen by the dozen. Those were great days. He laughs when he is asked about the Senate scandal: "Oh, that was the cleverest of all Jonathan's tricks. He wanted a panic and, by God, I panicked them for him." He tells the story as if it had been his own scheme. They remind him that the rumor was that Jonathan had double-crossed him. He denies this, boasts about his speech: "And out of the panic Jonathan had the railroad by the throat and I had five million dollars." When they ask him what has become of all that money, he says: "I put it into the hotel, bad cess to it; but I like horses better than men."

Sara has fits of senility when everything is confused for her. Ourni becomes Honey—much to Honey's disgust. Johnnie is Simon, and toward him she shows love and a bitter resentment. She'd like to burn his book. Then, "No, he's different, he's a poet and I'm proud to be wife to a man who has great dreams of beauty and is above giving his life to cramming gold into his belly." Josie is herself, but Sara is frightened by her ugliness—*she* was pretty. Leda she either doesn't know at all or confuses with Abigail. But when she is not in one of these fits of senility, Sara is her old practical self again, the self who came to manage the farm after Simon's failure, full of energy and authority.

Ourni loves Josie, who appreciates this love and is drawn to him by maternal affection and by a feeling that their fates are the same, since his father is not really his father either. He is afraid of his mother (Leda), who alternates between fits of absolute indifference to his existence and spasms of devouring maternal tenderness, in which he feels like food she wants to eat—a throwback to her possessive desire for his father, Wolfe. Johnnie avoids Honey, who tries to be kind but cannot hide his conviction that Johnnie is a half-wit. He is drawn to his cousin, Ourni, but lives in terror of his kidding.

The family live entirely isolated socially. Sara has anticipated cuts by cutting everyone first.

The second scene of act one is at the livery stable.

The third scene, back at the estate, has Leda eating herself to death. She finally dies in a fall down the stairs after a midnight raid on the icebox.

Act two opens two years later at the estate.

The second scene is at the stable and bicycle shop.

The third scene is back at the estate. Sara is dying. In her senile lapses now she confuses her father going to the Napoleonic wars with the Mexican War, the Civil War, the Spanish War, and the homecomings therefrom. Her final vision is of a recurrence of the curse of possessions on the family via machines. The locomotive has become the automobile. Listening to Johnnie's dreams of the automobile's contribution to the social development of the country and to farmers only adds to this.

The fourth scene has Ourni, Johnnie, and Josie leaving Sara's estate. Josie, in her exultation that she is free of the past at last, starts to throw away the key, then stops. When the others ask, "Well, why didn't you?" she replies, "I'll keep it to remind me of mistakes."

Part two (acts three and four) follows, generally speaking, the rest of "Bessie Bowen."[2]

Further notes for this final play occupied O'Neill on 1 and 2 September 1935. On the latter date he commented in his *Work Diary:* "As this 7th Play follows in main plot-outline the old 'Bessie Bowen' theme, nothing further needed on its outline now beyond the revision notes I've done in past week" (p. 229).

chapter seven

In September 1935, as O'Neill now turned his attention to the other plays in the Cycle, he found once more that it was the earlier lives of his characters that most stimulated his imagination. Because he had always planned the action of "Bessie Bowen" to come up to the present, the obvious way for the "*magnum opus*" to expand even further in time was backward. On the seventh he recorded in his *Work Diary* that he was "Playing around with idea [for] new first play to precede 'Hair of The Dog' [*A Touch of the Poet*], to go back to 1806 and show Abigail [Deborah] as [a] girl— [her] marriage to Henry H⟨arford⟩.—and their house & parents— Henry's father big character—title, '*Greed Of The Meek*'" (p. 230). He proceeded to make notes for this new play—the first of an eight-play Cycle—which was forcing itself upon him. He devoted a week to its preliminaries, but then went back to describing the characters in "The Hair of the Dog," explaining in the *Work Diary* that he was "trying to put 'Greed Of [the] Meek' out of mind— God knows don't want extra play tacked on to this damned trilogy unless it absolutely must be written!" (p. 231).

But the play still pressed itself on him, and after just one more day on "The Hair of the Dog," O'Neill decided to go ahead at least with notes for the new project. From 18 September to 1 October he worked on the outline, description of characters, and sets. The first character described was Andrew Harford, who was to be the focal point of the play:

Fifty-seven but in spite of deep lines & sun-wrinkles in his face looks no more than 45—thick black hair gray at the temples—a powerful, striking-looking face—a long, jutting square jaw—a wide mouth with finely-chiselled lips, neither thick nor thin, set in an arrogant, mocking smile—large deep-set, black eyes, placed far apart—eyes slant just a trifle and with the heavy lids that come down over the pupils give his face a strange Mongolian or Indian cast which is added to by high, prominent cheekbones—naturally swarthy complexion a deep bronze from sun—an arrogant, cold Roman nose—a scar over left cheekbone (or forehead)—

He is well over six feet in height—an astonishingly youthful figure, with deep chest and wide powerful shoulders, small waist and hips. He moves as if always balanced on the balls of his feet like a boxer, so quietly that one does not notice how quick his movements are—he speaks with deliberate quietness, holding his powerful, resonant voice in order—

There is an atmosphere of arrogance about him as if, confident in his superior difference from others, he viewed them with a barely tolerant disdain, cynically amused & contemptuous—an air of authority, of a sea-captain's privileged isolation—something cruel, mocking & almost Mephistophelian—

Dressed with a flair for dandyism but clothes of a style dating back several years

A compelling personality, physically & mentally, impressing his authority on men and women alike

His wife is Kate Harford:

She is sixty but still a fine figure of a woman, her body full-busted and buttocked, but her flesh is still firm and sound, with no flabbiness or fat. Her pale face must once have had beauty of a rather masculine type, and it is still handsome with a long straight, rather heavy nose, a wide mouth rather thin-lipped and compressed, a strong obstinate jaw, steady cold blue eyes, a low wide forehead, thick, iron-gray hair.

She is dressed with a severe, prim good taste. Her smile and her manner are those of one constantly conscious of the conduct proper to a lady under all circumstances. She moves, speaks, sits in repose, seems to think with a disciplined politeness, a cold formally correct reserve, worn like an ironclad armor behind which she lives within herself, untouched.

There is something repellent about her and at the same time fascinating and compelling admiration, some mystery.

Andrew Harford's three half-sisters here make their first appearance:

Maggie Harford

A tall lean withered Scots woman type, with a strain of weird mysticism—a fierce will to possess beneath an outward seeming of meekness bowing before the will of God—dressed with a mythic-like ugliness, cheapness & plainness—a rasping sharp voice—dirty white hair—no ornaments of any kind—sallow complexion

The grim mask which uses religious conformity to get what its greed desires—to make someone else get it for them so it comes to them

She is 69

Eliza Harford

Medium height—a plump greedy health about her that offsets being delicate—an obvious endeavor to look younger than she is—polished shoes, gloves, dressed with care and style—thin face with small snobbish features, blue eyes, white hair—ultra gentle voice—everything about her meek, scrupulously neat, ultra-refined,—small round China blue eyes—a simperingly refined voice—

The social-conformity meek

She is 68

Hannah Harford

Short, squat, fat—a shapeless figure with short thick arms & legs—a swarthy broad face, long nose, big mouth, high cheekbones, small black eyes, heavy-lidded—very Mongolian, American Indian in appearance—wrapped around in heavy shawl like an Indian blanket—a husky guttural voice—a stolid resignation about her—earthiness—meekness as fatalism—it is Nature's law that I should possess—appears to notice nothing, to be stolidly indifferent, but nothing escapes her beady black eyes—

She is 67[1]

By 1 October 1935, O'Neill had completed preliminary work on the new play. He devoted a day to jotting down ideas for the sets of the whole Cycle and commented in his *Work Diary:* "Decide [I] have done all preliminary work on [the] Cycle [I] can do now and need a break & a change so C⟨arlotta⟩. & I will go to N.Y. . . . for our annual dentist, etc. orgy—also need medical going over to see what pain I have had for past 2 mos. is" (p. 232). They left Sea Island on 6 October and for three weeks renewed their friendships in New York. O'Neill went to his dentist, had his eyes examined and new glasses prescribed, and was ordered into Presbyterian Hospital for X-rays and tests. There were numerous lunches and dinners with friends before the return to Georgia on the twenty-seventh.

O'Neill felt no better, however, and on the thirty-first, described himself as "very depressed—can't concentrate on anything" (p. 234). In early November he made a start on the detailed scenario for "Greed of the Meek" but didn't like it. Although he read over the scenario for "The Hair of the Dog" (*A Touch of the Poet*), he could summon up no interest in writing that play, noting that it "needs to be reconceived in line with general theme of [the] Cycle" (p. 235). In desperation he again took up "Greed of the Meek" and finished the scenario for act one on 9 November. Because he had written it in a special morocco-bound notebook that Carlotta had given him, the manuscript was never destroyed:

The first scene of Act I shows the interior of Waldo [later Henry] Deane's study and a section of the garden of the parsonage, in a small inland town near Boston, on a morning in 1806. Deane, 58, is discovered at his desk in the study, trying to write a sermon on the text "Blessed are the meek." He goes to the window to watch Abigail [later Deborah], his daughter, 20, who is dreaming in the garden. In his thoughts of her, there is a minor conflict arising from his doubts about his motives concerning her forthcoming marriage with Henry Harford, 25. He can't guess her real feeling. His own feeling is of closeness and at the same time alienness to her: she is his child but not his child. He gives up. He can only hope for the best. He finally assures himself defensively that he is acting unselfishly—for her good.

Mercy, his oldest daughter, 30, comes in. She is prim, matter-of-fact, motherly. He starts guiltily, is submissive to her. She fusses over him: he mustn't stand by the window, it's cold; there's a draft. She looks out, sees Abigail. Surely he's not worrying over her! That's nonsense. She is one who needs marriage, children, responsibility—to settle down. She's so flighty and fanciful. Deane tells her of his self-doubts and she reassures him: after all, one has to take money into account; there's no sin in that; he's ill-paid; her sister Prudence is a widow with four children. This isn't the sort of reassurance he wants. He reminds her that she is going marketing and will need some money. He gets it for her, but it is the last: he doesn't know how they'll live till the end of the month. He has given some of it away. She reproves him, starts to go. Then they talk of her sister Sussanah, who has just arrived the night before, having come home to be at the marriage of her sister. They are letting her sleep late—that's a Southern custom. Mercy laughs about her accent. She advises her father to ask Sue for money, but he refuses. He never approved of her marriage. He has forgiven her, but he'll never take help from her husband, Stephen Dixon, because he is a slave-holder. Mercy gives in, says that Stephen spends every cent, is thriftless; she supposes there's no use expecting anything from him anyway. But she hopes the fact of Henry Harford's father's having been in the slave-trade won't set *her* father's conscience against any help that Henry may offer. Deane says that he wants no help from anyone. Mercy goes on her shopping errand.

Alone again, Deane goes back to the window. He is about to call Abigail, to tell her that she needn't marry, but stops and goes back to his sermon. He can't write on the text "Blessed are the meek": he *has* been meek, but what has he inherited except trouble? If he only felt sure of his vocation; but he never has. He has never received any advancement, and rightly so, for he's a poor minister. Once he had dreamed of going to sea, but he was too meek; he obeyed his pious father, who was a successful minister. It's in his sea-longing that Abigail takes after him; that's where she gets her dreams. Immediately he repents his rebellious thoughts; he is forgetting his blessings—four daughters. He's been unhappy since his wife's death. He forces himself back to his sermon: "I *will* be meek!"

Sussanah comes in. She is a stout, good-natured, lazy, intelligent young woman of twenty-five. There follows an affectionate scene between father and daughter. She tells him of her life in North Carolina, though there's little beyond what she has written in her letters. She's sorry she and her husband are not able to help him financially. He says that in any event he couldn't in conscience accept help from a slave-owner. She is a bit hurt by this, but laughs, rallies him—a mistaken notion Northerners have of cruelty and chains. The slaves are better off than Northern labor, than the crews on ships for example, who are free only in name.

She changes the subject, goes to the window, asks him about Abigail: "She came to my room last night, but would talk only about *me:* she was evasive about herself and her marriage. I couldn't make her out, but then I never could. She was always strange and withdrawn, in the clouds, an alien in the family. But I have always loved her, perhaps all the more for that, and I still do. It must be the Welsh strain in our family." Deane agrees. Sussanah comes back to the subject of the approaching marriage, asks about Henry Harford. Deane says that he is a sensible young man in every way, educated at Harvard, in business, ambitious, wealthy. Sussanah asks meaningly about his father, says that Mercy has written her there was some scandal about his having made his money in the slave trade. Deane is righteously indignant: "He made money privateering during the Revolution. He was in the slave trade for a while afterward, but then went into the Pacific-China fur trade." Then he confesses that Andrew is undesirable, a completely immoral ruffian, from all he hears, deplored by his family. "He has cut off from them, rarely sails home, and when he does he stays only long enough to re-outfit, and then puts to sea again. He has been gone this time four years. There are grave fears that Chinese pirates may have got him."

Abigail appears in the doorway. She says: "Fears? You mean hopes, don't you, Father?" She laughs. Deane is immediately strangely timid, apologetic, and embarrassed before her. His attitude is one of fascination and at the same time fear, as though she exercised some spiritual domination over him. She rallies him with affectionate whimsical teasing, telling Sussanah of their struggle over the garden, his endeavor to make her see the beauty in vegetables, penance for his sinful love for flowers, his attitude about slavery, her marriage. "He will be so grieved to lose me, so lonely without me, and yet so at peace, so infinitely relieved!" Her father tries to fall in with her outer mood of banter, and protests jokingly; but all the time it is apparent that underneath this he is all serious; he feels himself accused, stripped naked of his moral evasions, and condemned. And underneath Abigail's affectionate banter is a biting, disillusioned mockery and contempt. Finally she glances at the text for his sermon, "Blessed are the meek," and she laughs: "Oh, Father! And are you meek?" He answers: "I try to be." She says: "I would rather hear you preach on 'Greedy are the meek'—greedy to inherit the earth." Immediately after this, Deane makes excuses to go, and leaves.

Abigail looks after him: "Haven't you wished at times, Sue, that we could have had a father?" Sue laughs, shocked: "Why, what a thing to say! Poor Father!" Abigail: "Yes, poor in spirit. I am tired of being a spiritual mother." Then, banteringly: "Let's talk. I know you're dying of curiosity to hear all about the marriage." She then rattles on in an amusing, fanciful way, describing Henry, her meeting with him, what he's like, his home, the aunts, his mother. Here she grows almost serious, gives a vivid description of the strange atmosphere, the sense of inner struggle to the death, the feeling of waiting, the loss of identity. Sussanah is repelled: "I should think you'd be afraid." Abigail: "No, that's one thing I shall never be—afraid. Only the meek are afraid—that some of their possessions (stolen goods) will be taken from them. I look upon it as a great adventure, a sailing out upon a dangerous unchartered sea after too long a lifetime spent paddling a round tub 'round and 'round a duck pond. I feel I am to become a battle ground: charges from without and charges from within. I even hope their hopes are mistaken and Father Harford will come back. I confess he appeals to me most of all the family." Sussanah: "What?" Abigail: "He sounds like Father's description of Satan. I should like to meet Satan. Father's evident prejudice has made me feel there must be a lot to be said on his side." Sussanah: "Really, Abigail! And how about Henry?" Abigail: "Oh, Henry will be a very good husband, just as I shall be a very good wife. I won't disgrace you. But, oh, Susan, before you settled down to a lifetime of good wifehood with Stephen, didn't you wish, in your own mind, for one wild glorious, foolish, insane, sinful adventure, in which you would just let life explode in you?" Sussanah: "You mean, with Stephen? But our honeymoon was that." Abigail: "Oh, yes, honeymoon. Henry has ours all planned out. We are going to New York. And I suppose it must be exciting to get in bed with a man—and find out which of one's guesses are right and which wrong." Sussanah: "Abi!"

Abigail goes on: "But no, I wasn't thinking of marriage and a honeymoon." Sussanah: "You don't love Henry?" Abigail: "I don't know. Perhaps. He is very handsome. Perhaps there is some of his father's spirit which will come out. But how can I tell? What is love like? You tell me." Sussanah: "You'd know if you did. I don't see how anyone could sleep with a man without love." Abigail: "Don't you? I do. I can disassociate self from body, stand aside and observe. I have done it when Henry kisses me. It is easy to give the body: without the soul it is nothing to give; it cheats only the possessor; it does not fool the giver. In one way, I am alien in this life, inhabitant of some dream land I remember in dream. This life rejects me, but I also reject it: I pull my skirts aside so as not to be soiled." Sussanah: "Even by love?" Abigail: "Yes, perhaps love is the most soulbefouling of all contacts. But that is soul, because soul is outside, can be a spectator, can be loved without being possessed, can live as an actress playing parts automatically, part of social [?] living." Sussanah exclaims: "What thoughts!" Abigail replies: "Yes, I have had many strange thoughts in the garden—or dreams, rather—but don't misunderstand my attitude toward Henry. I am most fond of him; I can't imagine anyone it would be safer to marry—safe in the sense that with him I know that in the spirit, in which he is not interested, he will be only too glad to leave me alone and free." Sussanah is bewildered and a bit shocked, gives her sister up with a sigh. Abigail laughs, kisses her: "Don't bother trying to understand. I love you just the same, however evil I be. Do you continue to love me in spite of everything and all will be well."

Mercy comes in to say that Henry Harford is in the sitting room. Abigail comments, gaily mocking: "Why the man must be quite insane with love to come here in mid-morning, to leave his beloved counting house and drive miles—" Mercy: "Sshh!" Abigail: "To think, Mercy, that in a week I shall be going to bed with that man! It is an awesome thought, truly." Mercy is horrified: "I wish you wouldn't talk in that horrible brazen way. If you must have such shameless thoughts, keep silent. Really, instead of a piously brought up girl one would think you were—" Abigail: "A courtesan? Well now, Mercy, since you've said it—" Mercy: "I said nothing of the kind!" Abigail: "Since you've *thought* it, I must confess I've often dreamed that that must be a very romantic course to follow—that is, in the spirit! It is only that I do not wish to bring disgrace on Father and you—" Mercy: "Sshh! Henry will hear!" Abigail laughs: "Well, he might as well know what a hussy he's marrying. We must be truthful, mustn't we?" She laughs, gaily kisses Mercy: "There, you old Gorgon! Don't look so horrified! I'm only teasing you. Haven't I always been a good girl? Why, I was condemned at birth to be good. So don't worry!" She starts to go: "I must compose my face, be shy. Can I start a becoming blush? No? Well, Henry'll have to wait for the blush until my wedding night; but I can look demure by casting down my eyes. I'll call you in a moment, Sussanah, after the kisses are over. You must meet him. You'll be green with jealousy. He's twice as handsome as Stephen, isn't he, Mercy?" She goes out demurely.

Mercy fusses around, mumbling with loving exasperation: "Such a girl, how she talks! Wherever she got it, if one took her seriously, my goodness, what would you think of her?" Sussanah sighs: "That's what I'm wondering—what to think of her." Mercy: "It's time she was getting married, with such ideas." Sussanah: "Poor Henry!" Mercy: "Yes, indeed, poor Henry! But he's one of those quiet ones: he's not so meek as he pretends." Sussanah: "Meek?" Mercy: "He's certainly not so in business, young as he is, from what I hear. No one gets the best of him. He wouldn't be the son of that old pirate, his father, if he didn't have a will of his own. I'll wager he'll tame Abigail's fancy notions before he's through with her." Sussanah: "I wonder. In the flesh, yes. But in the spirit—?" Mercy (irritably): "Don't you start talking like her. What's the matter with you? It's not becoming to you. You've always had good common sense." She surveys her sister: "You've grown stouter, Sue. How are the children? Why didn't you bring them with you? I love children around, and so would Father."

Curtain[2]

On 10 November 1935, O'Neill reconsidered for the new play an "old many-scene idea starting at [the] Revolution".[3] He made some notes, but felt too ill for work, confessing on the fifteenth to "complete mental lethargy".[4] Thinking that stopping smoking might improve his health, he gave up cigarettes, later making a detailed report to his doctor:

It's now two weeks and a half since I quit and the old physical condition is very much improved as to nerves—tremor, when I hold two hands out straight in front of me is practically gone from right hand and very slight in left. Also I find I can do a lot of hard physical work in the garden without getting at all tired or winded.

All of which is to the good—*but*—as to mental condition I am slowed down to a crawl. When I try to work of a morning I feel woozy, stupid, entirely uninterested in plays or any ideas, and lazing along, attention wandering, from one silly day dream to another—can't concentrate at all! If I shut my eyes for a minute or two I start to fall asleep. And this applies to any reading I try to do at any time during the day—can't even concentrate on a detective yarn!

This morning feeling isn't uncomfortable—quite the reverse, it's relaxing!—but then afterward I get feeling guilty because I haven't worked, and am behind my schedule, and then comes depression, and I'm so mentally enfeebled that the depression meets no resistance from the quiescent brain—in short, the non-smoking, nerveless blues are, if anything, deeper indigo than the old ones when nicotine played the tremor accompaniment.

What I need now above everything for peace of mind is to get back on the job—to snap out of these morning stupors in some way. I don't want to go back to cigarettes. I'm leery about thyroid because I know it is liable to bring back nerves & tremor. So I thought I'd report all this to you. Your letter speaks of a known definite effect of nicotine on the adrenals. Perhaps this is what is doing it and there is something to counteract it—that is, until such time as my brain can get used to doing without the kick of the post-breakfast cigarette that used to start me on the morning job.

Funny, it wasn't so hard for me to stop, although this is the first time I've done it since back in 1927. My head swam a bit the first few days, I had spells of gulping deep breaths as if I couldn't get enough air, and my pulse dropped as low as 52 at intervals, but the general feeling was one of a welcome relaxed tension.

Queer about this sleep thing. I fall asleep over a book but once I'm asleep at night, I don't sleep well, keep waking up and have one nightmare after another.

I ramble on about this because, besides requesting advice, I thought these ex-nicotine addict symptoms might interest you. So few people ever give up smoking any more that I have the vainglorious sense of being a very special occasion indeed![5]

In his *Work Diary* O'Neill records such progress as his health allowed. With brain still sluggish, he turned to the actual script for "The Hair of the Dog" and worked for several days on a new first scene; but it didn't go well, and he soon decided that the scene was unnecessary, that it was better to begin the play as he had originally planned. He proceeded to take up the first act and worked on it a total of eight days between 12 and 23 December. After forty-nine days without smoking he set down on the thirtieth a "Pre New Year resolution to give up giving up smoking!—may be good physically but leaves me inert mentally!"

The first day of 1936 was gray, with O'Neill's "spirits even grayer!"; but by the tenth he felt well enough to resume writing "The Hair of the Dog." Even though he lost the cap from an eye tooth, he continued to work on act one and noted on the fourteenth that he was "pleased—really getting going on this now" (pp. 241, 242). But then, the very next day, the cap came off the other eye tooth! There was nothing to do but return to New York to see his dentist. He and Carlotta left on the eighteenth, arriving in

New York in a blizzard. Although O'Neill had four upper teeth extracted on the twenty-second, the next day he still managed to complete the first act of "The Hair of the Dog," totaling forty-two pages. He then took up the preliminaries to the second scene of act two, having decided to do "all Irish Inn parts [of] this play—then go back and do 'Greed of the Meek' & carry N⟨ew⟩. E⟨ngland⟩. straight through" (p. 243). Working from the twenty-fifth to the thirty-first he was able to finish the scene. He then went on to the second scene of act three, in spite of interruptions and a sore throat, and did more work on 5 February, even though he was in bed with a cold. An attack of gastritis on the twenty-first sent him to Doctors' Hospital. Discharged on the morning of the twenty-sixth, he and Carlotta, who had also been sick, took the evening train to Georgia. On the twenty-eighth he commented that it was "Good to be home—N.Y. trip was one long siege of troubles & bad luck!" (p. 246).

Depression and nerves kept him from any attempt at work until mid-March, when he began going over the first act of "The Hair of the Dog" and took up the second scene of act three where he had left off in New York. Although bothered by another stomach upset, he finished that scene in five days and recorded: "all I will do on this play now—will go back [and] start 1st Play now as per plan" (p. 247).

He worked on "Greed of the Meek" in spite of visits from Theresa Helburn, Maurice Wertheim, and Russel Crouse—all of the Theatre Guild. In the course of their visits he talked with both Helburn and Crouse about the eight-play project. A letter from Brooks Atkinson, the drama critic, arrived asking him to write something for the presentation of the Critics' Circle Award; O'Neill willingly spent the morning of the twenty-ninth on this but regretted the loss of a day's work from the Cycle. He was able to finish act one of the new first play on 1 April, in spite of another stomach upset, and got in a little more work before suffering a bilious attack.

O'Neill continued to work on "Greed of the Meek" as his health permitted and made more notes for the whole Cycle. On 10 April he thought it might "eventually be best to have Cycle title 'A Legend Of Possessors Self-Dispossessed'—II 'A Touch Of The Poet' VIII '[The] Hair Of The Dog'" (p. 250). (Nonetheless, until August of the following year he used the old titles in his *Work Diary* entries.) On 17 April he had finished act two of "Greed of the Meek," totaling forty-four pages and by the twenty-seventh had written the first scene of act three, amounting to thirty pages (pp. 251, 252).

After working fairly steadily, in spite of being interrupted by visits from Carl Van Vechten, the novelist, and his wife, the actress Fania Marinoff, and from Lawrence Langner and his wife, the actress Armina Marshall, he completed the third act on 21 May (p. 254). Immediately he went on to act four, although hampered by bilious attacks and bad nerves. Admitting on the thirty-first that he was "getting nowhere—baffled" he began to revise the outline of the whole play and went back to the original beginning of act four, adopting a scheme with more emphasis on the Three [Harford half-]Sisters. He made a new outline in accordance with this plan but had to admit that it "doesn't seem [to] solve problem of solution Abi⟨gail⟩. & Andrew". He began again on act four on 6 June, the day George Jean Nathan arrived for a visit. The next day he reported: "decide a 9th play may be necessary, preceding "Greed Of The Meek"—story of Andrew, Sisters, Kate from farm to French Revolution—write a plan of this" (pp. 255, 256). He got a possible title for that new first play, "Give Me Death," and began a revised outline of "Greed of the Meek" as it would be if a play preceded it. But after only a few days he found himself stuck, having decided that he could not complete that outline until "Give Me Death" was firm in his mind.

Accordingly, he worked on the new play from 15 to 23 June. He then took up "Greed of the Meek" again but, frustrated once more, he decided to put both plays aside for a time and finish "The Hair of the Dog." He ventured the hope that it might be possible to get along without the new plays as part of the Cycle, reverting to the original concept of "The Hair of the Dog" as the first of seven.

He took up that play on 27 June but promptly got a new slant on "Greed of the Meek" and made brief outlines that he hoped would solve his problems when he went back to the two new plays. Concentrating now on "The Hair of the Dog," he finished it on 17 July, except for the epilogue.

O'Neill brought Lawrence Langner up to date on the Cycle on 12 August:

> As for inside dope on the progress on my work, I have the second play ["The Hair of the Dog"] in good shape—beyond first draft—I can call it pretty well completed, unless I have to make minor changes in it later because of things in the other plays. The first play ["Greed of the Meek"] I have in first draft—but, damn it, it is two-plays long and will have to be entirely rewritten to condense it—or if it can't be condensed, then I may have to add still another first play ["Give Me Death"], making nine in all!

Try a Cycle sometime, I advise you—that is, I would advise you to, if I hated you! A lady bearing quintuplets is having a debonair, carefree time of it by comparison.[6]

He finished the second draft of "The Hair of the Dog" on 21 August and, still uncertain about the epilogue, decided to let the play rest without it.

The next day O'Neill made notes for the prologue for *More Stately Mansions* but then on 23 August returned to "Greed of the Meek," only to get stuck at the same old place (pp. 264, 265). On 8 September, he thought he had found a solution but was not completely satisfied and did some rewriting. By the sixteenth he had finished the first scene of act four and decided that, with revisions, this could stand as the complete act and end the play. But the next day he described himself in the *Work Diary* as "very depressed" and commented: "[I] don't like [the] end & this 1st draft is as long as 'Strange I⟨nterlude⟩.'!" (p. 266). In spite of his dissatisfaction with it, he decided to call the play finished, pending revision and condensation.

Although O'Neill subsequently made extensive notes for rewriting this second play of the nine-play Cycle, he seems not to have got around to making the changes he had planned. The manuscript of the play was destroyed on 21 February 1944 at Tao House, after the place was sold, but he preserved the title page and lists of scenes and characters, which provide evidence as to the state of the play at this time:

The characters were: Rev. Waldo Deane (51); Mercy (28), Sussanah (Mrs. Stephen Dixon) (26), Abigail (20), his daughters; Mrs. Andrew Harford (___) [O'Neill's blank]; Maggie Harford (69), Hannah Harford (68), Eliza Harford (66), her sisters-in-law; Henry Harford, her son (25); Captain Andrew Harford (57).

Act one was in a single scene: Waldo Deane's study in his parsonage in a small inland town near Boston—a fine morning in early spring in the year 1806. Act two was also in a single scene: the parlor of the Harford house—late fall, 1806. Act three was in three scenes, all showing the exterior and garden of the Harford house. The first scene occurred later the same day; the second still later that same day; the third that night.[7]

The weather during the summer months of 1936 and O'Neill's debilitated state were the reasons he gave at the time for his startling decision that he could no longer work at Sea Island. (A decade later, he gave Elizabeth

Shepley Sergeant a different reason: "Boom in Sea Island caused him to leave, too many people. It became solidly built up with rich social southerners in summer and northerners in winter.")[8] Carlotta was understandably upset when he informed her more or less casually of his verdict, but she accepted it resignedly, and the house that was to have been their final home was put up for sale. In spite of the disorder of packing, O'Neill spent 19 September reading over and making notes for the revision of the scenario for *More Stately Mansions.* He began work on actual dialogue for the play on the twenty-fourth and finished the first scene on 1 October. The next day, however, he began running a temperature and having chills, which persuaded him that he must go to New York again to see his doctor. On the fourth he wrote in his *Work Diary:* "will be glad [to] leave this place—hope we can sell it soon—climate no good for work half of year—and [I] feel [I] am jinxed here" (p. 269).

They left the next day. In New York Dr. Draper, after X rays and tests, agreed that O'Neill's whole person was sick but singled out no particular organ as responsible for his condition. The usual round of seeing friends followed, with no work possible. Later in the month Dr. Draper advised O'Neill that he must have absolute change and rest and not think about plays. On 30 October he and Carlotta left New York for Chicago on the 20th Century Limited and continued their journey on the Great Northern's Empire Builder. Sophus Winther, a young English professor at the University of Washington, whose critical study of O'Neill had been published in 1934, met them at Seattle. He and his wife drove the O'Neills to the house rented for them at 4701 West Ruffner Street, which O'Neill described as a "comfortable place, beautiful grounds on Puget Sound" (p. 271).

He and Carlotta had barely begun to enjoy life in the American Northwest after the heat and humidity of Georgia when, on 10 November, telegrams arrived from Russel Crouse, of the Guild; Richard Madden, O'Neill's agent; and Harry Weinberger, relaying the news that he had been awarded the Nobel Prize for literature. O'Neill at first refused to believe this (it had, after all, been rumored in 1935), but at 7:30 A.M. on the twelfth the word became official. Reporters from all the wire services—even one from Sweden—interviewers, and photographers swarmed around the O'Neill house; there were telegrams and cables; the moving picture newspeople would not take no for an answer. It was all too much for O'Neill in his poor mental and physical state. His

Work Diary of 15 November provides a record: "nerves all shot—hell of a chance to rest cure & forget plays!—feel I am on edge of breakdown—vitality exhausted—mental jim jams" (p. 272). Of course his ill health made travel to Sweden impossible, but it was obligatory that he write something to be read in Stockholm at the Nobel Prize banquet. He managed to finish the statement on the eighteenth.

After a few days the news became old, the reporters went off in search of fresher prey, and the O'Neills were free to continue their exploration of the country around Seattle—the Olympic peninsula and Lake Quinault, Whidbey Island, and Bellingham. Their old friend Kenneth Macgowan arrived from Hollywood for a brief visit. O'Neill was glad to see him again, and the two had "Much talk . . . over past & present". Among the many congratulatory letters was one from Earl Stevens, a mining engineer with whom he had gone to Honduras to prospect for gold in 1909. Stevens, who now lived in Portland, Oregon, came for an overnight visit; O'Neill found it a "pleasant surprise to have seen him again" (p. 274).

On 14 December O'Neill and Carlotta left for San Francisco in her daughter's Ford and arrived at the Fairmont Hotel on Nob Hill in the late afternoon of the seventeenth. He was under the weather most of the following day with a blinding headache; on the twenty-second, Carlotta took him to her old friend Dr. Charles A. Dukes, whom he liked immensely and who prescribed medicine for his bladder. On the twenty-third O'Neill commented: "feel very sick, weak & woozy . . . something all wrong, I'm afraid—getting to be a god damned invalid!—it's revolting!" (p. 275).

The day after Christmas Dr. Dukes sent O'Neill to Merritt Hospital in Oakland for tests and X rays. He awoke at 4:00 A.M. on the twenty-ninth with "terrible cramp, spasms" (p. 276). Dukes diagnosed appendicitis, and O'Neill underwent surgery at 1:00 that afternoon. He began to feel somewhat better, but the pain in his prostate and kidneys persisted, along with some nausea. On 12 January 1937 he wrote: "temp[erature] up to 102—chill—caffeine, adrenalin, codeine, morphine, atropine!—they give me the works!—C⟨arlotta⟩. & nurses up all night—⟨Dr.⟩ Dukes at 4 am—bad sinking spell with everyone worried but I feel too sick & ratty to give a damn whether I croak or not" (p. 277). He worsened on the fifteenth but then began to improve. A telegram on the twenty-sixth announcing the sale of Casa Genotta for seventy-five thousand dollars and his Sea Island lots for six thousand dollars cheered him a little. It was agreed that Carlotta would go to Sea Island to close the sale of the house and supervise the packing and shipping of their belongings. She left on February second, but O'Neill, feeling "lonely as hell!" kept in touch with her by telegraph and telephone (p. 279). When she returned exactly a month later, her mission accomplished, he got up from his hospital bed at six A.M. to meet her 7:45 train at the 11th Street Station in Oakland. He had arranged a second honeymoon for them, but when they arrived at the Fairmont, they were disappointed. He described the scene in his *Work Diary:* "shown to rooms & no double bed, in spite of my orders!—boys stand with bags while we kick & have bed changed!—a scene for farce but both of us deadly serious & determined!" (p. 281).

The honeymoon was soon over, and O'Neill went back to Merritt Hospital for more treatments, finally leaving on 12 March to return to the Fairmont. Now the search for a house to rent began in earnest. On the twenty-ninth they decided to take Woods House in Lafayette for six months, but since it would not be available until the first of June, there was still the problem of finding a place to live for the intervening two months. A happy solution became possible when Mrs. Harold Havre in Berkeley decided she would be glad to have the O'Neills as tenants. Her house at 2909 Avalon Avenue had a wonderful view from the heights over the bay to the Golden Gate Bridge, her family were fine people, and the Chinese servants who came with the house seemed good. So once more the O'Neills packed and unpacked. Loafing in the sun in Mrs. Havre's garden, he soon began to feel stronger. The Langners visited from Hollywood for tea and dinner and "much talk of ills of [the] theatre!" (p. 284).

But the family's bad luck continued: on 15 April Carlotta's daughter Cynthia also went into Merritt Hospital to have her appendix removed. Even so, on 18 May, O'Neill managed to make some notes on technique for the Cycle. They indicate how psychologically complicated his conception of the characters had become:

> Double characterization—two planes of dramas—
> Essential character in terms of compulsive thoughts—prejudices, hates, defiant & rebellious self-assertions of the uncompromising ego—going back to childhood—all this brought out in soliloquy
> Then the plane shifting to realism all this becomes hidden, shy, sly, compromising, opportunist, calculating, etc.

Characters introduced in soliloquy first—each alone—relaxed as far as surroundings are concerned—outer calm permitting free expression of soul assertion—

---

or on three planes—as Curtain rises—darkness—unconscious assertion—then half-light—characters dimly perceived—solil[oquy]. of conscious struggle living in part—then full light, realism, play begins in terms of surface life—[9]

On 22 April the O'Neills, searching for somewhere to live permanently, found the Bryant place, near Danville. O'Neill described it in the *Work Diary* as "just what we want!—most beautiful site ever!—158 acres" (p. 285). The title required a survey (the land was part of an old Spanish grant), and a right-of-way "kink" had to be straightened out. On 24 May Carlotta put up the balance of the money, and they purchased the property. On 1 June they moved, temporarily, into Woods House, and O'Neill commented: "beautiful place!—should get completely well here & able [to] resume work, please God!" (p. 288).

There he and Carlotta went over plans for the new house they would build on the Bryant property. After consultation with an architect, they decided on "the white with blue roof design—Cal⟨ifornia⟩. Gringo style!" (p. 290). He did a little work, "catching up on diary—letters", and bought a filing cabinet to facilitate arranging his papers (p. 289). On 18 and 19 June, after eight months of not writing, he set down a note for a new play "[of] 1 day—symbolical idea" and worked on it, recording in his *Work Diary* that it was "grand to feel creative mind alive again!" (p. 290).

The next day, O'Neill again took up the Cycle, making plans for the revision of "Greed of the Meek," "The Hair of the Dog" and *More Stately Mansions*. Notes he made at this time for "Nothing Is Lost but Honor" demonstrate how he was planning to enrich his portrayal of Honey Harford:

Honey brazenly builds up a legend of his heroic Civil-War record—when Jonathan and Sara point out that his story of having marched to the sea with Sherman can be easily refuted by facts & dates, he laughs—they don't know their voters—voters want to believe in heroes—don't reason, or no politician would ever be elected—facts mean nothing to them—what they demand are romantic lies—got to have a fairy story or they can't get to sleep—and what they want above all is to be put to sleep so they can dream—the leader they love most is the one who puts them most soundly to sleep and gives them the safest dreams—

But the irony is that in succeding plays Honey begins to believe his own lie—so does Sara—at last he believes it implicitly—and so does she—he has an imaginative narrative of the march to the Sea which is a real feat of tall lying—Georgia becoming a tropic wilderness infested with all manner of wild beasts & ferocious serpents—his tale is a sort of victorious tropical retreat from Moreno & Sherman a Napoleon—

Preceding this, and then paralleling it, is Sara's creation of the legend about her father—Honey laughs at this at first, and makes her laugh— but later he comes to believe it as she does.[10]

For a time in June 1937, O'Neill considered using "Give Me Death" as a general Cycle title but apparently decided to retain "Legend of Possessors Self-Dispossessed," at least for the time being. He worked on the outline for the new first play and also went over old notes, tearing up many of them. On 4 and 5 July he worked on the Harford family tree and name recurrence in the plays, and on the sixth once again took up "Give Me Death." On that day he bought drafting materials to help in drawing set designs. He continued to work on the first two plays but got stuck in the same old place with "Greed of the Meek." He was frightened for a while but commented in his *Work Diary:* "I'll get it this time!" (p. 293). By 22 July (his and Carlotta's eighth wedding anniversary), having worked every day, he finished notes for rewriting "Greed of the Meek." These notes pertaining to the second and third acts, summarized below, along with the scenario for act one already presented above, give an excellent idea of the plot of the play destroyed in 1944:

Jonathan [I, formerly Andrew] Harford, feeling that his wife, Kate, and his half-sisters, Maggie, Eliza, and Hannah, have stolen from him the love of his son, Henry, has left them, vesting control of his shipping business in Kate, to go on a series of voyages in search of freedom. Kate and the Sisters have approved Henry's marriage to Abigail Deane as a means of foiling his plans to be free of them. Henry will be bound to the business, therefore to his mother and his aunts so long as control is vested in Kate, and her will leaves it to the Sisters. The women are all in menopause; they have a new life, now that Jonathan has gone; but there's nothing for them to do but grow old and die.

Kate tells Abigail confidentially that she's glad she hasn't come to love

Henry. She resents his preoccupation with the business. He wants to take it from the sea, rid it of the ill-repute it has gained through years of the slave-trade, and make it honorable. Kate doesn't approve: business is business, and has its own code of honor. She and the Sisters picked Abigail out for Henry's wife because they were confident that she could hold her own. They wanted a woman who would help them manage Henry, one whose marriage would be a business arrangement, who would see to it that her husband did not cheat her of her rights.

After the marriage, the Sisters offer to let Abigail take charge of the garden, but she refuses: she has had enough of that at home. When *she* suggests that she might help Henry at the office or help them keep house, *they* refuse: they'll have no meddling. Finally she says she can just sit and watch and think—get to know them better.

Henry tells them all his plans to make the business a God-fearing one, in which it will not be necessary for his mother to be involved. His aunts rejoice at this—until he tells them he wants none of their advice either. When they say they'll disinherit him, he smiles coldly and points out that he knows them too well: they'd never leave their property out of the family. After he has made the shipping business honorable, he will sell out and go into textile manufacturing. Kate is at first happy at this, thinking in terms of an enormous store in Boston, but she becomes disgusted and hostile when he explains that he is talking about a factory. The Sisters, too, are hostile; they tell him his father would never consent. He replies that he is going to ask the court to presume his death, to declare him legally dead. Inwardly the Sisters don't approve (they are convinced that Jonathan is alive), although they pretend outwardly to agree. Abigail sees through this, and they admit it finally to her, but not in Kate's presence.

The Sisters and Kate see the need of the old defensive alliance against Henry. They must get Abigail on their side. They long for Jonathan's return: he'd soon put Henry in his proper place. They talk with Abigail, tell her that she mustn't be a slave to her husband. He'll do anything for her; he loves her madly. (Henry had confided to the Sisters an incident on shipboard during their honeymoon trip to France when he told Abigail that he loved her. She ridiculed this, because it wasn't what she wanted: it involved responsibility. She insisted that he had said it only because it was the proper thing for a husband to say to his wife on their honeymoon. He gave in and admitted that the marriage was to him only a good bargain. She said she was glad to have it all cleared up. In telling his aunts of this incident, Henry blamed them for his weakness.) And so now Abigail laughs, says that Henry loves no one, not even himself, only the business. The Sisters agree, but insist that he loves her second best. She must use her influence to make him fair to them. They offer to threaten to change their will to leave the business to her. But Abigail smilingly puts them off: she wants no possessions; she wants to be free. They tell her she talks like their half-brother, Jonathan. But they learned from him that those greedy for freedom must first own the earth. They must make everyone else slaves, or how can they feel free? Abigail senses that they still love and miss their half-brother, although they deny it. When she puts it another way, saying they hate him, they agree.

The news comes that Jonathan is returning home. The Sisters and Kate make excited dire predictions of the evil he will try to do to them. Abigail asks them why they pretend to themselves that this is not what they want. They deny it, but don't doubt *she* thinks she's got what *she* wishes. But she'll find out differently. See how she likes it when he tries to rape her. She thinks she's safe because she's his son's wife, but he'll have all the more reason to use her as a means of gaining revenge on Henry—for stealing Kate's love from him. Abigail is beaten down for a moment, then laughs at what minds they have. They remind her that she *would* pry into them, and warn her against prying into Jonathan's—if she doesn't want to drown in filth.

The Sisters wonder why their half-brother is returning. They suggest mockingly to Kate that he has heard the news of Henry's engagement and has come home to break it. Abigail points out that it is already too late: she and Henry are married. The Sisters ask if she thinks that will make any difference. They put it in her mind, and in Kate's, that Jonathan is coming home to take possession of Abigail, to add another slave. (They have always insisted that the Negro servant, Cato, is *his* slave, although he gave Cato to them when he left.) Abigail laughs, says she's no slave. And, of course, she is Henry's dutiful and faithful wife. The Sisters and Kate are at least glad that Jonathan is coming home because he will take back control of the business from Henry.

In the next scene, Abigail, alone, shows that she has been affected by the Sisters' suggestion that her father-in-law may be coming home to take her away from Henry. She is at first excited, happy, fascinated; then she be-comes angry, disgusted, shocked at herself.

In subsequent scenes, the Sisters, Kate, and Henry individually seek Abigail's aid against the others, assume that she will have influence with Jonathan because he will want to possess her. The Sisters tell her that she must make a good bargain. She asks if that means that they want her to sell herself. They reply, oh, no, only pretend, fool him, cheat him, give him nothing. He will be an old, lecherous fool by this time. She can twist him around her fingers. They are excited, elated; they feel young. Abigail, in spite of her boasted objectivity, is horrified—but also fascinated. She feels the same excitement—a bond with them. But she can't believe her father-in-law is such a monster as they say. They tell her, with relish, of the past, of Jonathan's unscrupulousness, of their father's murder, and their suspi-cion that Jonathan was the tramp who killed him. Kate tells of his kidnap-ping her. And Abigail sees that they all admire him. He takes what he wants, despite God or the devil. He's no pious fool, talking of myths like honor and honesty and virtue. He's not like Henry. They laugh with appreciation, and Abigail laughs with them.

They all get dressed in their best clothes. Abigail feels the atmosphere of excited jubilation at the return of their beloved and their triumph: Jonathan couldn't get on without them; he had to come home! Foreign lands are all right, but he belongs here, he belongs to America. But, of course, he'll never admit that: he'll boast how free he is.

In the next scene of act two, a few days later, there is jeering laughter outside the house from the crowd who have followed Jonathan, and a stone is thrown through a window. He enters, dressed in the yellow robes of a Buddhist monk. He tells his family of his conversion to Buddhism and of his plan to rid himself of all worldly possessions. They are at first amazed and dismayed, then laughingly scornful. He goes to his room, addresses Cato as his brother. Henry returns to his office. The Sisters and Kate taunt Abigail because Jonathan has taken no notice of her. Then they think it is all a trick on his part. But he can't fool them: they'll show him! "Give me liberty, or give me death," indeed; he has chosen death.

They predict to Abigail that they will win the coming battle. She is fascinated, then repelled, and asks them not to involve her. They tell her

The Harford Mansion. O'Neill's sketch of the façade. (YCAL, 20.3 × 22.4 cm.)

he'll make her involve herself. No man or woman who knew him was ever indifferent: you either hate or love, or both; but you can't stay outside him; you can't keep him from inside you. Among themselves they are vindictively glad that Jonathan will show Abigail up, take her down a peg: she's so confident because she's young and pretty, so sure of herself, as if she'd inherited the earth.

Henry brings in the newspaper, and is indignant when his father won't read it: it's his country, his duty. Henry talks of the Aaron Burr conspiracy: treason; all good citizens must unite to defend freedom against this threat to divide the country. He blames Jefferson for the Louisiana purchase: he's aiding the devil, Napoleon. They must stand with their mother country, England.

He tries to persuade his father to take back control of the business, to withdraw his denial of its value: he can't destroy his son's future, his life; and Henry explains why the business *is* his life and what his ideal is for it.

He suggests that they start on their own together, with the women out. Does his father still hold it against him that he stole his mother's love?

Henry appeals to Abigail to help him. It is she who has put the idea in his mind that his father may have come back to break up their marriage, as the Sisters have put it in hers. She asks if he is jealous. He denies it, says he loves only his business; and he knows her sense of honor and duty would keep her from letting anyone steal his property. But it would do no harm to cheat her father-in-law—make herself agreeable—for her husband's business's sake. She might achieve great influence, get him not to meddle, leave things as they are. She is alternately on Jonathan's side and on Henry's. Henry finally scorns her, tells her she is no help to him.

At the opening of the following scene, in the garden summerhouse, Jonathan and Abigail are in Buddhist contemplation. She yearns sincerely for him to convert her. But emotionally she resists it as death, giving up life without ever having lived, and she tells herself it is a trick to gain his confidence and then show him up. He reads to her. The Sisters and Kate come in, and Abigail pretends to them that she is being converted. They taunt her for her failure to attract him physically. The Sisters call her to go with them into the house; they want to give Kate a chance to win Jonathan over.

In the scene that follows, Kate's attitude toward Jonathan is at first only that of submissive, dutiful wife: if he comes to her bed, he'll be welcome. She confesses that she only pretended disgust when he used to take her: she *did* desire him in spite of feeling that she was just another whore. Now she's in menopause; it's a new life for a woman; she's free. Now that he too is free, can't they start again with her share of the property, and sail away? She'll go with him to the East, adore any God he adores, be his slave. But he remains silent. Then she flies into a rage; she knows he's only pretending. It's his cruel revenge: he knew he'd force her to humiliate herself, strip herself naked, and then his silence would spit disdain on her. She warns him to look out how he comes home to murder people's souls: two can play at that game. There was a time, as he knows well, when she would have killed her son— She is horrified at her own words: no, he put that in her mind again. But she would rather see him dead— He asks, than free? He gets up and goes.

Abigail has been listening, full of pity for Kate and of resentment, hatred toward Jonathan. The Sisters come and listen with her. They are glad that he scorns both Kate and Abigail, and are at the same time furious at him. They see that Kate has failed, and can't resist scornful satisfaction. When they and Abigail go to her, Kate says she changed her mind; denies she told Jonathan she'd let him come to her bed. She has pride if they haven't. The Sisters are scornful: does she think she can lie to them after all these years? They know what happened as well as if they'd listened. Kate breaks down and cries. They are genuinely pitying. They should have known better: they are the only ones who can manage Jonathan, bring him to his senses. They see him returning, and send Kate and Abigail away.

In the following scene, the Sisters begin by telling Jonathan they know he's only been pretending in order to get revenge on them. They admit that he has succeeded: they're punished; perhaps they deserved punishment—but not so much. They feel as if all value had been taken from life, as if all their living were worthless. They're getting older; they have moments of weakness; they'll never live to be a hundred. They're going to die. He says kindly that they all must die. After all, what is death? They are frightened at his mention of death; then react defiantly: he's trying to frighten them. They *will* live to be a hundred! He can't murder them! He starts to go. They stop him, pleading now that he not leave them alone with death. They were so glad to have him come home. It was like old times—the very old times on the farm, when he was a baby. He was such a pretty baby—when they were his mothers. They loved him so. They did a lot of wrong—of sin. It was because they loved him, wanted to make a man of him. And anyway he put it in their minds in the first place. Finally they confess that they didn't murder their father. They meant to—for love of him, Jonathan. They thought he'd believe them when they said it was for his sake, but he thought it was only their greed. Doesn't he believe? They wouldn't lie—so near death. Can't he forgive them? After all, he put it in their minds. Then they go on eagerly. They thought they could start all over—the four of them. They'd keep house for him. He's through with Kate. She's old. She can live alone on her share of the business. He doesn't need her. He can have all the wenches he wants. And Henry is married; he'll live on his share. Let him go into textiles. They'll all go back to the land—a big farm. He answers with kindly indifference that they don't understand: he has freed himself. All they speak of is earthbound greed, illusions. Their reaction is rage, jeering. They know he is pretending, and they, too, were only pretending. They *did* murder their father—to get the farm. And look out how he tries to murder them! When their lives are at stake—what they did once, they can do again! He goes. They break down and weep, feel old, dying: they can't even make him hate them.

In the next scene, between the Sisters and Kate, the situation is the same as in the previous scene between them, but with the roles reversed. They all weep together. Abigail is roused, loses her detachment, offers her sympathy. They reject it proudly. She denounces Jonathan, and then defends him. When they jeer that he has made a fool of her, is only pretending, cheating her, she insists that he is sincere. Why can't they let him alone? It won't do them any good, all this pleading for mercy, telling him how much they love him. Have they no pride? In their place she'd rather kill herself— or kill him. They must know it's either his life or theirs. They stare at her strangely, say, kill him? She says, well, they murdered his father in their mind; and Kate murdered Henry in her mind; and there comes a time when every murderer must kill again in self-defense, in order to keep living. She stops in horror at what she is saying, blames it on them: they put it in her mind! They stare at her. Then they turn and walk away—like nuns in a garden, their heads bowed in meditation. They mutter to each other: "Yes, perhaps that is the only way to possess our lives—in self-defense, but do it so no one would suspect. To hang for him would be a bad bargain. We must do it so we can accuse Abigail. She deserves it for failing us; anyway, she could say he tried to seduce her. Everyone would believe her: she's pretty, and no jury would convict her." They go.

Abigail, left alone, is torn by horror, fights to regain her mental poise, her mental detachment; but her emotions are uppermost: it serves Jonathan right for scorning her; but oh, she must warn him.

He comes in, and she does warn him, pleads with him to go away. He is calmly indifferent to the idea of death. She is angry at this: it denies the value of life, love. Then he says that he *would* go away, if it were not for— Greed is too strong here: it's hopeless to try to convert them. She asks what he meant when he said he would go away if it were not for—for what? He answers, for her. He sees that she is in great danger here of greed enslaving her, body and soul. Her spirit is rare and beautiful. He must save her first—free her spirit in truth so that they cannot touch her. She says that Henry may not consent to that: she is a dutiful wife. He replies that his son has the soul of a trader: he made a bargain for her body; let him keep that—but not her spirit. Abigail asks him if he desires to make her spirit his. He answers, to make it God's. She is scornful: her father tried that; she does not believe in God—only in the devil, in him. He turns away. She stops him. If she could only believe in him, in the purity of his love. He replies that he did not speak of love—except the love of the spirit. She goes on crazily: then she might be willing to have him possess her spirit, to give herself in freedom. But if he is free, why did he have to come home? He is struck by this, but smiles: since he is free, why not? Anyway, he wished to give them the property, free them. Abigail thinks he had to come home to prove to them that he *is* free, to prove it to himself. Again he is struck by this and angry: she doesn't want to be converted but only mocks at him; she is their conscious self, their slave. But as soon as she sees she has scored a point, Abigail is repentant. She blames the Sisters: it is they who put it in her mind; but she loathes them and all they stand for, and she does want to find new faith, a new God; since she turned from her father's God, she feels lost. He is drawn to her again, shows sympathy for her position, from his own experiences with his half-sisters. He begins to expound the Truth. But then she again has doubts, asks him what suddenly put it in his mind to come home? He thinks, remembers it was the news of Henry's engagement. He thought he might get here in time for the wedding; he knew it would be a long engagement. She suggests he may have planned to prevent the wedding; but no, that would not be right. He must be here so that he can steal his son's property, collect a debt—revenge. After all, it is only just: Henry stole love from him once. He reacts with harsh anger: what's that she's saying? It's a lie! He never loved— Then regaining calm, he says that he sees he's too late to save her: they already possess her spirit. He will go away. She grabs his arm, tells him he can't go. She needs him. She is poisoned here; her spirit is being enslaved; he must save her. She asks him to say he will stay for her sake. He consents.

There follows a scene with the Sisters in which Abigail tells them that Jonathan is absolutely sincere: they will waste their scheming on him. They ask if he has made love to her, kissed her? She is horrified and angry, tells them they put everything on the lowest plane. They reply that Jonathan taught them that was the only plane where they could live. She asks if they suppose she would let him make love to her. They reply that if he were the *old* Jonathan he'd *take* her. They leave her, hopelessly: he must have changed; he *is* free. They won't be able to rely on Abigail; they must act themselves.

She, left alone, expresses her resentment toward Jonathan: she will show him he can't despise her. Then she repents. She'll retreat into her mind, will not be involved.

The first scene of act three is set in the garden in the morning, some days (or a month?) later. The Sisters, now convinced that Jonathan is sincere, are in mourning: their brother is dead to them. Kate, too, is in mourning: her husband is dead to her. They all feel they are growing old, are dying, have lost interest in life. They hate Jonathan for murdering them. The plot to murder *him,* suggested by Abigail, begins to grow in their minds. They hate her because she has taken his side and defends him. Their taunts at her are in effect at him, but, as always, in spite of herself, they get under Abigail's skin: she tells them to wait and they'll see. Their hopes are momentarily aroused at this, but they soon sink back again into apathy.

The scenes are arranged to follow the pattern of Jonathan's meditative walks around the garden: as he comes to the particular spot, then walks out again (or they are all walking).

The next scene, the same afternoon, follows the same pattern: progressive deterioration, aging, desperation, the hatred of the Sisters and Kate. Kate had always felt before that, secretly, Jonathan desired her still: his refusal to have sexual relations with her and his throwing other women in her face were revengeful proofs that he still desired her. Now he confesses that he feels nothing; she is free. She takes this as contempt: she is old and unattractive; she is only the mother of Henry, who has grown up and no longer needs her, so she is dead. And so she too wants revenge on Jonathan: the death penalty for his having murdered her.

Abigail is being caught up more and more in this possessive-greed cycle. She feels slighted, begins to hate Jonathan—all this while maintaining before the Sisters and Kate her attitude of objective analysis and criticism.

To Henry, his father's attitude destroys honor, business, fair profit, patriotism, and family life. His indifference to Abigail is family nihilism: one should desire in order to marry, have children to inherit, found a family. That is what Abigail is pretty for, why God made her pretty. To deny this is to be a traitor to God, country, family. It is to murder life and so deserve death.

At the end of the scene Jonathan tells Abigail that she is indeed beautiful—and desirable. How came a girl of her spirit ever to love such a slavish, old young man as Henry? She replies that it is true she would have preferred a young old man of free spirit. Her manner becomes provocative: so he came home to kiss the bride, but he has not done so yet. He smiles and says that is easily remedied. They kiss, then, apart, stare at each other. She says, in horror, that that is infamous, unforgivable, for a father! He deserves death. He says that the Sisters and Kate have made her their creature; but he sees through her tricks, calls her a little slut. Then he repents. They exchange avowals of love. She says he must go away, and he agrees. The scene ends on the spirit plane.

Abigail feels at first a thrill, then disgust, hatred for Jonathan and hatred for the rest of the family for involving her. But when the Sisters come, she says there is nothing but all spirit between her and Jonathan. They taunt her with being worthless as a woman: she can't bear Henry a child. (Henry also shows contempt for this failure.) Then she reacts by boasting that Jonathan does want her. But they laugh, say that they've seen no signs of it. Why doesn't he take control of the business? Why doesn't he call them murderers? Why doesn't he force Kate to his bed?

In the third scene, it is night. Jonathan is in the summerhouse, reading the newspaper. He is fighting to recover his philosophic detachment, but has become obsessed with Burr, Jefferson, Napoleon, Louisiana—the issue of freedom or greed, the confusion in his thoughts with the personal issue as the reason for his homecoming: the Sisters, murder of their father, Kate, Henry, business, slave trade, Abigail, lust, love, his mother; hatred and love for Abigail.

His thinking is influenced by the passing of others outside the summerhouse. Every time he momentarily recovers his detachment he hears their voices and reverts to his old self. His final acknowledgment is that Abigail's analysis is right: he did come home to take her from Henry—and by God he will! Then he makes excuses for her: she's not a greedy bitch; it's not her fault; it's the influence of the family. She is a rare and free spirit; she loves him. He'll take her away from them, recover his old love-freedom dream that he had with Kate. Then he is bitter, foresees the same failure with Abigail that he had with Kate: if he could believe she loved him, but no, it's only greed.

The Sisters and Kate are on and off at the left, plotting murder. They are feeling their age; life is being drawn from them. They are justifying their contemplated crime by all that's happened in the past. The night is death; they are already dead and the dead can't be found guilty. But the blame is Abigail's: she put it in their minds. They are waiting for Jonathan's light to go out to kill him in his sleep. They don't want him to feel pain. It's the same plot as the old one for their father. Hannah has an axe; Kate has a knife.

Abigail comes in from the right. She can't sleep, is drawn in spite of herself, feels a terrific inner conflict, mental excitement, a feeling of power: they are her slaves. Then, as a reaction, she feels that she is *their* slave, Jonathan's slave; there's a feeling of joy at being his slave. Then comes anger: she'll make him adore her, then she'll spit on him. Then she fears for him: the Sisters and Kate will kill him and it's all her doing; she must warn him.

Cato comes to ask her to plead with Jonathan to take him back into slavery. (Jonathan has freed him on arrival.) She tells him she knows from her own experience that Jonathan will refuse; besides, she has no influence; she's detached. But Cato knows better. He has become more and more lost and bewildered since Jonathan's return. Jonathan's attitude makes freedom meaningless: Cato is only free to battle a hostile world. He wants his old security back—deliverance. Abigail is sympathetic, identifies his case with hers: it's cruelty. She subtly puts the idea of murder, revenge in *his* mind; then, when he has gone, she is horrified at herself. She must warn Jonathan.

She knocks on the door of the summerhouse. She enters, and she and Jonathan exchange declarations of love. Then each has the afterthought. Jonathan tells her to go away: he is meditating. He picks up the paper and begins to talk to himself about Burr. Abigail feels scorned, wants revenge: she'll go to the Sisters and Kate and make them kill him. She moves to the other side of the house, hears someone coming, hides.

Henry enters. As he does, the Sisters and Kate come in from the left. They see that Jonathan's light is still on and start to go back into the house. They are so tired; they're afraid they'll die before they can kill him. Henry talks more to himself than to them. He couldn't sleep, started to work in his office, Jonathan's old office, but his curse is there. Henry began to figure a deal to change the business from shipping to textiles, but the figures are meaningless, profit and loss are identical, honor or greed: he is bankrupt, a failure before he starts. His father has driven him into bankruptcy, ruined him; to save his pride there's nothing left but to blow his brains out.

Abigail comes forward to join them and says to Henry: or blow Jonathan's brains out, then they would all be free. The Sisters and Kate agree. Abigail adds that he can say his father tried to seduce her. No jury would blame him, as her husband. Henry goes to get his pistol.

Then Abigail is horrified; remorse sets in. She goes to warn Jonathan, or to threaten him with death if he doesn't—if he doesn't what? If he did, he should die; if he doesn't, he should die. She is bewildered, runs into his arms, calls him father, says she's frightened. He calls her a poor child, being possessed. He will save her, take her away. She is overjoyed. They kiss, but her dream develops into the old Kate dream. She kisses him in passion, then feels repulsion: she doesn't love him, she hates him; he is vile; she was only pretending so as to show him up as a fake. He agrees that, yes, of course, he's been pretending all along. He came home for revenge, as she saw, to take her back from Henry.

And now that's decided and all is frank between them, what is her price? She asks for the business. He writes out the gift and she accepts it. Then he says he doesn't want her. She replies that she doesn't want the business—and hands back the gift. There's a pause, as they stare at each other; then they kiss; then repulsion again. She says that he must be the devil. He answers that he supposes she thinks she's got him now, but he'll show her: he is leaving. She is dismayed, asks him not to leave. He answers that it is the only solution for them both. She agrees, tells him to go. There's danger for him here: there's murder in their minds. He laughs at this, says that death is nothing to him. She rejects this, accuses him of pretending again: she thinks death is what he came home to find. Then she taunts him about going: he's afraid, running away. He becomes angry: if one flees from the stink of a slave-pen, is that cowardice, or is it because one loves pure air? She tells him that he is a slave to his freedom, and leaves.

Jonathan, alone, in a rage, curses Abigail, but then gets her confused with his mother, his sisters and Kate, and all the sluts he has slept with. He'll fix her! And he dashes off a will leaving everything to her. He will join Burr: with him, by treachery and greed, and playing greed against greed, he can rise to the top. The only freedom is to make all others slaves, like Napoleon. He rushes out.

On his way out he meets Abigail, who has come back to save him. There is real love between them for a moment, then a recoil. He tells her she'll find her price inside—even if he didn't get what he paid for. And she'll rue the day she sold herself. She calls him a filthy old beast, tells him to go, with her curse. They start away from each other, then turn and together say, yearningly: if they could only believe their love was without greed. Abigail says that, at any rate, he was hers in his own mind; he can never forget that. He answers, no, he can never forget that *she* was *his* in the spirit. They laugh, strangely mocking, start toward each other, then turn, walk away without looking back, bid each other goodbye forever. He disappears. She whispers that she can never forget that she was his in her mind; now she will become pregnant.

The Sisters, Kate, and Henry gather at the right: the light is out, he will be asleep. It is time. They move toward the summerhouse.

The same action continues in act four. The Sisters, Kate, and Henry come in, find the summerhouse empty, and discover the will. Henry reads it to them, says that it is valid. Kate suggests weakly that they destroy it, but the Sisters are scornful: if they destroyed it, how Jonathan would laugh at their weakness! Kate says that they could do away with Abigail, but both Henry and the Sisters insist they can manage her: it will be a new game, give them a new interest in life. Each is glad the other didn't get the property: now they can be a united family again.

Abigail comes in. The others stare at her in silence. Henry hands her the will. She reads it, then starts to tear it up, but they all protest. Henry grabs her arm. The Sisters tell her that now that she's a Harford she will please remember that the Harfords have some honor. She agrees, pleads with them to believe that she is innocent. They ask if she is trying to make them think she swindled Jonathan—a pretty little fool like her. Oh, no, they know him too well. They boast with pride that he was one of the slickest traders on the coast: no one ever beat him at a bargain. Abigail repeats that she is innocent, then adds: except for a moment she can never forget, a moment in her mind. The Sisters are sympathetic, say they understand— who could understand better than they? They were like mothers to him.

They even murdered their father for love of him—that is, in their minds. Oh, not as he thought—if he ever did think so. He never knew what to think; he doesn't to this day. That's one time they fooled him and swindled him, but swindled themselves more because he never *could* believe. Kate asks, didn't she kill Henry for love of him—in her mind? Henry says he drowned a thousand Negroes for him; he can see them yet, in his mind, screaming as they were pushed over the side.

Then he suggests curtly to Abigail that they get down to business. What is she going to do? She says she'll give it all to all of them. Henry says, oh, no, she's a Harford; she must carry out his father's wishes. She suggests that she'll give it to charity. But Henry rebukes her: she can't do that, can't let it pass out of the family. She's a Harford. The Harfords don't believe in charity. They believe in no quarter given or asked, dog eat dog, and God help those who don't help themselves.

Abigail gives in: all right, she'll put Henry in control, but he must always consult with Kate; and Kate must consult with the Sisters. There are objections from all of them, but they finally agree, then ask: what about her? She answers, oh, she'll keep up the Harford garden with her slave, Cato. She loves gardens again now.

Henry leaves in a cold huff to get ready to go to the office. His final speech is addressed to his wife: she might have been fairer to him. Their marriage swindled him. She brings nothing—except her body—and he can buy as fair ones in town for ten dollars a night. He'll be giving her a child soon—not his. Kate, too, says that Abigail has swindled her, has taken her husband. She goes to her room.

Abigail is left alone with the Sisters. They become sad: they'll never see their brother again; they have a premonition that he will die, be free. They too will die soon and also be free. They become very feeble, self-pitying, and finally ask Abigail to give them a plot of ground in the graveyard for their own. Abigail softens, calls them poor old things. They change, call her weak, sentimental. She won't do; she'll never be a Harford. She takes this cue, says that she has reconsidered: their place will be in her burial plot, that's all. They call her a good girl, nicer than they thought: she understands.

Abigail, as she leaves, tells the Sisters that, anyway, they'll live to be a hundred. They answer that she can bet they will. But when she has gone, they confess to being tired of living: they don't want to be a hundred;

they'll die before Jonathan does; they'll know in time. They'll be over beyond waiting for him, beat him to it. He'll find he can't escape them. Dear Jonathan! They'll take care of him.

In the final scene, Abigail is walking in the garden. She is pregnant now.

The epilogue takes place about a year later. News has arrived of the wreck of Jonathan's barque, found in the Gulf of Mexico after a hurricane (or he was shot in a brawl with Burr's followers in Louisiana). The Sisters had died the very day before him. They had been waiting, growing older and feebler, then suddenly were in a great hurry to die, nervous and flustered, like aged brides. They looked so young in death. Kate has taken sick soon afterward: she feels a growing lassitude, weakness, is so lonely without the Sisters. She is resentful of them for leaving her. They got her into this, then deserted her.

The scene is set in Kate's bedroom. It is evening. Kate is dying, and Abigail sits by her bedside, nursing her baby [Ethan I, later Simon]. Kate asks if Henry is there. She doesn't want to die with Henry: Jonathan would feel cheated. He would want her dying to be his: his in death, forever his. She asks if the news of his death has been confirmed. Abigail says that it's undoubtedly true, but Henry has gone to talk to everyone on the ship, to make assurance doubly sure. He's getting each one of the men to sign a paper, with his lawyer. Henry is afraid his father will come back—to claim the child.

Kate's mind wanders: she relives the past, the honeymoon voyage and before; if only she could have believed. Then the episode of threatening to throw the child overboard. She thinks proudly that she would have done that for love—if only she could have believed. She feels that Abigail's baby is the heir, the child of love she wanted after Henry was born, who would have been Jonathan's child. Henry is only her own son—and the Sisters' son?—by her fear and insecurity; Jonathan was only the means.

Most of Kate's talk is before Henry appears—things she couldn't confess before him: he is so jealous; she would not have him know that she thought of murdering him; he would not understand—or how she has punished herself.

Abigail, too, is thinking of the past: she will never forget that she was Jonathan's. This baby is his in spirit, is only the son of Henry's body. She only used Henry as the material means to have a son by Jonathan. In

Henry's arms it was Jonathan she held. If she had not been a coward— She tells the baby not to listen. That is evil, but in the spirit all is good. She makes plans for the baby's future: he'll be a poet; he's the son of her spirit and Jonathan's. He will have the courage to sing that love is beauty, love is good; that love alone is good and beautiful, and that the highest moral duty is to claim and take what you desire in spite of all the world. He will be a poet, a Napoleon of the spirit.

Henry comes in, reports that all the papers have been signed: his father is dead. Now the business can go ahead, be reborn into textiles. All arrangements have been made to sell. Abigail will sign the papers, of course. He goes on talking of the future of the business, his own future. He is plainly exultant over his father's and aunts' deaths, and, by implication, the prospect of his mother's. He quotes Gray's "Elegy":

The boast of heraldry, the pomp of pow'r,
And all that beauty, all that wealth e'er gave,
Awaits alike th'inevitable hour.
The paths of glory lead but to the grave.

There'll be no more interference, no more greedy unscrupulousness and cheating. The business will be honorable, solid. He'll make the name of the firm a byword for honor, something the nation, the church, and the city can be proud of, an example to point to.

Abigail and Kate laugh together at this, so childish!—as if such things mattered! Abigail asks Kate if it is all right for her to give the business to Henry now. She agrees; they're all dead. Jonathan never really cared for property anyway, nor did the Sisters, nor does she. And she knows Abigail doesn't. Let Henry have his toy.

Henry is humbly grateful. But he is angry when the women laugh. He sinks into silence and begins to think aloud: now that his father is dead he can claim what is his. He calls to Abigail, but when she asks what he wants, he becomes embarrassed, mutters that it was only some business details, tells her, never mind.

Kate dies in silence. When Abigail says she thinks she is dead, Henry answers, yes, now he feels all free. Then he thinks aloud that he can now tell Abigail that he did love her on the ship—to be honorable, to clear up all the past. He doesn't love her now. He says to her that he wants at least one more son, to carry on the business, a reserve. He thinks aloud that he doesn't trust this one. Abigail says, yes, it's only a fair bargain that *he* should have *his* son. She is a dutiful wife. She's only too glad. He says then it's all agreed. He turns to go, to arrange for Kate's funeral. Abigail reminds him that he hasn't kissed his mother. He answers that he doesn't think she would have wished it, but since she is dead— He kisses her, then kisses Abigail, and is about to kiss the baby when Abigail says not to wake him. Henry goes to the door, turns, screams her name. She starts, irritatedly, tells him he'll wake the baby—might even wake the dead. He is stiff and polite: perhaps that was his intention; he doesn't know what made him do that—nerves, he supposes. Abigail tells him to go to bed: she will stay up with Kate.

CURTAIN[11]

O'Neill seems not to have carried out his intention to revise this second play of the nine-play Cycle in accordance with these elaborate notes. The list of acts and scenes preserved when the manuscript was destroyed in 1944 indicates that the changes were not made.

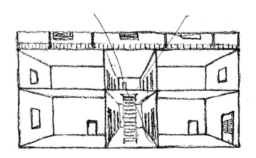

chapter eight

July 1937 to October 1940

With the help of new drafting equipment, O'Neill prepared a meticulously detailed Harford family tree on 10 and 11 July 1937. From the twenty-third to the twenty-fifth, he made notes on the whole nine-play Cycle and various of its parts. The next day he took up the final play, the old "Bessie Bowen," commented in his *Work Diary* that it would require an extra generation in the new scheme—" 'Honey' to live till [the] end?" (p. 295)—and made notes for it:

The play now opens in 1900, at Honey Harford's bicycle shop and livery stable (he has always loved thoroughbred horses). Act two is set at the factory as it becomes successful, and the final act three takes place at the old farm in 1932. (Lou Bowen, Honey's granddaughter, has inherited Sara's couple of acres on the river where Simon's log cabin stood—Sara having sold the rest of her estate—and has held on to them for good luck.) Honey, 67 in 1900, lives to the end, dying at 99. Sara II, daughter of Honey's wife Leda, but probably by Wolfe, is 37 at the opening. She marries Bowen and has an only daughter, Louisa (Lou), who is 18 when the play opens, 50 at its end. Lou marries the mechanic-inventor Ernie Cade (earlier Wade; finally Ward), who is 20 when the play opens, and they have four children: Jonathan III, Nora, Abigail, and Ourni. Lou successfully markets Cade's automobile and builds up a thriving enterprise. She gives a radio interview after she has sold the business and announced her retirement. This arouses tremendous interest because no one can understand why she should be taking this step at the height of her power and in the prime of her life. She has consented to give this first and only interview—

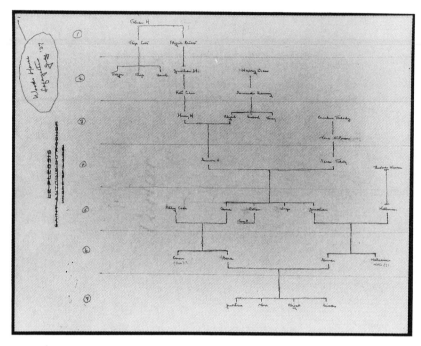

The Harford Family Tree. Drafted by O'Neill for the nine-play Cycle, 10–11 July 1937. (YCAL, 21 × 27.7 cm.) Many of the names were changed: for example, Ethan [I] H. became Evan H.

on condition that she can speak frankly, without sham. Her own attitude is an attempt to believe in what she says—and, on the other hand, a cynical materialism, a fear of insecurity, no goal.

She says that the second half of her life should have a different goal and be directed inside rather than outside. One should strive to learn the meaning of life and to know oneself. She has sacrificed everything for the business, has neglected her husband, letting him disappear into the background, although he is responsible for the car. (She knows no one will believe this.) She has neglected her children and wants to become a real mother now, wants to live in their lives.

But Lou's good resolutions come too late so far as her children are concerned. The younger son, Ourni, becomes "a hophead and Anarchistic idealist," who says at the end: "Sometime man will be able to live the Anarchist ideal—after he's grown a soul and is no longer nine-tenths the gorilla

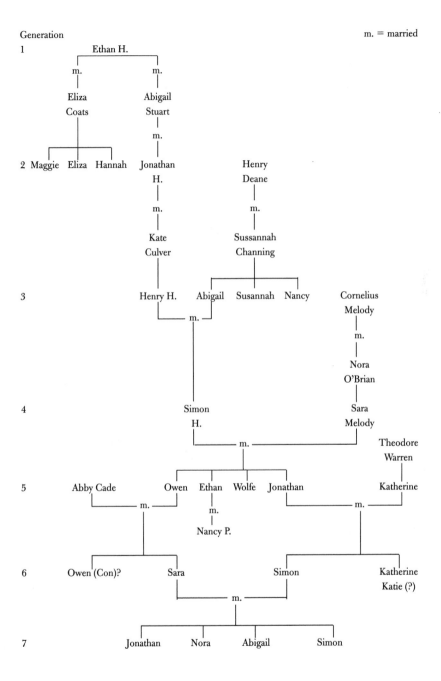

Generation   m. = married

1   Ethan H.

m.   m.

Eliza   Abigail
Coats   Stuart

m.

2   Maggie   Eliza   Hannah   Jonathan   Henry
                                 H.   Deane

m.   m.

Kate   Sussannah
Culver   Channing

3   Henry H.   Abigail   Susannah   Nancy   Cornelius
                                                 Melody
                     m.

m.

Nora
O'Brian

4   Simon   Sara
                         H.   Melody
                            m.   Theodore
                                             Warren

5   Abby Cade   Owen   Ethan   Wolfe   Jonathan   Katherine
             m.   m.   m.
                              Nancy P.

6   Owen (Con)?   Sara   Simon   Katherine
                                                  Katie (?)
                          m.

7   Jonathan   Nora   Abigail   Simon

as now." Then, cynical: "In a million years. In the meantime, let us sit and dream until death releases us. In death, what is time? Here's to being born again in that happy time, for, as you know, life might be of some significance across the belly then, it really might. One can imagine it—that is, with the aid of dope one can!" This son's wife is a Communist escapist. One of the daughters, a Lesbian who goes to Paris's Left Bank to live, is either to be a psychoanalyst or to undergo psychoanalysis, and is "left with a naked 'I.' "

Honey lives until 1932. He has stopped drinking in 1914 when told that he will die otherwise. He makes a virtue of this and becomes an ardent advocate of temperance when he sees the growing influence of the Anti-Saloon League. He becomes a power behind the scenes with that organization, sees war as a chance to put it across, foresees a great profit from booze under prohibition. He plans for breweries, distilleries, etc., tries to get Lou in on it as a favor to her. Then in 1920 he has a stroke and is ordered to cease all business activities or die. He wants to live—life is too good a joke to pass up—and so he resigns himself to playing the role of a cynical spectator. After another stroke in the late 1920s, he has to retire to a wheelchair. His mind begins to wander and he confuses the present with the past, but he keeps his old cynical immoral jests. His ambition is to fool all the doctors and live to be a hundred. His philosophy is a distortion of Wolfe's: life is all a gamble in which you are bound to lose; it's the game that counts; but the game is fine if you play it with enough zest.

At the very end of the play his is the last speech. He has reached the stage of being almost completely paralyzed, is rarely able to talk, but suddenly laughs with amusement at his family's vague gropings toward hope: "That's right! A hair of the dog that bit you! That's the ticket! We Harfords have been bitten by 111 dogs—and they're all the same dog, and his name is the Greed of Living and when he bites you there's a fever comes and a great thirst and a great drinking to kill it, and a grand drunk, and a terrible hangover and headache and remorse of conscience—and a sick empty stomach without greed or appetite. But take a hair of the dog and the sun will rise again for you—and the appetite and the thirst will come back, and you can forget—and begin all over!

He is silent—dead—they all stare at him—a long pause—curtain"[1]

O'Neill's plans for this final play, and especially for its ending, never became definite. Notes made at about this time indicate that he thought also of making Honey a successful writer "who cannot believe in the importance of writing. Words instead of opium—words are the opium of the spirit." He also considered making Lou's younger son "a successful novelist or playwright—yourself" and giving the final speech of the play to the author—"after he has bitterly stripped everything to mean nakedness": "What solution do you offer? Beautiful solutions, but no evasion over consciousness. We had every chance, brains, education, great teachers (Christ, Buddha, etc.)—have had them always with us. But greed checked us. Let us try ourselves, find ourselves guilty, condemn ourselves. And let us make the noble effort of our senses be to build a better character big enough to hold all the world, rid this earth of ourselves, give the insects a chance. They may prove as greedy and brainless as we. They may prove no better, but certainly, oh very certainly, they cannot be worse!"[2]

On 9 August 1937, O'Neill decided on some title changes that had heretofore been only tentative and set them down in the *Work Diary:* the new first play would be called "Greed of the Meek" and the second "And Give Me Death" (the title appears also as "Give Me Death" and "Or Give Me Death"). The third play would be *A Touch of the Poet,* and the ninth and last play, developed from the old "Bessie Bowen," would become "The Hair of the Dog." The whole Cycle would be called "Lament for Possessors Self-Dispossessed" (p. 296).

O'Neill began to write actual dialogue for the first play, "Greed of the Meek," on 11 August, but work was slow and he soon became discouraged: the play would not come to life. A new concept for its beginning gave him fresh impetus, however, and in spite of recurrent sinking spells, he managed to finish the first two acts by the end of October. Although he began act three, notes from Woods House dated 1 November show that his thoughts had again turned to the ending of the Cycle:

The younger son [of Lou Bowen and Ernie Wade], Ourni, says: "Truth is so simple, we've been taught it so many times—by Lao Tze, Confucius, Buddha, Plato, Christ—that everything would be solved. And why isn't it solved?" (in a rage) "Because not even God, if there was one, can make the soul of man out of the heart of a hog. You've got to murder the past in man, the hog. You might set an example by murdering the past in yourself." He shoots himself (?)

The elder son, Jonathan III, becomes a breakdown race-track driver, is disillusioned. Now he can't afford speed driving. He says: "That art-for-art's-sake is all bunk. It must have a purpose." He and his comrades form a mystic brotherhood; they unselfishly risk their lives to free men from machines. They drive and drive until they break the car, show its weakness—and then they make it stronger. "But still we break it, and, finally, they won't be able to make it any stronger—and we'll still break it."³

O'Neill resumed work on "Greed of the Meek," finishing the second scene of act three, but felt another sinking spell coming on, describing himself in the *Work Diary* as "very depressed mentally & physically". He read over the scene on the twenty-fifth and decided that although he didn't like it very much, he would postpone any rewriting until he had completed the play (p. 306).

Now, from mid-November 1937 until the end of March 1938, in addition to his other health problems, a painful shoulder and heat treatments for it interfered seriously with work. On 29 November O'Neill admitted that he was stuck on the third scene of act three of "Greed of the Meek." He didn't like this and other scenes set on shipboard (in this early plan) and on the thirtieth jotted down a new idea for them. He began a new second scene of act three on 6 December but soon decided that he had got off on the wrong foot and tore up what he had written. He managed to finish a new version on the tenth and completed a new third scene on the twentieth, recording in the *Work Diary:* "will call play finished now, because [I] feel too sick to work, but I know it is only 1st draft and needs a lot of rewriting before it can be what I want" (p. 308). On the twenty-third he looked over the first draft of "Greed of the Meek" again and commented: "is longer than "Strange I⟨nterlude⟩"—don't want this—but don't see now how it can be drastically cut without ruining it—trouble is [I] want to get too much in these plays for single length" (p. 309).

O'Neill tore up most of his notes for this first play of the nine-play Cycle. When he destroyed the manuscript in 1944, he preserved its title page and the listing of scenes and characters, as he had done with "And Give Me Death":

Act one was in four scenes: the first was set in a clearing at Evan Harford's farm in Massachusetts in the spring of 1775. The other three scenes were set at the farmhouse, the second a few minutes later, the third and fourth a year later in, respectively, June and July 1776.

Act two was in five scenes: the first was set in the street before Jonathan

" Greed Of The Meek " — $\text{Part One, Scenes 2, 3 + 4}$

Evan Harford's Farmhouse (with rooms). O'Neill's design for the set in "Greed of the Meek," Play One of the nine-play Cycle. (YCAL, Size of original: 10.2 × 15.2 cm.)

Harford's house in a seaport town in the summer of 1780. The other four scenes were set in the parlor of the house: the second also in the summer of 1780; the third a month later; the fourth over a month later, and the fifth a month later.

Act three was in three scenes: the first was set on Jonathan's barque, 1 January 1781; the second in the parlor of the Harford house in 1783, and the third the same, an hour later.

The characters were Evan Harford, 64; Elisa, 43, Dinah [formerly Maggie], 42, and Hannah, 40, his three daughters by his first marriage; Jonathan Harford, 21, his son by his second marriage; Thomas Knapp, a neighbor; Kate Blaine Harford, Jonathan's wife, who is 23 when she first appears (in 1780); Higgins, mate of the barque "Three Sisters"; Henry Harford, born in 1782, the son of Jonathan and Kate; Deborah Sykes, 25, unidentified; Caesar [later Cato], a [Negro] servant, who is 25 when he first appears (in 1782); Abigail [later Deborah] Deane, 9-year-old daughter of a neighbor in town; Rev. Simon [formerly Waldo, later Henry] Deane, 38, her father; the townspeople of the seaport, etc., and Robert MacNeer, unidentified.[4]

Apparently Evan Harford was murdered in the course of the first act, by a tramp. All four of his children seem to have had motives for wishing him dead, and the three daughters imply that they did kill him in their minds. They became convinced that he intended to disinherit them because they had played a part in encouraging their step-mother in her elopement. They also at times suspect that Jonathan may have been the tramp that killed their father.

Jonathan, educated at Harvard, becomes an advocate of freedom and of the American Revolution, and is engaged in running the blockade. After the war, he takes up the slave trade and makes a good deal of money. He becomes an apostle of France and Jacobinism, to the disapproval of the townspeople and his half-sisters, and finally renounces all property, leaving his wife Kate in charge, and sails off to the East in search of freedom.[5]

On 30 December 1937, the O'Neills moved into their new home, which they named Tao House. He recorded some of the events of those days in the *Work Diary*. Although the house was still a bedlam of "plumbers, electricians, carpenters banging", he tried to arrange his study tentatively (p. 309). On 9 January 1938: "walk over estate with C⟨arlotta⟩.—fine day—beautiful place with one of finest views ever seen—feel will be happy home once we're settled—and well!" (p. 310). But they were finding many things wrong with the house. They built a fire in their living room fireplace and found that it smoked up the whole area. To make matters even worse, a few days later the bad news came that the cost of the new house would be a good deal more than they had expected.

On the twenty-sixth neuritis was giving O'Neill "new hell—no sleep" (p. 311). On 2 February he went to the dentist for X rays to see if this new affliction was possibly caused by his teeth "instead of old [prostate] infection they have blamed so far" (p. 312). The verdict was that he must have more teeth pulled; he celebrated the tenth anniversary of his and Carlotta's elopement by having four teeth extracted. They were found to be badly abscessed, and O'Neill hoped that their removal would put an end to his neuritis. A month later he had four more pulled: "bad pyorrhea—thank God there are only a few left to trouble me now—teeth a curse for past ten years!" (p. 315).

In a letter sent that same day to his lawyer Harry Weinberger, O'Neill expressed his vexation: "This bad health stuff is a rotten bore. It busts up my working entirely. I only have to tear up the stuff I force myself to do when I'm under the weather. It just won't come right unless I feel reasonably fit. Rotten

Tao House, Danville, California. Built in 1937 by the O'Neills, who lived there from 30 December of that year until 26 February 1944. (YCAL)

nerves I don't count. I've always had those. But piling other ills on top of the rotten nerves gets me groggy. I haven't yet learned to take that extra punishment and go on regardless."[6]

The weather did nothing to help the situation, because from 17 January to 14 February it rained every day, setting a record. During that time O'Neill was able only to make a few notes for a play on Robespierre, indirectly connected with the Cycle, which now went back to the American Revolution. But at last, on 22 March, he felt up to reading the first three scenes of "Greed of the Meek." His opinion, recorded in the *Work Diary,* was that they "have real strange quality but need cutting & revision" (p. 315). Having read the entire play straight through, he commented: "needs a lot done to it—is as long as "Strange Interlude"!—and too psychologically involved in spots—feel I had better postpone rewriting 1st 2 plays until I've finished all others[:] easier [to] do then because of repeated themes first plays and last which complete [the] circle" (p. 316).

Toward the end of March, O'Neill read the scenario for *More Stately Mansions,* the fourth play of the nine-play Cycle, found that he liked it, and decided to go ahead with writing it. Better weather, the heat treatments, and the extracted teeth had cured his arm, and he felt he could work. He began with the usual preliminaries and started actual dialogue on the first of April. Work was somewhat interrupted by visits from his son Shane and Russel Crouse, but he finished act one and the first scene of act two before experiencing another sinking spell. Even so, he managed to work at least a little almost every day. He ran into difficulty in act four, reporting in mid-July that it was not going well and that he didn't like it. To clear up the trouble, he worked on a new scenario for that act and the epilogue and began again on act four at the end of July (pp. 324, 325).

Many of the notes for the revision of the play, including several that were not used, were preserved. The following, relating to Abigail (Deborah), reveal the complicated psychological states O'Neill was attempting to portray:

> Abigail's fear of what his [Simon's] coming to garden has done to her— has brought greed into it—the unscrupulous courage to face life, oneself, what one wants—to determine to get it no matter how, by any means, to steal it from another, to destroy one's enemy without mercy, to run any risk, to gamble for all or nothing, to bet one's soul, one's life, one's reason—she is afraid but at same time exultant—alive at last!—no fear of danger—and when Simon with her, no doubts—to gain love & hold it against world, that's woman's honor—like finally living her old dream of Versailles—and I'll drive her [Sara] out, destroy her, make her beg on knees for mercy and there will be no mercy—after all, it is just—she invaded, intruded, stole what was mine, drove me out to beg on the streets for life—only claiming what is mine—for what is more mine by every right and justice than my own son, born of my own body, blood of my blood and flesh of my flesh—I'll draw him back farther & farther into past—at my first word he becomes like child again—and it is what he wants, to be freed from her gross greed, the slavery to her hungry body which devours him— he longs for the old peace he knew in my body, as part of me, no greed, all tenderness, knowing my life was his life, that he had no life but mine—yes, I know he wants this—and I want only his happiness—then why afraid?—I am making him forget her—remember only past before she intruded on our privacy—but I am afraid it will destroy him—no, it is she who destroys him—and I destroy her peace & drive her out—[7]

On 8 September O'Neill could at last report in his *Work Diary:* "Finish Epilogue & 1st draft of 4th Play—but needs [a] lot of revision & rewriting—is as long as Strange Interlude!—but don't think [I] will be able to cut length much" (p. 328). He spent the rest of September and the first days of October going over the play and doing some rewriting. But on 12 October he had to take to his bed: both his doctors (Dukes and George Reinle, who was treating his prostatitis) made a house call that afternoon and decided he was experiencing another sinking spell and a "flareup of same old infection ⟨prostate⟩" (p. 331). He continued sick in bed until the fifteenth but celebrated his fiftieth birthday (on the sixteenth) by doing a little more work on *More Stately Mansions*. Although still feeling "punk," he worked on revisions from then until the end of December, going over the epilogue on the final two days of the year. Meanwhile, Carlotta, in spite of difficulty with her eyes, had typed the manuscript. On 1 January 1939, O'Neill began revising and making cuts in this typed copy and, even though beset by bad attacks of melancholia and neuritis, finished the revision of the first three acts—the "3rd Draft" of the play—on the twentieth (p. 340).

In this version a new first scene is introduced in act two: Joel Harford and Nicholas Gadsby, on the evening after Henry's funeral, get Abigail to leave the summerhouse and agree to try to persuade Simon and Sara to come to the rescue of the Harford Company. Other scenes are omitted or consolidated: the grandsons appear only once, all four together with Abigail in her garden in the second scene of act three. In the office scenes the Joel-Sara attraction is heightened; Abigail no longer intrudes there; and Sara deals with Simon's competitor, now named Tenard. In the end, Sara proves her love for Simon by agreeing to give him up to his mother. But Abigail, to show that it is she who loves him most, pushes him away from her and goes alone into madness. Sara, recognizing that Abigail has paid a price for love her own pride would never dare to pay, resolves now to give her life up to setting Simon free to become once more the dreamer with a touch of the poet in his soul, and the heart of a boy! She will smash the Company by letting Tenard know of its true condition. But she will take care first to get the Company's cash from the banks and put it in Abigail's name so that she will have it to keep her, comfortable, safe in her dream till the day she dies. In the epilogue Sara reports for Simon, who is recovering at last from his long illness, the story of his mother's last days.[8]

O'Neill now turned his attention to *A Touch of the Poet*, setting down notes for revising this third play of the nine-play Cycle to make Abigail (later Deborah) a more important character, "bring her in contact with Melody" (p. 341). He spent the period from 27 January to 9 February rewriting and finished a new act one with Abigail in it. He began at once on act two but felt too ill to do much. On the nineteenth Carlotta went into Stanford Hospital in San Francisco to have an eye operation, the trouble, wrote O'Neill, "probably brought on by typing my handwriting!" (p. 341). She was operated on successfully the next day and was allowed to return home, but with a trained nurse.

Soon O'Neill had calmed down sufficiently to begin again on a new first scene for act three of *A Touch of the Poet*, although he continued to feel "woozy" (p. 344). On 10 March Dr. Dukes gave him an examination and checkup. His blood pressure was found to be extremely low, and he was advised to "take it easy or else" (p. 345). Even so, he continued to work on *A Touch of the Poet* and finished another second draft. Working a little almost every day, he completed a third draft on 19 May. The next day he set down an idea that had come to him for a new play: "one day, Paris, Napoleon's coron⟨ation⟩." Although when he made the notes he was thinking of it as "outside [the] Cycle" (p. 350), it occurred to him at once that he might be able to use the story material of "Greed of the Meek," the first play of the nine-play Cycle, in this:

> 3 sisters—old scandal of [the] death of [their] father?—young wife, A[bigail]. & minister, (retired) father—Henry, Henry's mother—Jona[than I].
> Period play—1890 [i.e., 1790]–1805? (from start Jac[obinism].—to Emp[eror].) (put crown on own head—God blessing himself)
>
> ────────
>
> If joined to Cycle, then becomes story of Jona[than].—3 sisters—Kate—Henry—Abi[gail]—In Abi[gail]'s mind: Identification [of her father] Deane with Christ—with Napoleon—Identification [of] Jona[than]. with devil, with Robespierre, with Napoleon— . . . 1st trip [to] France '93 2nd trip France 1806[9]

O'Neill began to write the prologue for the fifth play, *The Calms of Capricorn,* on 24 May and finished it, "far from satisfied", on 3 June. But only two days later he reported in the *Work Diary:* "Decide what I've done on 5th Play is n⟨o⟩. g⟨ood⟩., so tear it up. Feel fed up and stale on [the] Cycle after 4½ years of not thinking of any other work—will do me good [to] lay [it] on [the] shelf and forget it for a while—do a play which has nothing to do with it" (p. 351).

He summarized the situation in a letter written at about this time to his friend Dana Skinner:

The Cycle of plays? The score is four down and five to go. However, of the four, two—the first ["Greed of the Meek"] and second ["And Give Me Death"]—are still in first draft and, for reasons too complicated for a letter, it is better not to try and finish them until I have gone on much farther with the whole thing. A matter of keeping them in their right place so they won't anticipate too much of what must appear again when the curve completes its circle. That will do for an explanation, although it doesn't tell all the story. A devilish job, this Cycle! It involves problems of adjustment between parts and whole for which there is no precedent in playwriting. And how this element, which I only dimly foresaw, or I might never have attempted the thing, devours time and labor! Rewriting and then rewriting some more! I work and work and time passes while, in relation to the whole work, I seem to stand still. Most discouraging, at times, like being on a treadmill. And then, the attempt to get a deeper, more revealing, more complicated motivation into character—to get at all the aspects of the inner struggle of opposites in the individual which is fate—keeps me constantly overreaching the medium. Confidentially, of the four plays written so far, three were double length or over! Which means I have really written seven plays, judged by length and labor. I say "were double length" because one, the fourth play [*More Stately Mansions*], I am bringing down to normal. Only the third one [*A Touch of the Poet*] wrote itself as naturally an ordinary length play. This is all most deplorable! I don't want any of them to be double length, except the last which will have to be, and I'm damned if I'll let them get away with it! So you see how it is. Yet I'm not really complaining. It's all extremely interesting and stimulating, and I'm glad of the excuse to have a long creative vacation from the Broadway theatre racket. As you know, the glamour of the Showshop and the fascination of casting and rehearsing and performing were never glamorous or fascinating to me. To put it mildly! I didn't tour with "Monte Cristo" the first seven years of my life for nothing!

But I would like a vacation from the Cycle and I may try writing a single play which is quite outside its orbit. Have quite a few ideas I like. So far, however, the Cycle just won't let me concentrate on anything else. It evidently doesn't approve of vacations, of that sort—or any sort![10]

The *Work Diary* documents O'Neill's progress in getting away from the Cycle. He read over various ideas for single plays and decided on 6 June to outline the two that seemed to appeal most to him: "the Jimmy the P⟨riest⟩.— H⟨ell⟩. H⟨ole⟩.—Garden [Hotel] idea—and N⟨ew⟩. L⟨ondon⟩. family one" (p. 351). He made notes for the first and got a "fine" title, *The Iceman Cometh,* instead of the tentative "Tomorrow" (the title of his published short story) that he had used in earlier notes. From 8 to 19 June he worked on the play and had finished an outline of the action through the first scene of act three when he felt another attack of weakness coming on.

The report from the doctors was "very low blood pressure—told to rest", and the O'Neill reaction was characteristic: "to hell with that!" In spite of feeling low, he resumed work on *The Iceman Cometh* and though he got little done, he expressed himself as "enthusiastic about this play's possibilities" (p. 352). He completed the outline on 24 June, felt better, with more pep, and made notes for the "N⟨ew⟩. L⟨ondon⟩. play idea—'Long Day's Journey'" (p. 353), finishing its outline on 3 July.

O'Neill decided to write *The Iceman Cometh* first and at the end of the month was able to report twenty-five working days devoted to it. He completed both act one, over forty pages, and act two, "long but grand!" in August (p. 357). In spite of another sinking spell early in September, he finished the first, longhand draft of the play on 12 October, the second draft on 26 November, and the third draft on 14 December. Six days later he wrote in his *Work Diary:* "will now call 'The Iceman Cometh' finished—one of [the] best plays I've ever written!" (p. 367).

The next day his publisher, Bennett Cerf, arrived for a visit, and they talked until two in the morning. Christmas interrupted work to a certain extent, but O'Neill managed to finish "trimming" *The Iceman Cometh* on 3 January 1940. He made notes the next day for a comedy with the tentative title "The Visit of Malatesta," and on the fifth reread his outline of *Long Day's Journey,* commenting: "want to do this soon—will have to be written in blood—but will be a great play, if done right" (p. 368). On 6 January, he reread the longhand draft of the first two acts of "Greed of the Meek," the first play of the nine-play Cycle, and liked it better than he'd thought he would (p. 368). On the seventh he finished the rereading and then made notes for its revision.

O'Neill did some further reading in January in connection with this and the second play, and from the tenth to the twenty-second worked on notes for use in rewriting the latter, now called "And Give Me Death." Some of these, dated 10 January, escaped destruction:

Jonathan[I]'s previous visits have come every five years. What he is and does each time is a symbol of his inner conflict: whenever he feels confident that he has solved it and become all one thing, he has to come home to boast—as the Sisters think. He feels the necessity to prove it to them, but they never believe him, or admit that they believe, because it is always like a revenge on them, proving he hasn't freed himself from them, and he has to go away to search for freedom again.

His first return had been in 1788, with a Hindu concubine. He was the immoral pagan pirate sailor, freed from love and law, with a wench in every port. He begins to corrupt the town, throwing money away, while obliging his family to live on a small allowance. Kate, now with a strong ideal of propriety, reacts as he desires her to, protects Henry from his influence, but she is really jealous: the Chinese mistress brings back the past. Kate wants to ask the authorities to make Jonathan leave, but the Sisters dissuade her by saying that the authorities wouldn't do this—too much money and influence of the company. They also taunt her with jealousy, give him satisfaction, etc. So they stop her, and Jonathan winds up defeated and leaves. He goes to France this time for the Revolution.

His second return comes in 1793, when he starts a Jacobin Club in the town. He is back to what he was at the beginning of "Greed of the Meek": a rights-of-man idealist. But, again underneath, it is defiance of the four women to prove that he is free of them. He is a ruthless fanatic idealist now, believing any crime is justified—including his father's murder. He attempts to convert them, and Henry; he is the extreme aesthetic Robespierre, the Saint Just type, cold, aloof, incorruptible, free of women—except the goddess of Liberty and Reason.

On his third return, in 1798, he shows his reaction of disillusionment at the failure of the French Revolution. In mockery of the rights of man, he has turned his ship into a slave ship. He betrays the beginning of his secret admiration of Napoleon. He tells the Sisters that he has come back to show them that he is completely converted to their philosophy. He has reverted to his father, a sensualist, with greed for property, the slave-trade profit. He has a female slave with him and flaunts her before the Sisters and Kate. Africa has fascinated him and has had its effect: he feels kinship with the primitive himself.

On the fourth return, in 1806 [the time of "And Give Me Death" as written], he comes back for Henry's twenty-fifth birthday and to distribute the property. He wants to convert them to what he thinks is his sincere belief in the vanity of possession. Abigail [later Deborah], 19, is at first disappointed in Jonathan, then drawn to his ideal of non-possession. They are all drawn to it, but, led by the Sisters, cannot really believe. There is a constant struggle between longing to believe and a failure to do so. Abigail and Jonathan himself are drawn into this struggle. Henry tries to stay aloof, to withdraw into his ideal of the upright, leading citizen, who believes it is his social duty to use his business for public service, for the development of the country. At last all the past comes alive for all of them and becomes the motivating force.[11]

O'Neill continued these notes on the twenty-first:

Jonathan has come back sincerely meaning forgiveness and greedlessness. They doubt, then believe. Then the past begins to take possession. Jonathan moves out of the house to avoid it. Suspicion grows. Abigail feels this and is terribly disturbed. She takes it upon herself to become reconciliator and mediator. The Sisters and Kate are at first grateful and eager, then suspicious. They hint at the sex motif. Abigail is horrified and fascinated, only half understanding. They take it back, say that they meant Jonathan. They warn her of what a ruthless beast he is underneath.

Her contact with Jonathan follows the same trend. Jonathan has the same struggle within himself. The past makes him want to possess Abigail as revenge compensation against the Sisters for his mother's desertion of him. He sees Henry as Kate's first husband, as his mother's lover, Abigail as his mother, Kate. He fights against them, tries to cling to his philosophy. He finally admits love for Abigail, but only on a spiritual plane.

As the past assumes control, the Sisters revert to unscrupulousness, which will use any means—even murder—to defeat Jonathan. And so Jonathan, as the past becomes more powerful, begins to see Abigail as his means of revenge, compensation payment in kind.[12]

In these notes the basic elements of plot remain more or less the same, except that O'Neill apparently contemplated having the scene of the crucial meeting between Abigail and Jonathan take place on Jonathan's ship, with the Sisters and Kate spying (as in *Mourning Becomes Electra*). He also had the idea of having the Sisters, Abigail and Deane go to France to find Jonathan before the play opens and of sending Henry and Abigail on a honeymoon trip to France to see Napoleon—ideas he used later in his plans for rewriting "Greed of the Meek" and "And Give Me Death" into four separate plays.

Saxe Commins, his editor, arrived for a visit on 19 January 1940 and was allowed to read *The Iceman Cometh*. O'Neill continued to work on his Cycle notes in the mornings but relaxed with Saxe and Carlotta on walks in the afternoons and over cards in the evenings. There was even a holiday on 2 February for a trip to San Francisco, where the three visited the Grabhorn Press and Golden Gate Park, with dinner afterward in Chinatown. The next day, O'Neill made some notes on the "*Cycle as whole*/mythological background—Sisters as Fates)," elaborating on the basic undertheme of the "frustrated meek to whom greed becomes a fate which they pass on as a destiny to the family":

At the opening of the first play ["Greed of the Meek"], the fate goes back to their own dispossession and that of their mother (with whom they identify themselves) by their father's second marriage to Janet [later Naomi]. They are the goddesses of Jonathan's birth: they possess his fate when they help and encourage his mother to desert him. They pass on fate of their own inner conflict in all its manifestations (for example, love of farm as free nature, beauty and their greed for farm as enslaved earth, profit. Janet brings them, through identification with her, love of flowers, garden as willful greedy cultivation—love versus lust—dream versus material reality—God versus Satan—meekness versus pride—free will (will to freedom) versus acceptance of predestination).

At the start of "Greed of the Meek" they affect their father through Janet, and Jonathan through Janet, representing fate out of the past. They come to realize through their own slavery to the past in themselves that the secret is that there is no present except in the past as it moves on: the past is the future. Those who know the past in others can use it to control the future. They deliberately resolve finally to identify themselves with the past, to be its agents and use it to be fate to others.

The only books belonging to Janet left in the house that their father didn't burn are mythology. The Sisters have become intrigued by this subject long before Janet elopes, fascinated to identify themselves—behind their meekness—with the Fates, the Furies, Houris, Graces, etc. They get revengeful satisfaction in going over to paganism in secret, since God has given nothing to meekness. They love spinning as a symbol (of their identification with the Fates).

There is a struggle throughout the Cycle of free will versus destiny (the past which is oneself) and therefore to conquer oneself in order to be free, to conquer outside one the symbols of the past that are in one (or evade, escape them). The Sisters hold Jonathan through his past, Kate through hers; they are again goddesses of birth over Henry. They get to know Abigail's past and become its agents in order to direct her destiny to their purpose.

But always they feel slaves to their own fate. They long to escape from it, to help others escape.

Through Abigail, they are again goddesses of birth over Simon's coming into the world and through what they have made Abigail and Henry; they pass on after they are dead into the family past that directs Simon's falling in love with Sara—its spiritual and material components—her past having made her into a complementing destiny.

In "Greed of the Meek" act one, they comment that their book learning concerning mythology came from Janet. The three Moirae were by some accounts daughters of Cronos and Night—Time and the goddess of the underworld and the dead (of ghosts and nightly apparitions). "Our father swallowed his children." They think of themselves as sisters identical with Hecate.[13]

O'Neill suffered another attack of weakness just before Commins left on 6 February and was in bed through the ninth. Gradually he began to feel better, and on the twenty-second he made more notes for the New London play and got the full title, *Long Day's Journey into Night.* This and the Malatesta-comedy idea alternated in his mind. On 3 March he decided to write *Long Day's Journey into Night* next but admitted to his *Work Diary* that he was "too low physically now for long stretch [of] work". But he continued to make notes for the play in spite of feeling "exhausted" and "all in". On the eighth, his doctors found his blood pressure "down in my boots" and decided to try some new shots (p. 373). Feeling much better, O'Neill began to write *Long Day's Journey* on 21 March and found that it went surprisingly well. Although work was interrupted by a siege of the flu during most of April, he managed to finish a first draft of act one on the thirtieth. But then he painfully threw out his sacroiliac and was again confined to bed. He was still feeling "too disorganized" to work when on 10 May came news of the invasion in Europe. O'Neill commented in his *Work Diary:* "to hell with trying [to] work—it's too insignificant in this madmen's world" (p. 377).

Because the war news had caused O'Neill to feel "spiritually completely disintegrated" (p. 378), Dr. Dukes took Dr. Edward Rynearson, of the Mayo Clinic, to Tao House to look O'Neill over. The two advised a three-week course of new daily shots. On 28 May O'Neill began administering them himself and reported on 9 June that they were "having fine effect—feel much better than in years—blood p⟨ressure⟩. up" (p. 379). Mentally, however, he could think of nothing but the war. Through most of June he began his *Work Diary* entries with the monotonously recurring words "War obsession" (pp. 379–81), but on the twenty-fifth he wrote: "am determined [to] shake this off—[it] is becoming neurosis—can't save even myself by not working and despairing about the future of individual freedom" (p. 381).

The next day he forced himself to read the first draft of act one of *Long Day's Journey into Night* and was surprised to find that he was "deeply held" by it. On 4 July he finished going over what he had done and commented: "am ready [to] go ahead with this play, deeply moved, convinced I can make it one of my best" (p. 381). Work on the play progressed steadily, although both O'Neill and Carlotta were sick intermittently, and because of eye troubles, he had to be fitted for new glasses. O'Neill again interrupted work in the middle of the month to make notes for two plays outside the Cycle "re present world collapse & dictatorships—no titles yet," one a "timeless timely, ventriloquist play," the other later called "Time Grandfather Was Dead" (pp. 385, 387). In spite of the tempting plans for new plays, he finished the first draft of act three of *Long Day's Journey* on the twenty-ninth. The next day, another new idea came to him for "duality of Man play—Good-Evil, Christ-Devil—begins Temptation on Mount—through to Crucifixion—Devil a modern power realist—symbolical spiritual conflict today & in all times" (p. 386).

The same day, O'Neill wrote optimistically to George Jean Nathan: "I think my putting the Cycle on the shelf indefinitely will prove to be a damned good thing. Particularly for the Cycle. When I do take it up again, I hope to be not only somewhat older but somewhat wiser. It can do with a bit more wisdom, and it needs a new orientation inspired by the fresh insight the present world revolution should give its author—if he can be wise!"[14] But he continued to stick to *Long Day's Journey,* completing the first draft on 20 September and the second draft, much pruned, on 16 October.

chapter nine

In July 1940 O'Neill had written sadly to Lawrence Langner that "The Cycle is on the shelf, and God knows if I can ever take it up again because I cannot foresee any future in this country or anywhere else to which it could spiritually belong."[1] But on 18 October he did return to the nine plays, surveying the first two and recording in the *Work Diary* on the twentieth: "both as long as 'S⟨trange⟩. I⟨nterlude⟩.'—& too complicated—tried to get too much into them, too many interwoven themes & motives, psychological & spiritual". And the next day: "Continuing study 1st & 2nd plays—question abandon and go back [to] old 7 play cycle, starting with what is now 3rd play—material too valuable for that—only other way is to break up 1st & 2nd into more plays than two". On the twenty-second: "Having slept on it, awake with idea for four plays to take place of 1st & 2nd, expanding Cycle to eleven!—1st to go back to 1755 when the Three Sisters were young girls". And the next day: "Decide [to] go ahead & make notes & outlines for the four plays of new idea which would replace present 1st & 2nd plays—very interested, as it is worth the time & trouble" (p. 391).

From 24 October until 13 November 1940, O'Neill worked on these notes and outlines:

The first play, tentatively titled both "The Poor in Spirit" and "The Pride of the Meek," and referred to, in 1947, as "Give Me Liberty And—," opens at a New England farmhouse, in 1754 (?), with three sisters, Eliza, 23, Dinah [formerly Maggie], 21, and Hannah, 20, spinning. Jonathan [I] Harford, 23, stops at the farm, seeking a temporary job in order to earn some money to enable him further to explore the American wilderness. He explains to the three sisters that he came over with General

Braddock's army, but was wounded and captured by the Indians. When they ask why the Indians didn't kill him, he says that he really doesn't know but thinks they saw that he liked them. He wasn't afraid, and honestly considered it was only just and natural that they should kill him. He had come to realize that the Indians are the victims of the war between France and England, seeing which nation is to own their lands. They decided he was honest and wanted him to join their tribe. He liked their idea of the land: use just enough to support them—no ownership. They wanted him to marry one of their young women, but he refused. The wilderness was too much for him, however, and he finally asked them for his freedom. They inquired if he wanted to go back to the white men; he replied, no, he wanted to find himself.

The Sisters ask Jonathan what he plans to do, will he settle down on the land? He replies that he aims to remain free, to travel, to see the wonders of the New World. He tells them of his family's slavery to the land in Wales. That was why he enlisted. He had no hard feelings for his family, although they did have against him: they see life one way; he sees it in another. Now he wants to rest a while, do the work he is used to on the land, get his bearings before he starts out again. They warn him not to tell that to their mother, Naomi [formerly Janet], and advise him to pretend that he wants to stay, since all their hired men leave. He asks why none of the sisters has married; he hears that girls usually marry early here. They answer that it's because they're plain. No one wants them unless he can get a piece of land as well. Their mother won't give that. Dinah did marry, but her husband ran away after a couple of months. Their father was worked to death. They finally urge Jonathan not to stay: they would like him to, but their mother will work him, too, to death.

Jonathan meets Naomi, still handsome at thirty-nine. She offers him employment, and he accepts, tempted by the fertile land, the fine house, and this handsome woman. In a short time he has proven his worth and established himself as a member of the family. He tells Naomi that it's the beauty of the valley and the land that attracts him—not the productivity of the farm; and he accuses her of not seeing it. She replies that she does, but she doesn't think of it except on Sundays in church.

She expresses to Jonathan her contempt for her first husband. He was the son of their nearest neighbor and the marriage had been arranged by her parents when she was eighteen in order to join the two farms. Eliza was born the next year and her two sisters within the next three years. Her parents died, and she came to dominate her husband, who was meek, a maker of daughters, an ex-vagabond. He became her slave, shared her greed for the land. Their three daughters grew up with a contemptuous tolerance of their father because of his usefulness, but without love or respect for him. He died when Naomi was thirty-six. Right after that she began to try to marry her daughters off to the farm's advantage, but their homeliness made this difficult. Being herself handsome, she feels disgust for their ugliness and has never troubled to conceal it. She hasn't wanted to marry again herself, was glad to be free. But Dinah's brief marriage changed her attitude. Dinah's husband was soon unfaithful, and even tried to seduce his two sisters-in-law, just for fun. When he realized that his mother-in-law had no intention of giving him any of the land, he left. After his departure, Dinah found that she was pregnant and deliberately brought on a miscarriage. Her two sisters' attitude toward her is a mixture of respect for her sexual experience and a jealous jeering.

Ever since the fiasco of Dinah's marriage, all three daughters have united in a meek, implacable defiance of their mother. She has come to see that remarriage is necessary for her. It will be her punishment on them to leave the farm only to the children of her second marriage. All the daughters will get is permission to live on the farm and be buried there. It is for this reason that she has decided to propose marriage to Jonathan as a strictly business proposition. She wants his labor, and a son. Finally, she does ask him to marry her. He accepts, but tells her honestly that he doesn't love her. She's a free, handsome animal and he wants her, and he supposes marriage is the only way to get her. She says that it is: she's no fool. He warns her that marriage won't hold him, but she replies that *she*'ll hold him: she'll have her looks for years. And she'll have a son by him. A son is a man's continuance and the continuance of his possessions. And the farm will hold him: she'll make a will leaving it to him. But, of course, she can always change her will.

She tells him that all three of her daughters are in love with him. He could have them by crooking his finger. He says that he knows he could. And he'd like to—to give them joy, if they really wanted that. But they want *him*—not pity. They're proud. She asks, sarcastically, if it's the pride of the meek; she's never heard of it. He replies that the meek can be terribly proud.

The Sisters have been listening to all this at the door. They comment that their mother is in love with Jonathan. She may fool him but not them. They feel a strange joy at his saying that he'd like to have them: so, in a way, they have been his—in spirit, which she doesn't understand. But they're glad he sees that they are proud.

Jonathan makes one other stipulation: Naomi must leave the managing of her daughters to him. They must no longer be slaves: they must be set free from spinning, must have a little leisure. She tells him he's a fool. Spinning is all they're good for. But she agrees he can have his way. He'll find they'll spin because what else can they do with their lives?

The marriage takes place, and a son, Ethan [I], is born the following year. But the birth is a hard one for Naomi, the last straw, added to overwork, and it leads to her collapse, her loss of her good looks, and rapid aging. She hates the baby as the cause of her ill health, and makes his three half-sisters nurse him, keep him out of her sight. She fears that Jonathan will leave her now that she is no longer handsome. She becomes jealous of him, nags, frets, and eventually worries herself into an early grave. She dies at forty-two.

Now that he is free of his bargain, Jonathan feels that the time has come for him to return to the wilderness. He has a deeply religious nature, but free from all cant. He explains to his stepdaughters his theory about life and the soul—hidden, suppressed, as God gives it: you've got to find it—make it your own in freedom—and at last you've got to give it away. His favorite Bible quotation, impressed on him by his father, is: "What shall it profit a man that he gain the whole world and lose his own soul?" He has brought them an appreciation for the spirit of freedom, a sense of beauty and love of the land divorced from ownership. The Sisters come to see the farm through his eyes. Although they would like to have him stay, they understand his need to be free, and they are happy to have sole possession of his son. He tells them to bring him up to be free: he must achieve liberty of mind through education. Jonathan has always been conscious of the handicap of his ignorance, and can only be free on a primitive, savage, Indian plane. He laughs at his stepdaughters, sees, with affectionate derision and pity, the greedy meekness in them: Ethan will profit by their bad example and will learn not to be one of the greedy meek. He promises to make over the farm to them and his son, equally, one fourth to each, provided they do not marry. This will protect them from themselves and his son from them. When Ethan is twenty, it will be for him to make the decision as to what is to be done about the farm.

The Sisters resolve to work the farm without help. They want no intruders. And so the first play ends, with Jonathan's departure, in 1757.

The second play, "The Rebellion of the Humble" (tentatively titled both "The Rights of Man" and "The Patience of the Meek"), opens eighteen years later on an April evening in 1775. The setting is the same as in the first play, but there is much evidence, exterior and interior, of an attempt to beautify the surroundings: an arbor, flowers, ornaments. Eliza is now thirty-eight, Dinah thirty-seven, Hannah thirty-six, and Ethan nineteen.

Inside, just after supper, Dinah, the cook and housekeeper, is clearing off the table. Eliza, the overseer and business manager, is at her desk. Hannah is the laborer. They discuss the growing excitement in the village over the news from Boston, reflecting a vague uneasiness. Ethan has sent warning of trouble, but they have always been reassured by the thought that nothing will ever affect them. They are uneasy, knowing that Ethan will be deciding the future of the farm, now that his schooling (at Harvard) is over and he has been admitted to the bar.

Eliza has been drawing up a summary of all they've done for the farm. If Jonathan ever comes back, he will be proud of them. And he *will* return some day, if he is still alive. They are afraid he may be dead: they haven't heard from him in ten years. He was then living in the wilderness, but had met someone who could write, and had sent letters out. They have obeyed his last admonition that they make Ethan an educated free man. He is a prodigy of brains, was head of his class at Harvard. They admire him tremendously, but show their regret that he has escaped from them in books. It's all in his mind; there's no feeling. But they quickly excuse this: he is their baby and they're proud of him. Feeling will come in time. He has had to concentrate on learning.

Hannah goes out to take care of the livestock, and her sisters discuss her love affairs. They disapprove, but excuse her: she can't help her desires; Jonathan wouldn't blame her, he'd understand. But Ethan, beneath his refusal to acknowledge that he knows about his half-sister's promiscuity, has shown that he is sternly disgusted. Dinah recalls her own brief marriage. She now insists that her husband did love and want her for herself, that she did respond to him. It was their mother's fault that he ran away. She has come to believe this ever since the news arrived of his death.

A scene outside the farmhouse shows Hannah and a farmhand. They discuss the news of Lexington and Concord. She goes in to tell her sisters. They wonder what the war is all about. Hannah reports that the farmhand has said it's for freedom. They vaguely approve of this, say that Jonathan would approve, and Ethan must approve. The farmhand has brought a letter that has come from Ethan. They read it together. He will be home soon. He tells them that he, as legal next of kin, has made application to have his father declared dead; but he will do nothing final without their consent, for he considers that he and his half-sisters own everything jointly. The Sisters say that he knows they love him. He knows they will do anything he asks. He says he has a plan. They hope his plan will be theirs: to come home, practice law in the village and county, make speeches, read books—but they are afraid.

Act two opens a week later, again at the farmhouse. The Sisters have continued to worry about what Ethan will decide about the farm. They know he will do the right thing, but they fear his idea of right. He is so different from anyone else in the family: his solitude as a boy; his courage; his timidity with girls (there was one who led him on and made fun of him). He has been extremely sensitive about his father's absence and the lies he has had to tell to explain it away: that he was sent to fight the Indians and explore the wilderness. The Sisters are tender over Ethan's dependence on them, and yet they resent that dependence—as if he was afraid he might love them: it isn't fair not to get a little love in return for all their love. Jonathan loved them, in his way.

Ethan arrives, and plunges right into the business of the farm. He considers the property three-fourths theirs. He knows they will see their duty to the cause of Liberty as he sees it: he knows they feel a sentimental attachment for the place; that's all the better—the nobler their sacrifice. They also have a greedy profit attachment. It will be good to purge their souls of that dross. He knows their souls are pure in essence, just as all men are good (Rousseau), and it was they who taught him to love liberty. They try, feebly, to protest, explain, persuade: he doesn't understand. But Ethan replies coldly that they will do as they wish—buy him out. They ask him what he will do. They point out that he is a lawyer without a practice. They see themselves as losing him. Won't he live with them, let them work, spin again? He appreciates their offer, but says he wants nothing done for his sake; all must be for the cause of Liberty. They give up meekly, try to make him accept a document assigning their interest in the farm to him, but he refuses. He has found a purchaser for everything, a man named Knapp. They resent his lack of interest in the farm: he sees neither the beauty nor the utility of it. Concealing his feeling, he asks casually about his pet bird, a thrush. He goes in to see it, comes back, overjoyed: the bird recognized him, hopped on his hand.

Act three opens a few hours later. Jonathan has come back, much to the delight of the Sisters. He was actually on the same stage with his son, but did not let Ethan know. The Sisters are uneasy at finding that Jonathan has changed. He seems sad, looks much older than his years. But they reassure themselves: it is only because he is tired. He asks what they have done. They tell him all about the farm. He says they know he doesn't mean that. They answer that they have brought up Ethan. He thinks they've made a mistake loving meekness: they've made a tyrant who needs to own a slave in order to be free. He asks if they love Ethan. They answer that they do. He says that's too bad: they had two poor choices to love—his son and him. They insist they will never regret loving him: he's opened their eyes to beauty.

He tells them of his experiences. At times he registers an Indian-like silence, followed by a burst of released inarticulate speech. There has been a conflict in him: he discovered he could never belong in the wilderness, or among the Indians. Just when he'd think he had begun to belong to their life, the slave in him would crop out, the tug back to hearth and home and tilled fields. He would start back for the farm but never get farther than the nearest town. There he would go on a drunk and soon become sick of civilization again. The only thing he's got out of it all is a love for America, Indian America, the vastness and beauty and freedom of it. Even the Indians don't own it: it allows them to crawl on it like insects, that's all. And he has come to a belief in war for war's sake as the proper activity of man. The war outside is the symbol of the war within—war as freedom from fear of death, of pain, of loss—from the cherishing of our individual life as if it were a property, as a declaration of the soul's independence. His idea of revolution is to chase the British out, then join with the Indians to shove the Americans out, then a grand war of extermination among the Indians themselves. Finally the land will be left alone, free and unconquerable, far from men's greed. But he says all this means nothing to them. They're thinking of the farm. The Sisters reply, no, they're thinking of him.

Ethan comes in with his caged bird. Father and son meet. Ethan registers a stilted formal politeness. Jonathan replies in kind, amusement in his eyes. He tells his son that he has an advantage over him: he heard him talk, watched him, on the stage when he thought all eyes were on him; he caught a look at his face when he thought he was alone. He thinks he knows him. He takes the cage from Ethan, shows sympathy for the captive thrush, asks, with some contempt, why not set the bird free? His son answers that the bird couldn't stand it. His father replies that that's what he thinks of man. This leads into a long argument between them about man's natural state. Ethan argues that human beings are naturally good. Jonathan expresses scorn for this point of view: what *is* good? Ethan goes out with his bird.

Jonathan and his stepdaughters discuss the future of the farm. He believes that they will be glad to be free of it: they'll get a chance to live before it's too late; they'll be able to stop being meek. They are sad: he no longer understands them. He wants to reaffirm the document by which they own three-fourths and Ethan one-fourth; but they refuse: they love Ethan; he's their baby. They will not be paid. He answers that he had forgotten their pride. They say, yes, he's forgotten their love, too. He asks what they want him to do. They ask him to stay here with them, in his home. They recall the beauties of the farm to him. But he says that now it's they who have forgotten him. One day he'd go, and then another day in the wilderness, just as he'd begun to belong, the tug of home would reassert itself. No, it's war for him now; he'll fight until he's free. They accuse him of being in love with the fear of death; it's himself he wants to kill in battle. He admits that may be: who knows? Anything.

They return to the subject of the fate of the farm. The Sisters will accept whatever Ethan wants. Jonathan asks them impatiently, will they never get over their damned meekness? He's going to see that they get their rights. It's time they ceased being meek slaves. He wants to set them free. They can't make him see that they love the farm creatively. But he has come to despise labor, tilling the earth: he'll make Ethan give them what is rightfully theirs. They reply that he has already offered it to them and they wouldn't take it. Jonathan says that Ethan made the offer because he knew they wouldn't accept it. They reply that he doesn't want it for himself, but

Jonathan insists that Ethan's goddess of Liberty is himself disguised as a Greek woman. He asks them to listen to reason. They, as women, were never made to mingle in men's arguments over the meaning of liberty. They were made to know that it means either being a slave to man, or having him for a slave. They've tried the first; now they can do as they please. They've got to live in the civilized world and there's only one way to be free in it—put money to work for them. He suggests that they take up privateering as an occupation, with motives of both patriotism and profit: that would give them a chance to inherit something besides hard labor; it would set them free. He insists on this, says he will tell his friend Mardo, a ship captain, to help them. Ethan, when he is told of this proposal, reluctantly agrees, because they will be engaged in an attempt to destroy British commerce and thus help the Cause.

The act ends outside the farmhouse with Jonathan saying goodbye to Ethan and the Sisters. He is going back to the army; he smells a battle soon. At the very last he realizes what the farm has come to mean to his stepdaughters, and asks Ethan why he doesn't stay here. But Ethan is inflexible: his half-sisters may do as they please, but he must go. He wants nothing to do with ownership of land. There'll be no ownership in the ideal State. Jonathan tells the Sisters to stay here and be damned to Ethan. Let him go his way into the slavery he calls Liberty. But they ask what they would have. They've given their lives to their half-brother. Jonathan doesn't know him. Ethan is really weak; he needs them.

After his father has left, Ethan is petty, jealous. He says he's glad he's gone: everything was arranged, and he did his best to spoil it. The Sisters ask if he's jealous, and he asks coldly, of what? He goes into the house. They are bitter: they were going to give him their share, weren't they? Perhaps they'd best wait and see how he behaves.

At the opening of act four, at sunset of an evening in June, the Sisters reveal growing rebellion, disturbance, and bitterness toward Ethan. He has gone to the village to conclude arrangements for the sale of the property. Each of the three says goodbye to her activities on the farm, while the others try to sympathize with her. Then they think they hear Ethan coming. They stiffen: they can be as hard as he is. They won't let him see, won't give him that satisfaction. They see through him. He begrudges the love they gave to the farm, wants it all. But then they feel regret, try to excuse him. They begin from another angle: they could make war, too. He needs them more than they need him, he'll find. They hate Knapp's having the place. They plan a surprise for him—for Ethan too (they have freed his pet bird). But they still cling to their devotion to Ethan and a vain hope of regaining Jonathan: maybe he'll be wounded, need nursing. If he lost a leg he couldn't wander any more. But they don't really mean that, of course.

News comes of the great victory at Lexington and Concord. There's a bonfire in the village. The Sisters hear Ethan coming and go and get the empty bird-cage, putting it in a prominent position. He comes in. He has got cash from the sale of the farm to Knapp. He gives each Sister her share, then begins an harangue on the Sacred Cause, the Rights of Man. He hopes they will see their duty. He has engaged a carriage to come for them right after supper. They ask, so soon? Then they agree, the sooner, the better. They're sick of this place: they want to get away and be free. But why a carriage? Why waste money? The stage is good enough. He explains that he has made a good bargain; he can afford the extra expense, and otherwise they would have to wait until morning. He is needed in the city, must make a speech at once, pointing out to all true patriots that independence from England should be only one aim of the war: it is necessary also to gain independence from domestic tyrants, greedy landowners like Knapp. He thought also that they would want to be alone with him in the carriage in their mutual bereavement; and he doesn't like at any time being forced to rub elbows with just any Tom, Dick, or Harry staring at him, prying into his affairs for no decent reason. You never know who may be a Tory, a British spy. And then, too, he'll be carrying his bird: there's too much fresh air on the stage, and people might regard his having such a pet as a sentimental weakness in a patriot.

The Sisters ask Ethan what he meant by "bereavement"? He pays no attention to their question, sees the cage, discovers that the bird is gone, breaks down. They tell him they let the thrush go, knew that it would be his wish to set him free. He flies into cold, arrogant fury: how dare they? The bird was his. They should be sent to prison, condemned to death. Then he asks them where the bird went, which way? If he calls, the bird will come. He rushes out to the gate, calls, whistles, coaxingly, then commandingly, in a rage, then pleadingly, breaks down and sobs. The Sisters gloat, then break, rush out to comfort him contritely: they'll buy him another bird. He says aloud to himself: the only thing he has ever loved. They freeze, draw away from him. He collects himself, becomes the incorruptible fanatic again. He thanks them: he is freer now. A patriot should have but one love—the love of liberty. They ask him again about the bereavement. He says that that is a bad word: it's cause for rejoicing rather. Word has come that Jonathan was killed in the Battle of Bunker Hill. The Sisters are overcome with grief. He is strangely jealous: he knew his father was the only thing they loved—except the profits of the farm. Then, angrily, he says it's improper to grieve: his father made up for a misspent life by a glorious death. His was a life of selfish individualism in which he deserted his only child, left his step-daughters enslaved to the land. He died just in time, too. He was an undisciplined force in the army. His acts, and things he said to his son were treason, corrupting the ideal. Ethan would in conscience have had to disown him, to wish him hung. It would have been a terrible test of his love for liberty to have had to wish his own father hung. He shows exaltation. The Sisters stare at him. He breaks off guiltily: he'll go in and collect his books. Are their things packed? They reply, yes, but they've decided not to take them—not to take anything to remind them—only the clothes on their backs, and they'll throw those away as soon as they can buy others. They'd like to leave naked. He asks about supper. They answer, no, they're not going into the house again. He goes in.

The Sisters say that he'd have been glad to denounce his father to prove how patriotic he is. They won't forget that. They can't. Something has gone, besides Jonathan. It must be love. They're free. They look around the farm deliberately: Ethan got a good price. Yes, nothing much here except beauty. You can't eat beauty. Anyway, they don't see beauty now: that is something that Jonathan put into their heads.

At the very last they remind themselves not to forget to light the candles.

The epilogue of the play is titled "The Fire Dance." The setting is a hilltop overlooking the valley and the farm, at midnight of the same day. There is the noise of a carriage stopping, and Ethan and the Three Sisters appear. He says there's a big fire—it seems to be their farm. They say, yes, they left candles burning. He asks them how they could be so careless. They answer that they also left some wood shavings soaked in whale oil. Ethan denounces them. They explain that they wanted to be free from the past and all means were justified. He doesn't object to that, does he? He admits that it *is* man's duty to free himself from the past, from ignorance and superstition. The Sisters reply, that's right. They believed in love and unselfishness and beauty and the soul and God and all such stupid things. He asks if they mean that religion is a stupid lie. He is a Deist; he believes there is a God, a Supreme Being. They answer, yes, and they bet he knows who his only son on earth is!

Ethan changes to an appreciation of what they have done: it must have been a great sacrifice. He knows they had a deep sentimental attachment for the house and barn. They will make fine patriot women. Yes, let it burn—a lesson to landowners. He becomes fascinated by the fire. They say, yes, they'll be patriots. That's common sense: make patriotism pay. They're going to see his father's friend, Captain Mardo; they'll build him privateers. They're tired of being meek and waiting on God's promise. They're going to grab all they can, make money work for them, make it be their slave. Ethan does his little dance, his exalted harangue. They stop him. He is foaming at the mouth, his eyes glazed. They say they'd better hurry, take the back roads in case they are followed. They jeer at him with a sinister possessiveness: he's not a Deist. He loves fire: he's a Satanist. Well, they're glad to have one pure patriot in the family. Nobody will ever accuse them of being impure while he's with them. And he's going to be with them: he's going to be their little pet bird.

The third play, "Greed of the Meek," opens in Newport (or Providence) in December 1783. The Sisters are alone in the parlor of their mansion as news of peace comes with the ringing of bells. They talk of the past, of Ethan. They express satisfaction at their complete revenge on him, at his failure and embittered retirement, and his entire dependence upon them. He spends his time studying languages, wants to make speeches and write pamphlets in every language, advocating revolution in other countries. But underneath the Sisters are still not completely satisfied. There is something in him that they have not possessed. They have a secret wish that he should at least try to free himself, become human, a man, see some woman as desirable—a wish that their stepfather Jonathan's son might become like his father. Then they remember the farm and that Ethan was glad at his father's death, and they become all hard and revengeful again. They will smash the little spirit he has left in him yet, will make him of some use to them—a slave. They are sick of treating him as a star boarder, fixing up his study, buying him books, seeing that he's never disturbed—but that's all part of their scheme: now that they're rich, they're getting on, they want an heir, a baby. It'll be a great joke to make him give them an heir who will cut him out. The scheme Mardo suggested ought to shake him up.

There follows a scene between the Sisters and Mardo. Hannah drinks rum, Dinah a glass of madeira, Eliza nothing. Mardo, Jonathan's associate, has become their intimate friend and in many ways has taken Jonathan's place in their affections. He is a coarse bull of a man but a daredevil, rollicking, immoral, irresponsible. They discuss with him plans for the next voyage, first to France, then either empty or with a cargo of trade goods to the west coast of Africa, then with slaves to Charleston, and cotton home. They plan with Mardo the shanghaiing of Ethan. Mardo shows his contempt for Ethan, living on his half-sisters, and for his theories and pride. He says he can't believe he's Jonathan's son—meaning no disrespect to their mother. The Sisters say that he's like her. Jonathan turned *her* into a slave—not that he wanted to, but through love. Mardo says he'll make a man of him or else. They insist he mustn't hurt Ethan: they make him promise not to lay a hand on him, give his word of honor. He promises, but says he doesn't understand their attitude: one minute they seem to hate and despise him, the next you'd think he was their spoiled baby. They laugh; admit that he is both.

And speaking of a baby, they explain that they want Ethan to marry and have a child. They ask Mardo to try and get him interested in some woman. He agrees, but doubts. Sailors' women in the port are a bit too rough. But maybe his mate's widow, Kate Blaine. The mate was a dirty dog but a fine seaman. He treated his wife like a slave. She was above him, a school teacher, romantic about a seafarer. By God, he took the romance out of her. He was a lustful one, but so is she beneath her ladylike manner, although she hated herself for it—according to his tales. She's a stupid woman behind her learning, but a good looker. All men's eyes follow her and want her. The Sisters have seen her; he suggests that they cultivate her, use her husband's death on their ship as an excuse. They can easily twist her around their fingers: they can anyone—even him. Doesn't he know they've swindled him on his share! They all laugh. Eliza protests that he only throws money away.

Ethan enters. He addresses the convention, so to speak, on the subject of his own incorruptible love of liberty and the rights of man. War has failed; peace means nothing, because greed has stopped man's ears; no one would listen to him: "What shall it profit a man if he gain the whole world and lose his own soul?" He condescends to approve of Jesus as a revolutionary leader, not as a man. But there is a Supreme Being, he decrees: the soul that loves liberty purely is immortal. Even Jesus was corrupted. "Give unto Caesar" was a compromise with Tyranny. When there is liberty and justice, the pure lover of liberty then is Caesar. He leaves them. Mardo comments that he's purer than Jesus; he's Caesar; he's the only one fit to have an immortal soul, and he's created God. He laughs, says you can't beat him. Wait till he gets Caesar on his ship and makes him toe the mark! The Sisters are delighted, agree, but tell him again not to hurt him—they need him. And again Mardo wonders at their attitude.

At the end of the scene they tell Mardo that he will find Ethan's door locked, but they have a duplicate key that he has never known about. Mardo says he will come around himself before dawn-sailing with two men to take him away.

The first scene of act two takes place two months later, in February 1784. The Sisters have transformed the mate's widow Kate into a fourth slave sister, who has affinities with the other three: her lust equates her with Hannah, her social propriety with Dinah, her piety and liking for accounts with Eliza. Her great weakness, which fits in with the Sisters' plans, is her longing for a child—as justification for lust.

In the second scene, two months later, the ship has returned from the voyage. Mardo comes to report to the Sisters. He has gained a grudging respect for Ethan. He couldn't break him or make him shut up. He put him in the forecastle, where he made speeches and almost caused a mutiny. But Mardo finished by making him mate. Then he got afraid Ethan would push him overboard some night to be captain and start a Utopia under his command. He was fascinated by the sea, a mixture of love and hate, of defiance and fear. Mardo noticed the looks he'd give women, but he was too timid. He went to Paris—trouble was brewing there—and came back gabbing more than ever. Mardo sees Kate and sardonically grins with appreciation of what the Sisters have done with her—especially after Ethan comes and looks at her. He makes a speech forgiving the Sisters for having him shanghaied. They have taught him to know the world, that oppression is everywhere. Revolution must be worldwide.

In scene three, three months later, Kate, prompted by the Sisters, convinces Ethan of her love of liberty, and he finally proposes: a life of comradeship, no sex, purity, self-sacrifice, poverty, devotion to the ideal. They will take a honeymoon trip to France, borrowing money from the Sisters, who will of course charge him the usual interest rates. Kate mentions the child they hope for. Ethan is repelled. She hastens to explain that this would be a son to carry on his ideal—as heir to liberty—to carry on his teachings. He shows he thinks he has no need of a son; he himself can do it all; but she sides against him. He finally stammers bashfully that he would like a son to bring up in his teachings as the perfect free man of the future. The Sisters seem hurt: he's getting the better of her—she may fall in love. They decide to go on the honeymoon trip.

Act three begins in the spring of 1785. The ship is at anchor off an island, having been blown off course by a hurricane. Repairs are necessary to the topmast. All of them, except Mardo, have been changed by the sea. The Sisters, shaken, feel that it was a mistake ever to have come. They see their hold on Ethan and Kate weakened. He, though green with seasickness, was roused to reckless ecstasy by the storm, delighted in its wild destructive force (as at the fire on the farm); the storm was for him a symbol of revolution. This leads to unrestrained passion with Kate—destructive possession, a love of hate. She responds to this wildly. She is again enslaved as a female, but with aroused hostility. The Sisters see what is going on; they lose control of her—they are weak—not sea women. Kate fights a return to them—the only escape from Ethan's destructive uncreative possession is pregnancy and return to land. The Sisters pray with her for her pregnancy—salvation from the barren sea.

The setting shows the deck and cabin, the Sisters' stateroom below [as in *Mourning Becomes Electra*]. The land-locked harbor is the Sisters' sea. With land near, things return to normal. The Sisters again become dominant. Ethan reverts to his cold, dry-as-dust incorruptible self. He resents Kate's having taken advantage of the storm to corrupt him. Kate discovers she is pregnant. Ethan is resentful. The four of them put him back in his place, give him back to his ideals. They don't need him now, but he must work for his son on their return—no more loafing. They decide he isn't good for much but will serve as a clerk to help Eliza, or help Hannah check cargo, or help Dinah with the housekeeping accounts on afternoons at home. The Sisters say that he can keep on making speeches. Whenever they have company, they'll have him make one to their guests. Captain Mardo is in and out during all this; he gets the obvious currents, but most of it is over his head.

Act four opens with the ship at a wharf at a port in France in early 1786. Kate's baby, christened Henry, has been born at sea. There's much worry just now on the Sisters' part because Ethan has been on shore all night. He's never stayed away since his college days. Kate, possessed by the baby, is indifferent. The Sisters resent her attitude, show their contempt. She's like a cow or a sow. They taunt her. Her husband is ashore with Mardo, probably with prostitutes. Kate doesn't resent this. She explains she used to mind with her first husband, because she felt she was being cheated, but Ethan has given her what she desired. She doesn't want his lust; she's glad to have other women set him free of it. Then she adds, she's afraid of Ethan now too. Once when she was on deck with the baby in her arms, he bumped into her, almost knocked the baby out of her arms or both of them overboard. He pretended it was the roll of the ship, but it wasn't. The Sisters ask why she didn't tell them—before? Two can play at that game. Then they are horrified at themselves: maybe it would be better if Ethan never came back. Kate agrees.

Mardo arrives with a letter, enormously long, written to them all by Ethan. He has decided to give his life to the revolution starting in France. This will be a pure one. He calmly announces that he has taken all the ship's money, and justifies the theft as the means to an end. He orders the Sisters to see that Kate brings his son up right. He doesn't trust her. She is impure, easily becomes a slave to lust. But two of the Sisters are pure, and Hannah is at least a free spirit. The letter ends with a long speech of admonishment to the Sisters to free themselves from greed for material possessions. He says he can support himself as agent for their ship— provided there is no slave trade.

Kate says simply she's glad he's gone. He was dangerous to the baby— jealous of it. They are furious with her—taunt, sneer at, revile, threaten her. She hasn't a nickel. They'll make her sweat. She says she'll do anything for her baby. Then she becomes sly, points out that he's their baby, too. If they're nice to her, she'll let him love them, too. The Sisters see her scheme and tell her so. But she says she's not trying to hide it: they were partners in this. They group themselves around the baby and say, scornfully, anyway Ethan will come back.

And Ethan does—along the wharf, up the gangplank, along the deck. He shows great agitation on the wharf, fear of the dark. He hurries toward the group, then stands without speaking. They don't notice him and go on talking. He'll come back. They'll get tired of his speeches; they won't believe his love of God. They'll rotten egg him. There won't be any liberty. What is liberty? A word. There is no such thing—and even if there was and he had it, what would he do with it? He'd have to shoot himself. He'd go crazy. He'd burst out crying: he'd be so afraid of the dark.

Ethan's face hardens. He turns back, retraces his steps. He walks along the wharf, at the edge. Just before his exit, he meets a stranger, button-holes him, starts an harangue: "Death to tyrants!" The women on board don't hear him; they are admiring the baby: he looks like our stepfather Jonathan—the only man we ever loved. He didn't have to free others. He *was* free.

The epilogue takes place in the early autumn of 1794. In the first scene, in the west parlor of the Sisters' mansion, are Kate and Henry [later Waldo] Deane, a minister. Kate and Ethan's son, Henry, now eight, and Deane's eight-year-old daughter, Abigail [later Deborah] are in the garden. The ship with the Sisters on board is coming into the harbor to the family dock. They have gone to France on receiving the news that Ethan was arrested as an adherent of Robespierre. It is evident that Deane and Kate are sentimentally attached. She is in a distracted state and confesses to him that she hopes the Sisters have failed in their effort to free her husband, that he was executed; then she would be free. He rebukes her shakenly, but she goes on to wish that the Sisters were dead, too. She is their slave. If they were dead, and Ethan were dead, all their money would come to her for little Henry. They would all be free. Again he rebukes her, sternly. She breaks, becomes contrite, sobs on his shoulder. Abigail peers in the win-dow, interrupting them. Deane says he's afraid she is a mischievous child, needs a mother. All her sisters have married and gone away. Abigail just stares. Deane continues, says she's such a silent child—always thinking, day-dreaming. Then he asks her what she is thinking. She wonders why Henry's mother is crying. Is she sorry her husband is coming home? They send her back out to the garden to play. She goes dutifully. Kate says that the child does need a mother. Perhaps she and Henry will grow up to love each other and be married. Then she says, repentantly, that she's sorry she gave way. She didn't mean it about the Sisters, but the situation is a hard one to bear. She *is* a slave; she owns nothing; she is nothing to them but

Henry's mother. Her only protection is to threaten to take Henry away. They idolize him. Then she appeals to Deane's prejudice: she hates the Sisters for being in the slave trade, as he does. He says he doesn't *hate* them; he's sure he can make them see the error of their ways. They give generously to the church. Kate says she's afraid they'll see it's a wicked trade only when it becomes unprofitable.

The Sisters arrive home. Deane goes into the garden, telling Kate that it's better that she sees them alone. They come in. There's the sound of Ethan being taken upstairs. They explain they have bad news for her. Ethan's alive, but suffering from starvation in the top of the prison. They admit to a strange conflict in themselves: they had to take every step to rescue their step-father Jonathan's son, but at the same time they hoped they'd fail. If Ethan had been executed for his faith, that would have been a fitting end. They hoped that, for his sake. But still they are proud that his spirit was not broken. He's washed his hands of the world. He renounces it and everyone in it. He renounces them, says he's going to live in the summerhouse in the garden.

The Sisters had gone to Mme. Tallien and Josephine, had paid a bribe. He cost them a lot of money, Ethan did, and he's a dead loss. His final tragic futility was that he was so unimportant that they put him in prison and forgot to guillotine him. But he has made himself believe he was on the eve of being guillotined when they rescued him. He refused to be rescued, but they gave him the bum's rush out of prison. Later on, it becomes a legend that he was about to be executed for his Jacobinism. They have enough contemptuous pity to encourage this belief, and insist that Kate does so too, treat him as an outcast, family disgrace, because of it. This keeps his pride and self-respect alive and justifies his isolation and his idle dependence upon them.

There's a change in the Sisters. They are all unscrupulous acquisitiveness on the surface. Their weakness is their affection for Henry—and a growing secret fear of death, which makes them—especially Dinah—favorable to Kate's ambitions for respectability and church-going, her union with a minister's family. They are attracted to Abigail yet puzzled by her. She runs through their possessive fingers when they try to grab her. Their attitude toward Kate is one of cynical amused insight and contempt, combined with jealousy of her re Henry. They are glad at Ethan's return because that puts an end to her threats to run away with the child. They jeer about her and Deane, are ribald about it. Also in Kate there is a disappointment that Ethan is not going to claim his conjugal rights so that she can be a martyr. Kate, with the Sisters, always takes their attitude of hard, practical scheming. The end justifies the means. There's negation, and denial of any emotional motive.

At the end of the epilogue they are all on stage, including Mardo. Then Ethan enters, grim, dryly dictatorial. He announces his decision as to his way of life in the future, in a wordy speech. The Sisters begin to talk with Kate; no one is listening, having heard it all before. Ethan greets Deane. He wouldn't have allowed a minister in the house once, when he was an atheist, but now, since Robespierre decreed it, there is a Supreme Being and man has an immortal soul. (He quotes Robespierre's words.) He shakes hands with Deane and again gives a speech. He's conscious of the rude ignoring chatter of his wife and half-sisters. He turns on them, denounces them. He *has* no family, no sisters, no wife or child: he abjures and denounces greed, fake religion, fake respectability, gross animalism, fake modesty, hypocritical purity covering unbridled lust. Kate is terribly embarrassed and denies this bitterly.

Deane shows the children into the garden. Then Ethan goes on to denounce the profits of the slave trade. Deane joins in a diffident agreement, reproaching the Sisters. They reply that they're planning to get out of it, get off the sea altogether. They're going to invest in land, city land, rents, and sit back in leisure. They'll give the ship to Mardo; it needs so much repairing. Ethan denounces this. He is for the distribution of the land.

Then Ethan boasts to Deane that he was rescued against his will; he was about to go to the guillotine, his martyrdom more secure than Robespierre's. It was torture, waiting for death, day after day. He would have died gladly: his last words would have been: "*Mort aux tyrants! Vive la Revolution! Vive la Liberté!*" He suddenly turns appealingly to the Sisters, asks them if that isn't the truth? They stare at him at first, then say, pityingly, yes, of course. Kate comes in vengefully, says that it's not true. They turn on her, tell her to shut up. What does she know? Deane cuts in that he cannot agree with Ethan's admiration of Robespierre. He was a villain. Ethan insists that he was the greatest moral leader since Christ— greater than Christ. Deane is outraged. They argue furiously, and the

Sisters send them both out into the garden, telling Ethan to show the minister what he's going to do to the summerhouse to make it into a temple to liberty. They go out.

The Sisters tell Kate to get Deane to come often: he and Ethan can amuse each other, saving the world from each other. Kate is resentful, asks them why they lied about the execution. They are grim: they don't like Ethan; he's a big disappointment—a crazy fool. But he is a Harford. Kate isn't. It's true that Ethan faced death in prison day after day, bravely. It wasn't his fault that they didn't think him important enough to kill. It's taken a lot out of him. His mind is broken. It'd kill him if he knew the truth. So they tell her never to say that to him again, or they will think she is trying to kill him—and she would—and if she did, they'd kill her. They've got brains: they wouldn't suffer. They'd do it so no one would know. They hope she knows that they'd do it, and think no more of it than crushing a fly. Kate is terrified, tells them they needn't threaten her. They know her affection and gratitude. She feels like a fourth sister.

The Sisters suggest that while they're at it they decide about Henry. They got her Henry, and he's theirs too. The money he'd get is theirs. He's a Harford. Kate can arrange anything she likes about his personal life, but they'll take care of training him to be able to handle his fortune. When he's twenty he'll be worth a lot. She agrees heartily; she knows they love him and he loves them. They reply, yes, she wants him to be their heir. But they're not going to die anytime soon: they're going to live to be a hundred!

The fourth play, tentatively titled "And Give Me Death," opens in the summer of 1804, in the parsonage, the set showing Deane's study and a section of the garden. The Sisters arrive, to tell Deane and Abigail of a scene between Kate and Ethan in the house that morning. Ethan fell down stairs, might have broken his neck or fractured his skull, but was unhurt. They heard Kate's screams, rushed out, found Ethan unperturbed. Kate denies she pushed him, but admits that she did slap his face when he accused her of vile actions, and he lost his balance. Ethan says he made no accusation, told Kate she was a fool to be slave to guilt. The Sisters ask Deane to go to see Kate, who needs the comfort of spiritual advice. She's hysterical, blames them. Deane had better tell her such conduct shows an unbecoming lack of meekness in a Christian woman. Deane tries to control his agitation and dread, keep an outer appearance of ministerial manner. He goes out.

The Sisters turn on Abigail as if Susan, her sister, weren't there. Strange that Kate was up outside Ethan's room: she must have gone up to see him. What for? He denounced them and warned them that the day of retribution was at hand: the greedy possessors of the earth would be punished with death for trampling on the rights of man. They suppose he meant their making him come into the house, stop living in the summerhouse, with his rheumatism. Then they say that Susan isn't really interested in this; Abigail keeps herself apart—even when she's marrying into the family. They go, and Abigail and Susan talk. Susan questions her about their father. But Abigail asks how could she know what her father's thoughts are, except that he denounces Napoleon so bitterly she suspects he admires him—just as he admires the Devil more than God. She'd like to know what he's thinking now. Yesterday, he, the Sisters, and Kate all started to think thoughts they wished to hide; it was plain on their faces. They've had no practice in concealment, no thought for years that was not such a resigned, contented acceptance of each day's twenty-four hours, you could give it to the town crier. (Deane has already said to Susan that he has given up trying to discover what Abigail thinks or wants; perhaps she'll talk to her.)

And so Abigail does for a while talk to Susan in a gush of relieving herself, but not for long. The change that she senses in her sister stops her. Susan has become a contented cow—her husband's wife, his children's mother—possessed. Abigail retreats into fantasy, Susan into thoughts of her children at home; she will rush to leave right after the wedding.

Susan notices a Paris newspaper on her father's desk and Abigail explains that she persuaded him to subscribe, told him he ought to keep track of what Antichrist was doing. He really wanted to do it—he said, to please her, but she notices he always reads the paper first.

Deane returns. Abigail goes out into the garden, and Deane discusses her with Susan: every once in a great while she speaks out; she is sometimes so outrageously frank. She admires Napoleon. He supposes many young girls do—and not only girls: so many men admire him. He can understand. He appeals to an old sin in human nature: power, take what you want, no matter how. But Henry will cure Abigail of her romantic dreams. He justifies the approaching marriage: Henry is a very matter-of-fact young man, but an honorable one. He will bring her down to earth. She's a difficult girl; you can't tell what she thinks or wants. Deane sometimes thinks she wants nothing from life except to be let alone to dream whatever it is she dreams. Abigail comes back in and her father leaves to work in the garden.

Abigail and Susan talk of the Sisters. Abigail sees their mistake in stirring up Ethan, bringing him back into the house for meals. Everyone had forgotten him. For years he had been making notes on a life work (Abigail has helped him). He is writing two books, one a biography of Robespierre, the second a vision of Utopia called "If Robespierre Had Lived." But Abigail had seen that he was contented to remain the incorruptible free man, that he never would have dared the test of actual writing. He lives in dreams of the past, the lie of his having been about to be guillotined, and of being Robespierre's disciple. (He dresses in a sky-blue coat like Robespierre.) He had renounced the world, happy to be free of that test, contented to be an eccentric character; but now he has been brought back into the house, he is forced into everyone's calculations. He is furious against the Sisters, but as always abstractly "the tyrants, the oppressors." He inspires rebellion with his Robespierre-filled speeches. He becomes the center of a domestic Jacobin Club in which each hopes to use him and then get rid of him. His constant call for "Death" puts ideas into their heads. Kate and Deane and Henry are forced to think that if he killed the Sisters, he would be hanged, thus setting them all free. The Sisters sense this: they begin to feel that in bringing Ethan into the house, they have brought Death.

Abigail, too, senses all this: she has an admiration for Ethan, because of his untouchableness—a pity, too—and for the Sisters, a real affection and pity. She feels she can control the situation, work everything out for the best, by getting all the power into her hands, as a detached participant who wants no gain. She is excited and thrilled by the danger and the prospect. When she tells this to Susan, her sister points out that she runs the risk of being murdered. Abigail is scornful: "There's no such risk in domestic intrigue." But then she says fancifully: "If it were on a great scale, perhaps, like the rise of Napoleon." Susan is astonished. Abigail admits, teasingly: "He's the only man I love." Then she says, seriously: "No, I want to free them all from this fate they have built up and can't escape from by themselves. It is my duty to Henry, to their father, to Kate, too, I suppose; although I don't like her—particularly because I do like the Sisters and want them free to die naturally in their beds at peace."

Susan asks her why she is marrying Henry, whom she doesn't love. Abigail answers: "It's because he is handsome, because he is honorable and fair, because I know him; because I can prophesy everything he will do and what he will be; because there is no greed between us. Our marriage is an honorable bargain—there's no deceit. We'll leave each other free. He doesn't want passionate, possessive love, and neither do I. I can help him. I respect his belief in his lifework even if I scorn it as lifework. I'm marrying him because I can always feel and be superior to him; because there'll be no more poverty. I don't want possessions, but I do want comfort and leisure and protection. I will not be my husband's wife nor my children's mother, any more than I want Henry to be my husband, and the children my children. There's been too much of that in the Harford history—or at least the attempt to achieve it.

Act two opens later on the same day in the parlor of the Sisters' mansion in Newport (or Providence). Conspicuous among the furnishings are various portraits, busts, and even statues of Napoleon, evidence of their close following of his career. They began admiration for him simply to provoke the Harford family and the community, but it has grown on them with his success.

In the first scene the Sisters have summoned young Gadsby to write their will. It is a week after "The Jacobin" (Ethan) has been forced to come into the house for his meals, and with him Death. The will is a placation and a defiance. An excuse for the occasion is the fact of Henry's approaching marriage. The will provides that everyone will get something, economic freedom; but again it is a promise in future, provided each one remains meek. On the surface it is fair to all: the house goes to Kate on condition she take care of Ethan and he have freedom of the garden as now; Deane will get a new church and parsonage; the bulk of the estate will go to Henry, who is to maintain Kate in the house as befits her station in society and her support of Ethan. He is also to provide funds for the upkeep of the garden for Ethan and for the publication of Ethan's books when they are written.

The Sisters, dreading death as dispossession, are conscious of the death wish in the house. Eliza feels an attack of pain around her heart. She doesn't tell her sisters at first; they find out about it only when she faints. Then they both admit similar symptoms in themselves. All three are determined to conceal the symptoms, but they let it out in various ways, pretending mockery. They seek reassurance from Deane regarding the future life; from Ethan regarding his failure to feel fear when on the guillotine (without a belief in a future life); from Kate, a woman's affection in time of sickness (she used to be a fourth Sister).

Then, when they get nothing from all this and see they have aroused hopeful suspicions, they turn in defiant rage to the opposite extreme. They insist they'll live to be a hundred, will go back into shipping, into the slave trade, force Ethan into it to earn his keep in business, force him and Kate into resumption of their marital relationship, force Henry to go to learn the slave trade as supercargo with Mardo, get Henry and Abigail married at once to have children and insure continuance of possessions against the risk of Deane's death: it's time she stopped living in daydreams, and took life seriously. (The Sisters suspect that Kate and Deane have arranged the match between Abigail and Henry as a substitute fulfillment and they are, ironically, in agreement with it.)

The Sisters cling to Abigail. They feel she knows and understands and pities them. They reject the pity, but are fascinated by her detachment, her inviolate self-sufficiency. She is meek without being meek. She lacks all sense of possessiveness, apparently. They wish they could find out what she dreams about (her fantasy life as Josephine—her dream of making Napoleon get all the world and then—to show his contempt, as a lesson to the world—relinquish it and go to live in a hut in the forest).

When the Sisters tell her of their purpose, she shakes her head, says that isn't the way. It will only give them more reason to fear death. Still, it will bring things to a crisis which may force them to see. But it's very dangerous: they may force the worm to turn into a poisonous snake.

The next scene takes place in the garden of the Sisters' mansion. They come there to rest in the sun. They discuss Dinah's fainting before everyone, and talk of the same symptoms in themselves. They are conscious of the death wish in first Kate's and then Henry's solicitude. They react with defiant frankness and mockery. Ethan joins them and in the conversation that ensues shows that he takes a secret interest in world affairs, gaining his information from Abigail. To them he adopts an indifferent pose that since Robespierre has died, nothing matters. He admires Burr for killing Hamilton. But his greatest interest is now the espaliered pear trees he has trained against the north wall. He loves to cut, prune, train, to crucify the trees. He has theories of compulsory diet to go with it, to abolish hunger by decree— fruit and nuts. He also raises chickens, has placed lamps in the hen house to increase laying. He has really come to a point where he is quite contented, forgetting the French Revolution and Robespierre.

The Sisters cannot bear to see him degenerate into a futile crank, puttering about the garden. His one quality has always been his unconquerable dream of revolution. This was one thing their beloved Jonathan admired in his son, one vestige of his spirit, and they miss his defiance and denunciation when they go to the garden. He is indifferent to them now, even friendly and garrulously eager to explain his hobbies and have them sympathetically interested in what he is doing.

He is coldly philosophical about Dinah's fainting spell, tells her she's getting old, will die soon, and advises stoicism in face of death. They accuse him of wanting them to die because he thinks he is their heir. He is astonished and insulted. All he wants is to stay in the garden. They ask how long he supposes Kate would let him stay? She'd have him declared irresponsible, put away.

At the end of the scene, the Sisters announce that they have decided the wedding will take place at once and they will all go with Abigail and Henry on a honeymoon voyage to France. This they propose as a way of placating the growing hatred they feel about them. They will witness the coronation of Napoleon. The Sisters insist that they'll go anyway, and everyone feels compelled to join in. The idea of Napoleon grows: they all secretly want to see him; and the women, thinking of him, begin to feel a secret scorn for the men.

Act three opens in a Paris hotel, where the Harford party has a suite of rooms from which they view the parade. It is Napoleon's coronation day, 2 December 1804. The voyage over, with them all crammed together on the ship, has developed antagonisms and intrigues. The sea also has had an effect. Ethan has claimed his marital rights from Kate and she has submitted, partly to keep on his good side, partly to rouse Deane to take some action against him. Kate has made an attempt to push Ethan over-board—just as he once did her long ago. Deane has seen this, but neither he nor Kate admits it. Kate is now conscious of what she had become contented to ignore—her marriage to Ethan, forgotten in her ambition to achieve respectability in a marriage to a minister of old family.

Their admiration for Napoleon has had its effect on all of them. It has stirred up the battle, conquest, intrigue, unscrupulousness. The murder of Prébigru, the Duc d'Enghien, seems to justify any means for an end. As the band plays and the parade marches past, Ethan now sees Napoleon as still Jacobin at heart, the heir to Robespierre's dictatorship. The Sisters resolve to go back into business. Ethan's "Death to tyrants!" seems now to be directed at the Sisters. And they respond that they will live to be a hundred. As the Emperor goes away and the music recedes, they are all deflated, confused, weary, guilty, suspicious—all but Abigail. Outwardly she is untouched, but in her dreams she is the rival now of Josephine. She condemns Napoleon. She sees how terrified the Sisters are beneath their defiance, and yet they are excited, alive. They have put the threat of Death where they can fight it—not something inside themselves, or something at the whim of God, before which they feel helpless to defend themselves. Abigail says she will stay with them on the ship, and they accept her offer of aid immediately. Then they become scornful and resentful, reject her proposal. They express their self-confidence.

Abigail suggests that they take the shortest possible voyage home. The Sisters react defiantly, will choose the most profitable one: cargo to New Orleans, cargo from there home. Abigail compliments them on their fine spirit—if what they want is a battle for conquest and survival. They reply, yes, that's they: they *are* the damned meek! They'll live to be a hundred! They'll see them all buried. Abigail is unimpressed: but if what they want is peace and freedom and the calm acceptance of death as part of life—the peace which makes death leave them in peace, in which they might live to be a hundred, because in it would be no worries, or fear, or greed to murder—then they are making a big mistake. They are impressed but scornful: teach grandmother how to suck eggs! What does she know of life or death? She's not even pregnant yet, is she? She says, no, but she will be, now that she has seen Napoleon— They all smile, and she says, but it won't be their child, nor hers, but his own.

Act four is in three scenes, which take place in the Sisters' mansion, all on the same day in spring 1805, morning, sunset, and midnight. There has been an incident on the voyage home: the dropping of a marlin spike from the yard near Deane when Ethan has gone aloft to help furl sail, to the terror of the minister and Kate's scorn. The Sisters have not been well on the voyage. They are really terrified at the prospect of returning to the mansion, but outwardly are making plans to deal with the rebellion. The rebels come back united, all with a secret plan in mind, which is excused on the ground that the end justifies the means: they will use Ethan to get rid of the Sisters. He will be judged insane and they will be rid of him. The principal motive in all minds is to free themselves from the tyranny of the Sisters; after that they can settle other accounts. The whole rebellion is under the guise of support for Aaron Burr.

The Sisters sense the coalition against them and adopt repressive measures. The housekeeping is taken out of Kate's hands; Ethan is forced to give up the garden, live in the house in two rooms with Kate: it's time they stopped that scandal. Deane is ordered never to come to the house again, under threat of withdrawal of old support from church and public statement of the reasons. Henry is to become accountant under Eliza, leave business and go into slave trade (with Mardo taken into partnership), and will live in the mansion with Abigail.

The Sisters intend to try to divide and conquer, encourage antagonism, but find that each takes a stand. They'll settle that score afterwards. Then they change their will to leave all to Abigail, but that also doesn't put an end to the conspiracy. She tries to foil this plan by saying she will immediately distribute the estate. The Sisters are at first triumphantly and bitterly derisive, but then are won around to her plan. She calls a meeting of them all, advises that they turn everything into cash and build a big bonfire. Then they could all start a new life with a knowledge of the value of money. Henry tells her dryly not to be a fool. She answers, well, then, she'll allot so much to Kate to build a house of her own and income to keep it up until she dies; so much to her father, for a new parsonage and church and so much a year; so much to Ethan so he can join Burr's expedition and outfit a regiment; the rest to Henry to set himself up in an honorable conservative export-import business.

The final scene of act four is again in the Sisters' mansion, at midnight.

Gadsby has been summoned from bed. He prepares a simple agreement. The Sisters agonize about signing it, lament their beautiful land and gold. They grasp at a straw—that it may not be legal? But Gadsby assures them it is. They grin wryly; they thought it would be theirs a few hours more. Then Abigail gives it all away—to Kate, to Deane, to Ethan, to Henry. The Sisters gasp at each step, get heart attacks. They are miserable at last, but recover. Gradually they have a feeling of peace, well being. They grumble at Abigail, good-naturedly. "It's left us stripped." Hannah says: "I feel like an old hen in moulting season that's lost all her feathers and is cackling around with a bare behind." Abigail laughs: "Never mind. You're old rogues, with not a care in the world. You'll live to be a hundred." They answer emphatically: "Yes!"

Then Henry comes to protest against giving money to Ethan for Burr's revolution. "I don't mind the money, but the purpose. It's treason. He'll get into a disgraceful scrape, etc." The Sisters are mockingly indignant: "Burr's going to fight for liberty. Ethan knows what that means? Hasn't he got a soul?" They recall their stepfather Jonathan: "He never could learn anything except by experience—and that never taught *him* anything either."

At the end, Abigail says that one reason she's done all this is that she's pregnant. "I wanted a better, freer world for my son to be born into. I want to teach him to love the spirit, beauty, poetry—to scorn the world and give birth to his own soul." The Sisters are affectionately teasing: "So you know it's to be a son, do you?" She answers that she's sure. They say they know why she's sure; and they know who the father really is. She asks them what they mean: they're so wicked. They reply: "Oh, it's Henry all right—in that way, in the flesh. You used him—but not in the spirit. Henry couldn't be father to anyone in the spirit. His soul is only a sense of decency. Of whom were you dreaming when the baby was conceived? But you needn't tell us: it must be nice to bear a son by Napoleon. We wouldn't have minded that ourselves. He is the only man except Jonathan we ever took to—that is, when we used to be alive." Abigail laughs it off. The Sisters grow suddenly greedy again: "So you're going to have a baby?" Abigail answers: "No, you don't! Remember!" They say: "Yes, we're through with all that. You can keep him. He's yours." Abigail replies: "No, he's going to be his own." She speaks of her ideal of freedom for her son. The Sisters are benevolently sceptical and wistful: "It may be possible. We hope so. We'll help you to save your son from your love. We can do that, now that we've retired from life."

Ethan comes down in his French National Guard uniform, prepared to sail to join Burr. He goes to look over the garden, comes back in a dictatorial rage: "The espaliers are growing all over the place. They're free! I can't go yet: there's too much to do here. I must restore discipline. Mardo can take the money to Burr."[2]

chapter ten

November 1940 to November 1953

From these rough outlines for the first four plays of the eleven-play Cycle, it is apparent that O'Neill has altered radically the characters of both the original Harford and his son. One of the first notes made for the new plan in October 1940 (and marked marginally to apply "throughout Cycle") reflects this changed concept: "Jonathan becomes family legend, more & more distorted, of the Great Free Pioneer—spirit of rugged individualism—while his son, Ethan, becomes in legend the Great Idealist, the Revolutionary, the lover of Liberty and defender of the Rights of Man."[1]

Because so much of the material relating to the first two plays of the nine-play Cycle, as written, was destroyed, it is difficult to determine the role of Evan, the Harford progenitor, in the first play. It seems not to have been an important one, and his murder in the first act removed him early from the scene. The founder of the family in the eleven-play Cycle is a far more charismatic figure. A much younger man, he becomes the stepfather rather than the father of the Three Sisters and takes over much of the role of the former Jonathan (son of Evan) as man-of-action. In altering his concept of the second-generation Harford, now named Ethan, O'Neill expected to simplify his problems in dealing with that character's love-hate relationships with his stepsisters and his daughter-in-law (Abigail, later Deborah)—relationships that had been in large part responsible for the excessive psychological complications of the first two plays of the nine-play Cycle as written.

But as he thus eliminated some of the difficulties presented by Simon's grandfather, O'Neill became even more intrigued by Simon's great-aunts, the Three Sisters. They had seized hold of his imagination to such an extent that, in November and December

1940, he made extensive, detailed notes for revising *A Touch of the Poet* and *More Stately Mansions* in order to carry them into those two plays.[2] He went over his notes and outlines for the last five plays of the eleven-play Cycle and revised them in accordance with his plans for the first six as now projected. He worked also on the new scheme for *More Stately Mansions*, introducing the Three Sisters into the plot, and experimented with drawing set plans for the different plays.

On 29 November the *Work Diary* records a new idea for a series of short monologue plays, "for book more than stage, perhaps—scene, one character, one marionette (life size) The Good Listener", to be called "By Way of Obit." O'Neill did brief outlines for eight of these (p. 395). In early December he worked on notes for the last act of *More Stately Mansions* and arranged those already written for the first six Cycle plays. Then his nerves put him to bed for several days.

On the morning of 17 December, Blemie, the Dalmatian, died and O'Neill commented: "C⟨arlotta⟩. & I completely knocked out—loved him for 11 years—a finer friend than most friends!" (p. 396). O'Neill came down with a sore throat on the twenty-third and was in bed, first with influenza and then with bronchitis. In spite of illness he wrote *The Last Will and Testament of Silverdene Emblem O'Neill* on 26 December, but continued sick until 7 January 1941. He was able to make a few notes on play ideas, but then a new attack of weakness put him back to bed. Notes for *A Touch of the Poet* and *More Stately Mansions* occupied him on the twenty-seventh, and he worked a little with other ideas, spending six working days in January on a new project called "Blind Alley Guy" and eleven working days in February on notes and an outline for the Malatesta play, now called "Malatesta Seeks Surcease." On 2 March he commented: "like this idea but have lost grip on it—trouble is too many good ideas—can't settle on one—(the war, perhaps)" (p. 401). He switched to "The Thirteenth Apostle" and between 3 and 13 March succeeded in completing an outline for that play.

On 17 March he began to cut and revise the script, typed by Carlotta, of *Long Day's Journey into Night* and on the thirtieth finished the "second & I think final draft—like this play better than any I have ever written—does most with the least—a quiet play!—and a great one, I believe" (p. 403).

Early in April he returned to "The Thirteenth Apostle" but came to the conclusion that he was "not in right mood for this—will put aside for while" (p. 404). He made notes of new conceptions for the Cycle, the religions of the characters, the Three Sisters as Quakers; but the new series of one-act plays, "By Way of Obit.," suddenly recaptured his attention, and he wrote a scenario for one of them, *Hughie*. Unfortunately, he got too enthusiastic about gardening, overdid, and suffered another spell of exhaustion during which it became impossible for him to write. He eventually decided that he would have to give up such physical work around the grounds because swimming seemed to be the "only exercise I can take without fear [of a] bad aftermath" (p. 405). From the middle until the end of April he concentrated on *Hughie* and managed to finish a first draft, completing a second draft on 16 May, remarking that "in spite of interruptions [I] had [a] lot of fun doing this and like it" (p. 407).

But he could not for long keep his thoughts from returning to his biggest project. Later in May he made further notes for the new first play of the eleven-play Cycle and commented: "have not told anyone yet of expansion of idea to 11 plays—seems too ridiculous—idea was first 5 plays, then 7, then 8, then 9, now 11!—will never live to do it—but what price anything but a dream these days!"

He briefly took up the "By Way of Obit." plays and drew sets for several of them, noting that there "will be 8 in all, I think" (p. 408). On 27 May he went back to "The 13th Apostle" and began to write its prologue, finishing a first draft in mid-June. He went over it and on the twenty-third observed that it "needs still more condensation but that can wait" (p. 410). He began to write the first scene but got bogged down: "[I] lose interest, not in [the] play, but in working, writing anything—war!" (p. 411).

He did take up "The 13th Apostle" again early in July 1941 but soon had to confess that he had "gone dead on it . . . will put aside, try something else". He set down a few notes for "Blind Alley Guy," but his health was too poor for much work: he commented in his *Work Diary* that, given the way he was then feeling, the play's title would be a good one for his autobiography.

Oona O'Neill, aged sixteen, had arrived on 11 July for a week's visit. What her father felt was a change not for the better in her he blamed on "damned N.Y. school—or maybe she's just at silly age" (p. 412). "Blind Alley Guy" and "Time Grandfather Was Dead" vied for his attention: he was enthusiastic about the latter play, but still full of plans for the former, and had difficulty deciding which to work on. Notes and an outline for "Time Grandfather Was Dead" won out from the fourth to the eleventh, and then on the twelfth and thirteenth he made more notes for the Cycle.

The O'Neills at Tao House. Inscribed by Carlotta Monterey O'Neill on verso: "Eugene O'Neill—Carlotta & Puss!—1939/*Tao House—California*—/At our backs the San Ramon Valley & Mt. Diablo." (Photo: Fania Marinoff Van Vechten, probably taken July 1941; DCG)

The servant problem had been giving Carlotta endless trouble: some new servants did not care for country life and left, with the result that the "house routine [was] all upset". On 21 August "Blind Alley Guy" came to the fore again and O'Neill commented: "this can be [an] unusual, thrilling play" (p. 415). He worked on its outline for several days, but then Gene, Jr., came for a visit. O'Neill wanted his son to read *Hughie* and started going over the typed script to make final alterations, finishing them on 7 September. In addition, Gene, Jr., read both *Long Day's Journey into Night* and *The Iceman Cometh* and was "greatly moved" by all three plays (p. 416).

After his son's departure, O'Neill returned to the outline for "Blind Alley Guy" but on 29 September admitted: "can't move it—same old stuff again—too many ideas in head—lose interest not in idea of play but in writing it—a why bother in this world feeling—too much war preoccupation (which doesn't help anything)" (p. 418). The next day he reluctantly decided to put "Blind Alley Guy" aside for the moment and made additional jottings for various Cycle plays.

The notes he wrote at this time reflect various ideas O'Neill was then entertaining. Some concern possible divisions of the eleven plays. The first four would have a general subtitle, "The Three Sisters" or, possibly, "The Blesséd Sisters," with separate titles for each play based on the beatitudes: "The Poor in Spirit," "Rebellion of the Humble," "Greed of the Meek," and "And Give Me Death." The next two plays might have the subtitle "Sara & Abigail [later Deborah]," with the title "Brahma or Nothing" taking the place of *More Stately Mansions*. The next four plays would be "The Four Brothers," and the last play, retaining, presumably, the title "The Hair of the Dog," would be "the prayer for a Savior to lead . . . [the Harfords] out of Wilderness and debacle."[3]

On 1 October 1941 O'Neill had given up the plan of carrying the Three Sisters into *A Touch of the Poet* and *More Stately Mansions*, but he set down some ideas about those characters for possible use in revising the two plays:

[The Sisters] died when Simon was 12(?), but their influence is still alive and their ghosts dominate the Harford house. Abigail remembers them with conflicting emotions: an affectionate humorous appreciation (and secret admiration), and, at the same time, a fear and a repulsion. She believes that she has learned a great lesson from them—that non-possession is the only way to spiritual self-possession: the way to freedom is to set others free; liberty is others' liberty: "What shall it profit a man if he gain the whole world and lose his own soul?" But she admits in a scene with Simon, that she encouraged his going away because she thought he would fail in his efforts to make a success of the business and would then return to her forever.

As for Simon, he remembers his horrified fascination with the Sisters' waiting for death. They planted in him an expressed poetic pantheism, a longing to dissolve into Nature.[4]

O'Neill had decided to cut out of *A Touch of the Poet* the scene of Sara's seduction of Simon and have her merely tell her mother what happened (as she does in the play as published). He contemplated shifting some scenes between *A Touch of the Poet* and *More Stately Mansions*, removing the inn and cabin scenes from the latter play and beginning with a prologue in Abigail's garden after the death of Henry:

She now has freedom, an opportunity to live, to end her quest for Brahma, which has become for her the death wish. She expresses her longing for normal healthy activity, devoting herself to others, to grandmotherhood. She wants wealth for her grandchildren, so that they can be free. She has been wondering of what use freedom was for her after the release of her husband's death; but at the end the Napoleonic daydream suddenly forces itself on her. She renounces it.

In the cabin scene between Abigail and Simon [then in *A Touch of the Poet* but eventually transferred to *More Stately Mansions*] there is further talk between them of Napoleon, whom Simon denounces as a bloody tyrant. Abigail calls Simon a Jacobin, like his grandfather Ethan [I]. Simon denies this, points out that Napoleon was once a member of the Jacobin Club. Abigail replies: "Oh, he used any means." Simon answers: "I never understood why you always admired him for that—you who are so scrupulously honorable." She says: "Being honorable is the minister's daughter in me. I can't help it. Maybe I wish I weren't." Simon is shocked at this, but Abigail goes on: "I've been unscrupulous about you; I've encouraged you to take any means to gain freedom." She recalls her memories of Napoleon: "I was always reading books about him, had a bust of him in my bedroom." Simon says: "I always suspected that your daydreams were about Napoleon. I remember the Sisters and you discussing him." She laughs: "Yes, they used to say he was the only man they ever loved. I have always justified Napoleon's greed—for power and glory, to become a God—while despising the material greed."

In this scene with Simon, Abigail at first doesn't like being reminded of Napoleon, resents Simon's scorn at her odd romantic foolishness. Then when he says that he is glad, and intimates that she was silly, she is aroused to vehement defense. At the end, she jokingly apologizes for the intensity of her feeling; it must be because she has come out into life.[5]

In both *A Touch of the Poet* and *More Stately Mansions,* O'Neill contemplated emphasizing Abigail's Brahmanism:

In the period between the two plays, she sinks further and further into the practice of Brahma. Feeling herself getting old, she feels that her daydream of Napoleon becomes ridiculous, especially after Simon goes. She made herself set him free, but she knows that he would have gone anyway. Brahmanism makes all this without meaning: she jilts life before it can jilt her, turns her back on it and walks out, thus keeps her superiority. She learns self-hypnosis, contemplation alone in the summerhouse, until at last she knows that she has reached the point where she can escape the Opposition, can lose the Self. But she can't do this: she is afraid. It means death to her. She cannot overcome this fear, flies out of the summerhouse in terror, is afraid to go into it again.

This is just before her husband's final illness, which offers her temporary escape. She nurses him night and day, but after his death, she is forced to face her fear again. Lonely, missing her activity as a wife, she longs for Brahma now even if it is death. Then the news of the condition of Henry's estate comes and makes a demand upon her for action. She rejects this at first, but suddenly sees it as salvation, opportunity, and in the end she finds herself unconsciously daydreaming her old fantasy of being Napoleon's mistress. She jokingly renounces this—a fine daydream for a grandmother!

The admiration and longing for the Leader of the Meek who takes possession of the earth—Robespierre, Napoleon, all or nothing Caesarism—is part of a recurrent overtheme for the whole Cycle: in Robespierre, Napoleon, Brahma, the fanatic idealist, the cynical opportunist and realist, the escapist into more-life; in the United States Napoleon dispossesses Christ. At the end of the eleventh play, the Harfords, in their defeat and bewilderment and faithlessness, again want a leader to save them—Christ, Stalin, Hitler; that is part of the Hair of the Dog symbol. It is women who always yearn for the ruthless possessor who sets them free from themselves by enslaving them; and in a time of the collapse of faith in life-meaning, the feminine in men becomes dominant; it is the spur to their manly, warrior virtues.

In *More Stately Mansions,* Simon, Abigail, and Sara disintegrate into split personalities; there is in them the conflict of the opposites, the shifting alliances of good with good, evil with evil, greed with greed, etc. In the isolation of Simon within the company, he becomes a means, with Sara's children and Abigail's grandchildren the end; it forces him to become one-sided, unscrupulous, to repress his better self. He feels frustrated: the more success he achieves, the less success means to him, and the more he becomes conscious of the home situation, for which he blames his mother. At last he determines to reconquer his home, with the same ruthless self who rules the company. It is a campaign of conquest that he maps out—of destruction, dispossession and possession—a Napoleonic conception. He starts an undeclared war, "Divide and Conquer," start rebellion within, find an ally within.

Abigail, on her part, has by now become surfeited with grandmother-hood, although she will not admit it; underneath her sincerely real normal values, of simple, affectionate grandmotherhood, she has also conducted a campaign to possess Sara's children. She knows now that she has done this; in the Jesuitical sense, she has stamped her image on their spirits. With this purpose accomplished she becomes restless, bored and resent-ful: she is an unpaid nursegirl, too young for the role of grandmother. With her looks going, on the threshold of age, she longs for one last fling at life, for conquest. With the return of her Napoleonic daydream, she thinks of Simon. So when he starts his war, she greets it with triumphant, inner satisfaction: she is sure of her victory.

The recurrent discussions of Napoleon show the admiration of Abigail and Simon for his unscrupulous ruthlessness. But Sara rejects Brahman-ism, because her version of non-possessiveness is the Catholic Christ who died to save us.

As the increasing tension of battle splits the personalities, the alliances form. At the same time, the longing grows in each for the lost peace of the past. Sara longs for her early married life with Simon when enough was enough. Simon, for his aloneness at his cabin with his Utopian dreams, after he was free from Abigail and before he loved Sara; Abigail for her father's garden before she married. The garden becomes a symbol of escape from the battle-to-the-death of life; the house-office becomes the symbol of that battle.

In the end Sara wins through the greater strength of her primitive unscrupulousness and ruthlessness. She can advocate that the useless aged, sick and insane be put to death, or compelled to commit suicide. She tells Simon how to fool Abigail into going into the summerhouse: "It's nothing but a summerhouse to you. Go with her." But then she pleads hypocritically with Abigail not to take Simon there. (Their going in be-comes for Abigail and Simon escape from Sara.) But at last Sara snatches Simon back; she makes him destroy the business.[6]

Also in October 1941, O'Neill noted *"Recurrent Fate-within-past-of-family aspects"* of the Cycle:

In the first play, Naomi, by fear of the death wish in Jonathan's and the Sisters' minds (a way to freedom—and possession) drives what is uncon-scious in their minds into consciousness. In the fourth play, the Sisters do the same thing to the family, and remember the past. But their mother quit; they won't! But they do in another way: they buy themselves off.

There's a "touch of the poet" in Jonathan [I], Simon, Ethan II, and, in the eleventh play, the inventor [Ernie Ward]. The dictator-fanatic appears in Ethan I, Simon, Jonathan II, and Lizzie [Lou] Bowen. Detachment (defense, flight, superiority) occurs in Abigail, Wolfe, and, in the eleventh play, the Yoga daughter. The courtesan-whore motif appears in Kate, Abigail, and Sara.

Scenes reach a subconscious level of non-realism, a united front of woman against man in the second play (the Sisters against Jonathan and Ethan), the third play (the Sisters and Kate against Ethan), the fourth play (the Sisters, Kate, and Abigail against Ethan, Henry and Deane in the coronation scene), the sixth play (Abigail and Sara against Simon), the seventh play (Sara, Elizabeth and Lenore [i.e., Leda?] in the justification of the captain's murder), the eighth play (these same characters against E [i.e., Wolfe?]).[7]

Early in the same month, October 1941, O'Neill made additional notes and then read over the outlines he had written for the first four plays in the eleven-play Cycle. He expressed himself in his *Work Diary* as "pleased—can be great stuff—and I mean, great—but too long, tough job to tackle now".

So he returned once more to "Blind Alley Guy" but got little done, describing himself on 14 October as "not up to work" (p. 419). He woke on the twenty-first with his mind full of "Rudie," the chambermaid play in the "By Way of Obit." series of one-acts, and made notes for it. From the twenty-second to the twenty-seventh he worked on rewriting what he had done so far on "Blind Alley Guy," but it still was not right, and he decided once more to put it aside "till its time comes".

On the twenty-eighth he recorded in his *Work Diary:* "S[haughnessy]. play idea, based on story told by E⟨dmund⟩. in 1ˢᵗ Act of 'L⟨ong⟩. D⟨ay's⟩. J⟨ourney⟩. I⟨nto⟩. N⟨ight⟩'—except here Jamie principal character & story of play otherwise entirely imaginary, except for J⟨amie⟩'s revelation of self" (p. 420). He worked on notes for the first two acts of this on the twenty-ninth and observed: "this can be strange combination comic-tragic—am enthused about it". He continued to work on it and by 3 November had finished an outline and got a "good" title, "Moon of the Misbegotten" (p. 421). He began the actual writing on 9 November, changed the title to *Moon for the*

Misbegotten ("much more to [the] point") on the twelfth, and finished a first draft of the first act on the twenty-sixth, recording that he was "getting great satisfaction [from] this play—[it] flows" (pp. 422, 423). He was working on it every day and making excellent progress when on 7 December the Japanese attacked Pearl Harbor: "now the whole world goes into the tunnel!—but this has to be—we should have beaten the bastards to the punch!" On the tenth he forced himself to resume work on *Moon for the Misbegotten:* "little done—but am determined [to] finish 1ˢᵗ d⟨raft⟩. of this play, war or not—the Archimedes viewpoint should be the artist's, (as long as he is physically out, anyway—stick to one's job)" (p. 424).

Some notes on the main recurring spiritual themes of the Cycle occupied him later in December:

> My old idea of wisdom is simple: the way to happiness is easy, all great teachers have taught it: give yourself to possess yourself, etc. In liberty, freedom, only he who has lost himself shall find himself—an enlightened selfishness, etc.
>
> In the first four plays, this is the wisdom that the first Jonathan brings back from the wilderness: that freedom is not gained by running away. It is not in nature, but rather in its opposite. Nature in him keeps him blindly survival-of-the-fittest selfish and conquering outside things.
>
> Jonathan approves of [the American] Revolution, [but feels it] is superficial, without deep meaning, merely a change of appearances, its success will leave real freedom ungained. He dies at Bunker Hill in his own fight: self-sacrifice because he hopes that America may become, in time, the Promised Land of Liberty, that the impulse toward freedom will eventually lead to insight into what real freedom is.
>
> The Sisters begin as the sacrificial meek, but always there is in them hope of a reward (love, that is, possession of love). At the end of the fourth play, they dimly see that Jonathan was right—in their relief at escaping the results of greed.
>
> Evan [i.e., Ethan I] is the result of the search for freedom on a realistic plane only, which inevitably, no matter how fanatically idealistic, leads to the opposite.
>
> Henry represents respectable "honesty-is-the-best-policy": freedom must be economically sound.
>
> Abigail [Deborah] is aware of the truth in one phase, but is determined

on detachment. She knows admiration for the free (unscrupulous, immoral) conqueror in her retirement into her fantasy dreamlife; her later Brahmanism is non-life, annihilisation. In the sixth play [*More Stately Mansions*] she projects her conflict into the Simon-Sara family, with an ally for each side in each of them.[8]

But O'Neill warned himself to "keep this on small scale—(change to she is forced come to live with them)—it all hinges on whether Simon shall unscrupulously expand or not, throw out partner, etc."

It is through Abigail that the teaching of Jonathan [I] (via the Sisters) and Ethan [I] is passed on to Simon. He turns back to Nature of Jonathan and Utopianism of Ethan (made simpler and involving a detached small community). This is on a material plane except that poets shall not only be allowed in but shall be leaders of his Republic.

In the fifth play [*A Touch of the Poet*], Nora as exemplar on a simple religious plane, the nunnery ideal, but with fear of the other world. Simon's influence on Sara. Melody as the tragic sordid defeat of all striving to possess the self via outside things; he is the embittered power-dreamer.

At the end of the sixth play [*More Stately Mansions*], Simon sees the truth and lives accordingly thereafter. His idea is to set an example; but people consider him a lovable harmless nut. He becomes resigned finally to saving only his own soul.

Ethan [II] represents speed, power, freedom from the land, but there is a poetical, mystic strain in him, in his possessive love for his ship, his love-hate for the sea, the overcoming of the inevitable victor, Death, the death-longing, the final belonging, a dissolving into the sea.

Wolfe has Melody's Byronic disdain, with Abigail's detachment, the denial of the value of life (as expressed in money), the denial of love. He is the poker-face gambler, without emotion, conquering the fear of hurt.

Honey is the complete lovable opportunist, the immoral rogue—America as trough.

Jonathan [II] illustrates the old concentrated strain of power pursuit, the Empire Builder, with a Napoleonic complex; his idealism the greatness of America.

In the last play comes the complete realistic divorce from all sanctions, with religion, morals dead. There is no feeling of need for any justification or goal for success except success. At the end, the hop-head son sees the truth, but he cannot believe that he or anyone else can believe in it. It is too late; they've gone too far along the wrong road; there is no turning back: "we must destroy ourselves so a few survivors, reminded by ruins of the wrong way, can start again". But they deny, grope for hope. Honey's ironic dying comment: "it's a hair of the dog you need".[9]

An idea for a new play occurred to O'Neill and was set down in the *Work Diary* on 20 December: "transcontinental train—all types U.S. cit⟨izens⟩.— the old man who is Uncle Sam—his scorn for their selfish attitudes— endeavors [to] inspire them with ideal, etc.—one-act?" (p. 425). But he stuck to *A Moon for the Misbegotten* until the thirtieth: "not up to it—Parkinson's very bad—can't control pencil this am—also in upper arm & shoulder—not so good, this progress!" (p. 426). He was able to make a few additional notes for the whole Cycle on the twelfth day of the new year, 1942:

Add, general theme throughout—tragic battle of the opposites—aspect expressed in Latin quote I remember—translated for this purpose—"I know the good way (Tao) and I believe it is Truth, but I follow the bad way"

The Harfords always know in their hearts what is Truth & salvation, but a demonic fate in them makes them deny this in their living, and do the opposite—a defiance, a pride—a "better to rule in hell, than serve in heaven" complex—and instinct toward self-destruction—revenge—[10]

Still he persevered with *A Moon for the Misbegotten* and on 20 January wrote in his *Work Diary: "Finish 1ˢᵗ Draft*—but had to drag myself through it since Pearl Harbor and it needs much revision—wanders all over [the] place".

He was in bed all the next day, and his tremor was bad, but his spirits soared on the twenty-second when Saxe Commins arrived for a visit: "no one I'd rather have here" (p. 427). They had had hardly any sun for Saxe's visit when it ended on 6 February, but O'Neill had enjoyed talks and walks with him and had even found time to work a little more on "By Way of Obit." From the ninth to the eleventh he did more work on that series but then had to fight off a cold.

On 16 February he commented in his *Work Diary:* "Cycle—A Touch Of The Poet (5ᵗʰ in 11) (think [I] may rewrite this to get at least one play of [the] Cycle definitely & finally finished)". He made notes for the rewriting and then read over the script, finding it "too involved" (p. 429). Working almost every day, he finished making cuts in the first act on 13 March. That same day came the shocking news of the death of Dr. Dukes; both O'Neills sadly attended the funeral. He tried on the eighteenth to work on a new act two for *A Touch of the Poet* but found that he was too low in mind and his tremor too severe. He managed to make a little progress, but then, in April, took up "The Thirteenth Apostle" again. He worked on it by fits and starts all through the month, expressing in his *Work Diary* his eagerness to do the play: "real deep propaganda value, spiritually speaking—but I work so slowly now" (p. 434).

On 12 April the news of his daughter's having become "Stork Club publicity racket Glamour Girl—at this of all times!" did not please him (p. 433). Then a toothache was added to his other troubles, and, as before, necessitated an extraction, on the twenty-fifth. The ill was compounded when the jaw refused to heal and all his old prostate symptoms were stirred up. No work was possible, but by mid-May healing had at last begun, although the prostate pain was no better and the tremor was still bad. O'Neill busied himself in getting his old scripts ready to give to the Museum of the City of New York, Princeton, and Yale. A visit to Dr. Reinle revealed that his blood pressure had fallen to a new low, and another series of shots was prescribed. In the middle of June he worked a little more on "The 13th Apostle," which he was now calling "The Last Conquest," finishing a second draft of the prologue, and on 22 and 23 June he gave *Hughie* a final going over. He then returned to *A Touch of the Poet,* working on the new second act as often as his health would allow, but commenting at the end of July: "Tough game—take sedatives and feel a dull dope—don't take, and feel as if maggots were crawling all over inside [of] your skin".

On the thirtieth Herbert Freeman, the O'Neill's chauffeur and helper, left for his Marine training base in San Diego. O'Neill and Carlotta were up at 5:30 to see him off and O'Neill commented: "hell of a blow to lose him—more a member of [the] family than employee—a real friend, loyal, fine & decent" (p. 442).

On 3 August 1942, the War Shipping Board requested that O'Neill write a message to be sent to the next of kin of dead merchant sailors. He worked on this task for several days but had difficulty getting it right. From the twelfth to the fifteenth he went back to the new act two for *A Touch of the Poet.* Early in August a painful hip had begun to give him trouble and later that month he began to wear a steel brace, which he found "damned trying at first" (p. 444).

In mid-September he again had to have new glasses. At last, on the sixteenth, he was able to finish the new act two for *A Touch of the Poet,* the delay due to "no lack of interest but just plain feeling rotten" (p. 446).

From 17 to 29 September O'Neill was feeling better except for his tremor and worked on rewriting the second scene of the old act two of *A Touch of the Poet* into a new act three, finishing on 2 October. From the third to the fifteenth he worked on a new act four—in part a rewrite of the second scene of the old act three. On the thirteenth the disturbing news had come that Mrs. Dukes was fatally ill with cancer, and on the seventeenth O'Neill's tremor became so bad that he couldn't write. Besides, as he wrote George Jean Nathan, "The world drama you hear over the radio every day, or read in the papers, is the one important drama of the moment, and one can't write anything significant about that because it's too close and the best one could do wouldn't be half as effective as a good war correspondent's story of the front line."[11]

Nonetheless, he was able to resume work on the new act four for *A Touch of the Poet* on 25 October and, finally, on 13 November could record: "Finish new version 'A Touch Of The Poet' ((5th play in 11 Cycle)—have made it [a] much better play, both as itself & as part of [the] Cycle—a triumph, I feel, considering sickness & war strain—still has minor faults—needs some cutting and condensing, but that can wait a while)" (p. 451).

In this new version the location of Simon's cabin has been changed from seashore to lakeside. He actually recuperates—from an attack of chills and fever brought on by the dampness of the lake—at Melody's inn. Deborah (formerly Abigail), coming to visit him there, meets all three Melodys and in her conversations with Sara tells her about Simon's grandfather Evan (i.e., Ethan) Harford.[12] The consummation of Sara and Simon's love takes place at the inn, rather than in the boat shed, and is merely reported by Sara to her mother. The commemoration of the battle of Talavera is introduced, along with Melody's wearing his uniform. The epilogue is omitted.

On 14 November O'Neill tore up the typed copies of the second and third drafts of the play. He tried again on "The Last Conquest" but found that he was held up by "some inner struggle about it" and commented in his *Work Diary:* "I think the inner conflict is because it is at its final curtain a declaration of faith by one who is faithless—like D⟨ays⟩. W⟨ithout⟩. E⟨nd⟩.—a hope for faith instead of faith—and also a futile feeling that no one will see the truth, not even the author". The next day he advised himself to "concentrate on it as play—try to be the objective dramatist—after all, many a thief sincerely admires honesty" (p. 451). He finished the scenario for the first four scenes at the end of the month and worked on the play again in December. Then more tooth trouble (this time pyorrhea) seemed to stir up all his ills, and he decided on the thirteenth that it was "no go" with "The Last Conquest": "will have to quit on this again—or on anything else—one of my old sinking spells is on me—lower than low—mind dead" (p. 453). At the end of the year he recorded: "Park⟨inson's⟩. terrible—got fit in a.m. when I thought I'd hop right out of my skin—just as well I have no will to work because [I] couldn't make it anyway".

On 3 January 1943, although the tremor was still bad, O'Neill read the first draft of *A Moon for the Misbegotten* and commented: "want to get this really written—real affection for it—can be fine, unusual play" (p. 455). He made notes on the fifth and started a second draft the next day, working steadily for three weeks. On the morning of 28 January he was all in, but that night he went over his files, destroying old notes for ideas of seven plays, dating back to Sea Island or to France, that he now knew he would never write. During the final days of the month he was able to finish the second draft of act one of *Moon for the Misbegotten* but complained: "what I am up against now—fade out physically each day after 3 hours—page a day because [I] work slowly even when as eager about [a] play as I am about this—Park⟨inson's⟩. main cause—constant strain to write" (p. 457). O'Neill continued to work on the play through much of February and on the twenty-first again attacked his old files: "tore up the part of Act One, "The Life Of Bessie Bowen", I had written—n⟨o⟩. g⟨ood⟩.—and this play is basis for [the] last play of [the] Cycle now (with many changes)" (p. 459).

On 2 March, his mental state was worse: "The calomel blues continue—in fact, are worse—first attack like this I've had in long time—'My thoughts on awful subjects dwell, Damnation and the Dead', as that beautiful old Puritan hymn puts it—and P⟨arkinson's⟩. very bad" (p. 460). His health improved, however, and he was able to work with some regularity on *A Moon for the Misbegotten*, finishing the completely rewritten second draft of act three on 10 April. When he came to reread act four he decided that it would probably have to be entirely rewritten in light of what now preceded it in the second draft of the play. He could do nothing until the twenty-fifth, at which time he made only a few notes, but he did continue to work on it, now and then, through 3 May.

On 4 May 1943, O'Neill stopped making entries in his *Work Diary,* and there is no longer the day-to-day account that gives such a detailed record of his progress—or lack of it. He had told Carlotta on 25 February that her diary was better, more complete, and he saw no use in continuing to keep his own.[13] But of course Carlotta gives few specific details about O'Neill's actual writing, although occasional references in her diary and in his own letters provide some evidence. In a letter of 5 August, he told Sean O'Casey: "All I've done since Pearl Harbor is to rewrite one of the plays in my Cycle. *A Touch Of The Poet* . . . This is the only one of the four Cycle plays I had written which approached final form. The others will have to be entirely recreated—if I ever get around to it—because I no longer see them as I did in the pre-war 1939 days in which they were written."[14] On the twenty-ninth of that month he told Barrett Clark, his biographer, that he had done no writing "lately,"[15] and on 9 October Carlotta noted: "We discuss the theatre—*& he is set on my acting again!!* He insists upon my playing 'Deborah' in 'A Touch of the Poet'! Of course, it is a mad idea—and he goes on & on about it—& claims if I love him I will do what he asks! Oh, Mercy. What next?"[16]

The Langners visited the O'Neills at Tao House in December 1943, and Lawrence Langner promised to investigate the possibility of getting a dictating machine for O'Neill, thinking that he might be able to dictate his plays. Early in the new year Langner reported that he had written to the manufacturers, whose San Francisco office would arrange a demonstration. The Theatre Guild offered the machine to O'Neill as a Christmas present, but because they were being used by the United States Navy, it was necessary to secure a priority from the War Production Board, which at first refused to grant it.

On 19 January 1944, Carlotta reported: "Gene works, lunches, takes a walk. Returns & works in his files tearing up papers & letters. When I suggest it might be wise to *not* destroy so many of his 'notes' on plays & scenarios—he replies, 'I want to destroy all these things—I'm through, I'll never work again'! I go in my room & weep my heart out!" And on the twentieth, after gasoline rationing and the impossibility of getting anyone to replace Freeman as chauffeur had forced the decision to sell Tao House: "Oh, dear, it's all so terrible, Gene's state [of] health, giving up our home, my state of health—etc. What will happen to us? Gene can't live unless he can work—*that is his life!*"[17]

Tao House was promptly sold. On 21 February O'Neill tore up the manuscripts of "Greed of the Meek" and "And Give Me Death," Plays One and Two of the nine-play Cycle, later explaining that he did not want to be too much governed by what he had written when he came to the task of making those two plays into four.[18] According to George Jean Nathan, O'Neill also felt that, as written, the Cycle "began at the wrong point and over-told the story. Though he appreciated that he could rewrite what he had already done, he preferred to do away with much of it and to start afresh."[19]

On 26 February the O'Neills moved into the Huntington Apartments on California Street in San Francisco. There, in mid-April, the outlook seemed better, and Carlotta commented: "Gene working—Thank God his mind, heart & soul are in his work . . . !"[20]

Lawrence Langner, meanwhile, had finally obtained a priority for O'Neill's dictating machine from the War Production Board, and the device was delivered on 2 May. The company demonstrated it for the O'Neills on the twelfth and reported that they were pleased with it.[21] O'Neill wrote to Langner the next day:

> . . . it is a wonderful machine. . . . I can't test it out on the main job of creating with it, simply because I just am not in a creative vein at present. The coming invasion is too much on the heart and brain. I can't think of much else. But I have tested my end of the Sound Scriber on the play form—read spots of "The Iceman Cometh" and "Long Day's Journey into Night" into it. The result is quite surprisingly effective, considering I am neither a ham nor even an articulate speaker. The voice that comes back fascinates me. It is not my voice and yet it reminds me of someone. . . . It has an impressive ghostly quality and I do succeed in making each word on it clear.

He goes on to say that he will also practice by reading some of the poems he has written recently: "By the time I am ready to create again, I ought to be all set."[22] He did record an excerpt from one of his poems, which he and Carlotta listened to on 15 May; but he was never able to use the machine for creative writing.

Carlotta reported another development on 21 May:

> Gene asks me to *try to get an apartment* overlooking *the Bay*!!! I, of course say I will—& *I will!* One thing I cannot understand about Gene is his *lack of intelligence!* He is *gifted* & *he works like a slave!* But that *slavery,* is like

the *slavery* of a man *wooing* a *woman he adores!* His "work" is his *love,* his *passion,* his *integrity,* his *joy,* his *achievement!* Anything else is a *step to* that *achievement,—*or giving him more *time & quiet for* his achievement! Anything else is a *help,* a *saver of time*—a *guardian*—a *mother,* a *mistress,* (when needed) so that he is ready, in all ways, for *his work!*[23]

In June 1944, the O'Neills did move into a larger apartment in the Huntington Hotel, where a nurse was engaged to help Carlotta, who was herself in poor health with an arthritic spine. There, on 22 June, Carlotta noted: "Gene looking over Cycle—has me retyping some scenes"; and on the twenty-third: "We continue on Cycle—going over 'A Touch of the Poet' ".[24] On 11 July 1944 O'Neill wrote to George Jean Nathan: "No news about work. I can't do any."[25] And on the twenty-fourth Carlotta expressed her concern: "Gene rather excited about a new idea, that he can throw this tremor off by exercising! And give up sedatives! Am afraid exercising will make it *worse!* (Everybody calls it "Parkinson's" disease—but 'Dukie' told me it was *not* Parkinson's & explained *why* to me! It is part hereditary & part caused by the deterioration of certain nerves in the cerebellum. I believe what Dukie said)".

By 29 August, she was describing the situation as desperate:

Gene nervous—gradually driving himself mad over his work—tremor—etc.—and being without exercise. He won't go to the beach because *people are there!* Or walk in the G[olden]. G[ate]. Park—for the same reason. I have offered to walk with him at night. This "mood" used to take hold of him at Le Plessis (with 50 acres of woods!), at Sea Island (with long beaches)—now he is worse on account of War & tremor. I have tried everything I know. Now he tells me I am not interested in his work! Is this a deliberate effort to hurt me? (He has much of the sadist in him!)—Go in my room & weep my soul out!—& take a big dose of sedative & sleep! God help us both.

On 11 September Carlotta reported: "Gene going over 'Hughie' ", but there was apparently no new writing.[26] On 19 October, O'Neill himself wrote to his Spanish translator: "During the past year or more, I have done no work at all."[27] And to Elizabeth Shepley Sergeant on 4 December: "I haven't done a line of work in a long while."[28] On 24 March 1945, he wrote to Frederic I. Carpenter: "For the past two years I've done nothing at all." In that same letter he referred to the Cycle by its final title, "A Tale of Possessors Self-

Dispossessed," and stated that the last play, the old "Bessie Bowen" would "never be written."[29]

The Langners visited the O'Neills again at the Huntington Hotel in the early summer of 1945. Against Carlotta's better judgment, O'Neill let Langner take away scripts of *A Moon for the Misbegotten* and *Hughie*. Langner wrote about them on 2 August, expressing his joy that O'Neill was "ready to come back into the theatre."[30] But by the fourteenth, O'Neill had reconsidered, deciding that it was wiser to postpone production of *A Moon for the Misbegotten* until the following season: there was not enough time to cast it right for the fall of 1945. (Of course any production of the one-act *Hughie* would have to await the completion of at least one more play in the "By Way of Obit." series.) Furthermore, O'Neill could not stand the journey East to attend rehearsals.[31]

But the talk of possible New York productions of his plays had given O'Neill the impetus he needed to agree to pull up stakes in San Francisco. On 17 October, he and Carlotta left for New York and moved into a small apartment in the Barclay Hotel. O'Neill still seemed to nurse some hope that he might be able to write again, for on the first day of 1946, he wrote to Kenneth Macgowan: "No, you can't grab my sound scriber [i.e., his dictating machine]. I have simply *got* to learn how to use it when I start being creative again, which probably means when we go to Sea Island for four months May first."[32] The discomforts of life in the southern summer climate had, for the moment, been forgotten, and only its pleasanter aspects remembered; but in any event the mad plan did not materialize. Instead of returning to Georgia, in the spring of 1946 the O'Neills moved into a penthouse apartment (formerly occupied by the playwright Edward Sheldon) at 32 East 84th Street. There O'Neill worked on revising *The Iceman Cometh* for production by the Theatre Guild. He discussed the play with his old friend George Jean Nathan and filled him in on the various writing projects that had occupied him since the last O'Neill production, *Days Without End*, in 1934.[33] There, too, on three Sundays in August, Elizabeth Shepley Sergeant, who had interviewed him many years before and had published an account of that meeting in her *Fire under the Andes* (1927), talked with him about his life and work.

O'Neill's references to the Cycle in his talks with Nathan and with Sergeant constitute two of the last firsthand descriptions of the magnum opus. Sergeant's rough notes, never shaped into an article, summarize his conversation. "The Cycle," he told her, "called for the present 'Tale of Possessors [Self-]Dispossessed' . . . has eleven plays either in scenario or script."

[It] seems to him to round out what he has had to say about American life and life itself. [It] tells the story of an American family, Welsh in origin, then reinforced by an Irish strain—the founder is a deserter from Braddock's army—and . . . deals with the whole American story of Revolution, mercantile expansion, clipper ships, railroad building, money making and accumulation, ending . . . with the gradual *reductio ad absurdum* of the American dream of liberty, and of the value, for life, of money *per se.*

First four plays make a unit. New England family, Welsh and scotch. Harford. A Touch of the Poet is the dividing line—here the Irish element is introduced name Melody. . . .

The difficulty, after he began to go backwards [from *The Calms of Capricorn*] was to find the starting point in all this—could never be sure of place where he ought to begin. Everything derived from everything else. . . .

Now . . . the [eleven-play] cycle begins with a man [Jonathan Harford, I] who enlisted in the British Army under Braddock to get to America. He has read tales of the Indians. Also wants to get away from his and his Father's slavery to the land. He has himself a passion for the land and a passionate nature. [In America he deserts and, in the first play, works for and then marries the widow, Naomi,] who has a very earthy sensuality and a strong possessiveness about the land, [and operates a farm with her three daughters. He fathers a son, Ethan I, but] . . . deserts the family [and] goes to seek pure freedom among [the] Indians. Does not find it; lives alone in [the] wilderness. . . . He then hears of the Revolution, joins up, and [eventually] dies at Bunker Hill.

[His stepdaughters] . . . are people with guts. When they feel negative [about the farm], they burn the buildings.

[In] *Or Give me Death* [the second play, Jonathan's] son [Ethan, I] becomes a disciple of Robespierre (whom O'Neill admires greatly). One of most fascinating of men—dictator who sets out to make men free. . . . [Ethan] doesn't care for business—the three [half-] sisters go on [to] make money in the shipyard. [He] calls the [American] Revolution the Traders' War, and thinks the real Rev[olution is] in France. Joins the Jacobin Club in Paris just before Robespierre falls. Then gets thrown in jail along with Robespierre. He [Ethan] is unimportant and they forget about him. He lies in jail. The three [half-] sisters come to Paris—find [out] where he is and get him out by slipping some money to [the] jailers. Yank him back to his home town—like Newburyport—Then [he] settles down and becomes a

N[ew]. E[ngland] nut. Refuses to have anything to do with his family. Has a Grecian temple to the goddess of liberty in the garden. Keeps his . . . Fr[ench] Rev[olution] uniform, Fr[ench] National Guard. . . . (In A Touch of the Poet there is a recurrence of this theme. . . . [Melody] wears uniform of the British Irish Dragoons—fought in British army against Napoleon.)

O'Neill summarized briefly the plots of *A Touch of the Poet, More Stately Mansions, The Calms of Capricorn,* "The Earth Is the Limit," and "Nothing Is Lost but Honor" and then talked to Sergeant at some length about "The Man on Iron Horseback":

> In the r[ail]r[oad] play [he] tried to show the absurdity of the liberals' point of view about the r[ail]r[oad] men [which held that they] . . . saw before them a m[oun]t[ain] of gold . . . that it was money that made [them] move. That was not it. [The] r[ail].r[oad]. men were poets, and their dreams of power were something more than concern for profit of getting across the country from N[ew] Y[ork] to Frisco. Their crazy dream was eminently practical.
>
> [E. H.] Harriman's dream was to cross the Pacific—had his own boats to Japan. He wanted to go in his own ship to Vladivostock—was blocked in Manchuria. But almost controlled the Manchurian R[ail]R[oad]. Hoped to get his hooks in the Trans-Siberian.
>
> Harriman in end had control of the Am[erican] Transport Line—he was going to make the circle of the globe in his own steamships—arms around the world—but in the end had nothing. Hero of play [Jonathan Harford, II] differs somewhat—[His dream was Harriman's dream, but] in gaining this great power, encirclement of globe, he loses love, because he wants to possess that. . . . [In the end he] Dies of overwork like Harriman. . . .
>
> O'Neill went into this material with radical prejudice about important people. Got new light from Gustavus Myers' [*History of the*] *Great American Fortunes.* Myers did endless research in files to get [just] one fact. Never got mixed up in a liberal suit though [he] also wrote *The History of Tammany Hall.*
>
> Sara [Melody Harford] runs through (?) because [she is] such a grand character. Has an immense palace in Newport. She is left up there alone, deserted in palatial grounds. Servants love her. Before, in other plays, [she was] right in it.

O'Neill gave Sergeant two differing views of the final, eleventh play—on the old "Bessie Bowen" theme. On 11 August, he sketched the action to her as follows:

> In [the] end, [the] last woman [Lou Bowen] marries [a] bicycle dealer [Ernie Ward] who has . . . genius for mechanics. He is not interested in money. Goes from bicycle to airplane [and is the] 1st one to invent a cheap car. The woman takes over, pushes him into the background. In the beginning, they really love each other. He ends up with a rocket ship which will go to the moon. It explodes and he is blinded. She is so ugly, [she] could not believe any man would love her—but when he is blind she cares for him and loves him again. He believed her beautiful because he loved her. [In the] Last act, blinded by the moon bomb [i.e., rocket?] and in [a] wheel chair, [he] can't walk again, she comes—he says, "You are beautiful"—She reacts with bitter hatred. But as he is blind, she can find a meaning for the rest of her life in taking care of him—really being in love with him [again].[34]
>
> The stockholders [of the company] say she can't go on making cars—no sale for them. Finally—this is her end—she hears this tremendous *hum* in factory—she sits there and crumbles to pieces—broken to pieces.
>
> But there is an Epilogue—4 children—2 sons, 2 daughters. Their craziness is sobered down—all is gone—[The] old man, Honey Melody [Harford] (grandfather?) lives thro[ugh] it all, dies in [the] Crash.

Two weeks later, on 25 August, the emphasis in O'Neill's mind is on the ending of the play, and the four children have reverted to the original six of the very first sketch of "It Cannot Be Mad":

> The cycle goes to 1932.
>
> It ends with a woman [Honey Harford's grand-daughter, Lou Bowen], whose husband [Ernie Ward] has an auto factory, which has put out a cheap car; she puts him out of the business and runs it herself.
>
> There are four sons. They represent utter possessiveness as to Fate—triumph of machinery. One goes in for speed for speed's sake—as art for art's sake. He has a private race-track, where there are no prizes—just speed, going round and round, a speed maniac. Youngest boy [is] a dope fiend—life [to him] is a river, you sit on the bank and watch it go by—never acknowledge you belong to it. Another brother becomes a gambler—to

show contempt for money—for it, work and everything else—to show his contempt for everything men believe in.

[One] Daughter goes in for fake Yogi stuff—search for Nirvana. She is made pregnant by the teacher of Nirvana. [The] Other daughter, Paris Left Bank, Lesbian.

The old man . . . who had begun as a politician of the type of [Honey] Fitzgerald in Boston—Honey Melody [Harford] is his name—Hair of the gods? [i.e., Dog]. When they go in to him, after the Crash he is dead.

They are the kind of people who go after success, and succeed, and then fall but never stay fallen.[35]

Both Sergeant and Nathan report O'Neill as having become convinced that the "dramaturgical plan" of his Cycle was faulty. They seem to imply that his dissatisfaction was limited to the first two plays of the nine-play Cycle as written and was, in part, the reason for their destruction. But O'Neill had come to feel that it was a major flaw in his plan for the first four plays of the eleven-play Cycle to give such a prominent role to the Three Sisters who, in that plan, were not blood members of the Harford family. Nathan reports him as saying that the Cycle "should deal with one family and not two".[36] In the *two* destroyed plays the Three Sisters had been daughters of the first Harford (then named Evan) by his first wife. It is only in the plan for the *four* plays to replace them that the Harford progenitor (now named Jonathan) becomes the second husband of Naomi (last name not given), already the mother of the three daughters. It is therefore not the first two plays of the nine-play Cycle but the plan for the first four plays of the eleven-play Cycle that is faulty in this respect. It seems probable that the major reconstruction of his plans for the first four plays that would have been required to correct this flaw became an additional, final reason why O'Neill, his energies at a low point because of ill health and depression at the state of the world, failed to do any further major new work on the Cycle during the last years of his life.

On 9 October 1946, *The Iceman Cometh* opened at the Martin Beck Theatre in New York and was, on the whole, favorably received. In an interview printed in the 21 October issue of *Time*, O'Neill is quoted as saying:

inwardly . . . the war helped me realize that I was putting my faith in the old values, and they're gone. . . . It's very sad, but there are no values to live by today. . . . Anything is permissible if you know the angles.

I feel, in that sense, that America is the greatest failure in history. It was given everything, more than any other country in history, but we've squandered our soul by trying to possess something outside it, and we'll end as that game usually does, by losing our soul and the thing outside it too. But why go on—the Bible said it much better: "For what shall it profit a man if he gain the whole world, and lose his own soul?"[37]

When the Theatre Guild came to send *The Iceman Cometh* on a road tour, Lawrence Langner tried to persuade O'Neill to make further cuts in the play and, at his suggestion, marked recommended cuts on a copy of the script. The dramatist subsequently inscribed it to Langner: "THE HELL with your cuts! E. O'N."[38]

The Guild had eventually decided that it would be best to open *A Moon for the Misbegotten* out of New York and fixed upon Columbus, Ohio. The play opened there at the Hartman Theater on 20 February 1947, but it was not well received. After a short tour, with brief stops—and encounters with censorship—in Pittsburgh, Detroit, and St. Louis, it closed, and plans for an opening in New York were cancelled.

During the summer and fall of 1947, O'Neill gave to the novelist Hamilton Basso what were to be the last of his interviews. "The Tragic Sense," the three-part profile based on those conversations, appeared in the *New Yorker* in February and March 1948. Part three contains the dramatist's final statement about the Cycle:

The ninth [i.e., eleventh] play, which, chronologically, was to be the first of the cycle, deals with America during the French and Indian War. Its hero is an Irishman who has joined the British Army to escape the slavery of agricultural life in Ireland. It is his idea to desert as soon as he gets to America and to go into the wilderness, where, liberated from the economic and social bondage of the Old World, he can live as a truly free man. Once in this country, he strikes out for the wilderness. On his journey, wanting food and shelter, he stops at a frontier farm. It is only a clearing in a forest, but it is nonetheless the most fertile and promising soil he has ever seen. The farm is run by a young widow, who badly needs a man. The Irishman, caught between his dream of freedom and his hunger for land, and attracted by the woman's physical allure, finally abandons his dream and settles for the land. The bleak mood of the play was summed up in its title, *Give Me Liberty And—*. According to O'Neill's scheme, the seed of greed that had thus been planted was to grow and flower throughout the cycle.

The cycle, although primarily the story of an American family, was also intended to be the story of America. O'Neill thinks that we have not done very well as a country. Looking back upon the original promise of American life and pondering what he takes to be the present reality, he gets bitter and discouraged. "Someday," he says, "this country is going to get it—really get it. We had everything to start with—everything—but there's bound to be a retribution. We've followed the same selfish, greedy path as every other country in the world. We talk about the American Dream, and want to tell the world about the American Dream, but what is that dream, in most cases, but the dream of material things?"[39]

Basso's report reflects statements by O'Neill that, like the identification of the first play, may simply have been misunderstood. It seems inconceivable that O'Neill could have planned to make the Harford progenitor Irish rather than Welsh and Scotch (as in the account given to Sergeant in 1946). Making him Irish would have vitiated much of the Harford-Melody antagonism so essential to the plot of *A Touch of the Poet* as written. About the dramaturgical plan of the Cycle, Basso explains that O'Neill had decided "by the middle of 1939" that it "should deal with two families instead of one." But it is unlikely that the introduction of two families in the outline of the first plays of the eleven-play Cycle in November 1940 was deliberate. Certainly O'Neill, by 1946 and 1947, when he talked with Nathan and Sergeant, had come to see it as a major flaw. Basso also reports O'Neill as saying that he had destroyed "three completed plays, three that were practically completed, and two on which he had done considerable work"[40]—a total that does not tally with the evidence of the dramatist's own, scrupulously kept *Work Diary*, and with Nathan's seemingly more accurate account: " . . . he destroyed two of the double-length, or four, of the plays he had written [i.e., "The Greed of the Meek" and "And Give Me Death"], preserving only *A Touch of the Poet*, the third double-header (*More Stately Mansions*) and one scene in another to be called *The Calms of Capricorn*."[41]

In 1947, not being able to write made O'Neill even more difficult to live with, and after a particularly violent quarrel, Carlotta moved into the New Weston Hotel and contemplated returning to California to live alone in Monterey. In January 1948, O'Neill went into Doctors' Hospital with a broken arm and remained there for several weeks. Carlotta herself was briefly in the same hospital. A reconciliation took place shortly afterward, and on 19 April the O'Neills moved together into the Ritz-Carlton Hotel in Boston.

In that same spring of 1948 they purchased their last home, a cottage that Carlotta had found at Marblehead Neck, on the coast of Massachusetts. Because it had to be winterized, they did not move in until the fall. O'Neill was still hoping to resume writing plays and reported to Saxe Commins on 26 July that his tremor was better.[42] His state of mind was not improved, however, by news of the arrest on 10 August of his son Shane, charged with the possession of three capsules of heroin. (The young man received a two-year suspended sentence.) On the eighteenth, Carlotta reported: "Lawrence [Langner] & Terry [Helburn] go to see 'Hamlet' (opening night [in Boston]—come here afterwards & we chat until 1 A.M. All very uninspired regarding the casting of '[A Touch of] The Poet'—I wish Gene would *not* produce. His health is not up to it—just publish."[43] Eventually O'Neill did decide against both production and publication of *A Touch of the Poet*.

On 4 December 1948, O'Neill wrote optimistically to the screenwriter Dudley Nichols reporting improvement in his tremor: "And now at last . . . I can hope to start writing plays again."[44] But the hope faded as the tremor once again grew worse: in February 1949 he admitted to his lawyer, Winfield Aronberg, that "I will never write another play and there is no use kidding myself that I will."[45] On 20 March he sadly confirmed to Nichols that "no play is being written".[46] On the same day, he expressed it more forcefully to his old friend George Jean Nathan: "As for writing a new play, that pipe-dream seems as remote and unattainable as memorizing the *Encyclopedia Britannica*."[47] In August he explained to Nathan that there was nothing more he wanted to say.[48]

A crushing blow came in September 1950 when Eugene O'Neill, Jr., committed suicide. The father, in anguished tones, asked Norman Holmes Pearson, his son's friend and classmate at Yale, on one of his visits: "Why did he do it?"[49]

In February 1951 bromide poisoning of both O'Neills seems to have been primarily responsible for a veritable Grand Guignol of horrors. Following a violent quarrel with his wife, O'Neill, lightly clad, left the house, fell, and broke his right leg. Subsequently both he and Carlotta were hospitalized. At one point in March, Merrill Moore, the poet-psychologist, acting as Carlotta's physician, expressed his opinion that both she and her husband were mentally incapacitated.[50] Each filed charges against the other, and O'Neill was moved from Boston to New York, where he was again admitted to Doctors' Hospital, this time for two and a half months. There Sally Coughlin, his day nurse, did her best to encourage him to try to dictate his plays, but he insisted that the ideas just would not come unless he was actually writing them down. She felt that O'Neill never tried seriously to cope with his affliction.[51]

In the confusion of those troubled days, items like the revised typescript of *More Stately Mansions* and all the other Cycle Papers that had not been torn up were sent to Yale for the O'Neill collection. Eventually O'Neill and Carlotta were reunited, and in May 1951, having sold the Marblehead house, they moved into the Hotel Shelton in Boston. There Carlotta nursed her husband through his final illness. On 27 November 1953 Eugene O'Neill, aged sixty-five, died, finally ending all hope that the vast enterprise to which he had devoted such a substantial part of his creative life would ever be realized.

Appendix: A Chronology of Composition

The Nine-Play Cycle

Play no.

3   *A Touch of the Poet*
    Scenario: 6–24 Feb. 1935.
    First title, 10 Feb. 1935–9 Aug. 1937: "The Hair of the Dog."

4   *More Stately Mansions*
    Scenario: 10 Mar.–26 Apr. 1935.
    First title, 27 Feb.–22 Mar.: "Oh, Sour-Apple Tree."

5   *The Calms of Capricorn*
    Scenario: 6 May–9 June 1935.

6   "The Earth Is the Limit"
    Outline: 21? Jan., 22–30 June 1935.

7   "Nothing Is Lost but Honor"
    Outline: 23 Jan., 3–28 July 1935.

8   "The Man on Iron Horseback"
    Outline: 24–25 Jan., 31 July–27 Aug. 1935.
    Tentative titles: "Hail, My Columbia!"; "My Gem of the Sea."

9   "The Hair of the Dog"
    Notes: 29–30 Aug., 1–2 Sept. 1935; 26–27 July, 1 Nov. 1937;
        1–3 Oct., 18 Dec. 1941.
    First title, 29 Aug. 1935–9 Aug. 1937: "Twilight of Possessors
        Self-Dispossessed."
    Decision to use the "Bessie Bowen" play: July–Aug. 1935.

2   "And Give Me Death"
    Notes and outline: 7–15, 18 Sept.–1 Oct. 1935.
    Scenario (act one): 4–9 Nov. 1935.
    First title, 7 Sept. 1935–9 Aug. 1937: "Greed of the Meek."

3   *A Touch of the Poet*
>   First draft: 25, 27 Nov., 6–13, 17–23 Dec. 1935, 10 Jan.–5, 10, 15–
>   17 Feb., 12–18 Mar. 1936.

2   "And Give Me Death"
>   First draft (with title, "Greed of the Meek"): 19 Mar.–26 June 1936.
>   Outline revised: 5, 8–14 June 1936.
>   Final title: 9 Aug. 1937.

3   *A Touch of the Poet*
>   First draft (cont.): 29 June–17 July 1936. (Probably burned 1953.)
>   Second draft: 20 July–21 Aug. 1936.

1   "Greed of the Meek"
>   Notes and outline: 7, 15–23 June 1936, 21 June–8 July, 1–10 Aug.
>   1937.
>   Outline probably burned 1953.

2   "And Give Me Death"
>   First draft (cont.): 23 Aug.–18 Sept. 1936.
>   Final title: 9 Aug. 1937.
>   Manuscript destroyed 21 Feb. 1944; outline probably burned 1953.

4   *More Stately Mansions*
>   First draft (act one): 24 Sept.–1 Oct. 1936.

1   "Greed of the Meek"
>   First draft: 11 Aug.–20 Dec. 1937.
>   Destroyed 21 Feb. 1944.

4   *More Stately Mansions*
>   First draft (cont.): 1 Apr.–8 Sept. 1938.
>   Second draft: 9 Sept. 1938–1 Jan. 1939.
>   Third draft: 1–20 Jan. 1939.
>   Tentative new title, 1941: "Brahma or Nothing."

3   *A Touch of the Poet*
>   Second draft (cont.?): 24 Jan.–20 Apr. 1939.
>   Third draft: 21 Apr.–19 May 1939.
>   Second and third drafts (typescripts) torn up 14 Nov. 1942.

5   *The Calms of Capricorn*
>   Prologue: 24 May–3 June 1939.
>   Destroyed: 5 June 1939.

3 *A Touch of the Poet*

> Fourth draft: 22 Feb.–3 Apr.; 24 June–17, 21, 29–31 July; 7, 12–
> 15, 19, 22–23 Aug.; 2 Sept.–13 Nov. 1942.

The Eleven-Play Cycle

1 "Give Me Liberty and—"

> Outline: 23 Oct.–9 Nov. 1940.
> Other tentative titles: "The Poor in Spirit"; "The Pride of the Meek."

2 "The Rebellion of the Humble"

> Outline: 10–11 Nov. 1940.
> Other tentative titles: "The Rights of Man"; "The Patience of the
> Meek."

3 "Greed of the Meek"

> Outline: 12 Nov. 1940.

4 "And Give Me Death"

> Outline: 13 Nov. 1940.

5 *A Touch of the Poet*

> See the Nine-Play Cycle, no. 3.

6 *More Stately Mansions*

> See the Nine-Play Cycle, no. 4.

7 *The Calms of Capricorn*

> See the Nine-Play Cycle, no. 5.

8 "The Earth Is the Limit"

> See the Nine-Play Cycle, no. 6.

9 "Nothing Is Lost But Honor"

> See the Nine-Play Cycle, no. 7.

10 "The Man on Iron Horseback"

> See the Nine-Play Cycle, no. 8.

11 "The Hair of the Dog"

> See the Nine-Play Cycle, no. 9.

Abbreviations

"As Ever, Gene"	"As Ever, Gene": The Letters of Eugene O'Neill to George Jean Nathan. Transcribed, edited, and with introductory essays by Nancy L. Roberts and Arthur W. Roberts. Rutherford, N.J.: Fairleigh Dickinson University Press; London: Associated University Press, 1987.
DCG	Collection of the author.
Floyd	Eugene O'Neill at Work: Newly Released Ideas for Plays. Edited and annotated by Virginia Floyd. New York: Frederick Ungar, 1981.
Letters	Selected Letters of Eugene O'Neill. Edited by Travis Bogard and Jackson R. Bryer. New Haven: Yale University Press, 1988.
"The Theatre We Worked For"	"The Theatre We Worked For": The Letters of Eugene O'Neill to Kenneth Macgowan. Edited by Jackson R. Bryer, with the assistance of Ruth M. Alvarez. With introductory essays by Travis Bogard. New Haven: Yale University Press, 1982.
Work Diary	Eugene O'Neill, Work Diary, 1924–1943. Transcribed by Donald Gallup. Preliminary ed. 2 vols. New Haven: Yale University Library, 1981.
YCAL	Collection of American Literature, Beinecke Rare Book and Manuscript Library, Yale University.

Notes

The Cycle Papers are quoted, wherever possible, in their entirety, because brief summaries, departing inevitably from O'Neill's phrasing, decrease the significance of these documents. Ideally, they should all be printed as written, but for the general reader, and even for scholars, the detailed outlines and scenarios require editing. Few individuals would have the interest, patience, and sheer perseverance to follow some of them in their often tortured grammar, ambiguity of reference, and almost total lack of conventional punctuation and paragraphing. O'Neill's setting down second and sometimes even third and fourth thoughts—possibilities, many of them entertained only momentarily but not always marked for rejection—means that some kind of selection process must operate. Choices must be made: to give all of O'Neill's alternatives in cases where he obviously hadn't made up his mind becomes simply too confusing; furthermore, some sections demand rearrangement into more logical order.

I have quoted the Cycle Papers chiefly in three ways:

1. Transcribed as written, except that erasures and deletions have been ignored. Such transcripts are identified in the notes as "transcript A."

2. Transcribed as written, except that abbreviations have been silently expanded; dashes have been replaced by conventional punctuation; understood articles and pronouns have been silently supplied; paragraphing has been introduced; and, occasionally, the order of phrases has been shifted, a word silently supplied, and a repetitious word or phrase omitted in the interest of clarity. Such transcripts are identified as "transcript B."

3. Condensed, often radically—by as much as two-thirds—with occasional paraphrasing for the sake of clarity and some rearrangement of elements in the interest of logical order. Almost all the operative words are O'Neill's. Passages of dialogue that do not forward the plot have been omitted. Such transcripts are identified as "transcript C."

Introduction

1. In "The Monastery and the Prison," one of the essays in his "*From the Silence of Tao House*," Travis Bogard suggests that "the characters in the Cycle are extravagantly clad versions of the figures that really haunted O'Neill's imagination—those of himself and

his family, and . . . the Cycle was a dark mirror that enabled O'Neill to get where he needed finally to be—to the autobiographical plays" (pp. 149–50).

2. He himself referred to his affliction as Parkinson's, but an autopsy revealed that it was actually another rare disease that subjected the cells of part of the brain to a slow, degenerative process.

3. Eugene O'Neill, typewritten letter to Winfield Aronberg, 4 Feb. 1949 (YCAL).

4. *"As Ever, Gene,"* 236. The letter is dated 27 Aug. 1949.

5. Travis Bogard, *Contour in Time,* rev. ed. (New York, Oxford University Press, 1988), 369.

6. *Letters,* 475.

7. Eugene O'Neill, typewritten letter to Robert Sisk, 3 July 1935 (*Letters,* 447).

8. Elizabeth Shepley Sergeant, typewritten notes of interview with Eugene O'Neill, 3 (i.e., 4) Aug. 1946, leaf 5 (YCAL, MS 3, Sergeant papers, ser. 3, box 16, folder 358).

9. *Letters,* 488.

10. Ibid., 546.

11. O'Neill had first outlined this play in August 1927 (*Work Diary,* 45). Then titled "It Cannot Be Mad," it was to be a "vast symbolic play of the effect upon man's soul of industrialism" ("1921–1931 Notebook," YCAL, O'Neill MS 82), planned tentatively as the third member of a trilogy with *Dynamo* and *Days Without End.* Working on it intermittently, and often changing its title, he decided early in 1935 that it "should be part of something, not itself" (*Work Diary,* 208). In August of that year, he made it the final unit of the seven-play Cycle and eventually titled it "The Hair of the Dog."

12. Eugene O'Neill, autograph letter (draft) to Frederic I. Carpenter (YCAL, O'Neill MS 118, vol. 3, 4 Feb. to 16 Sept. 1945).

13. *Letters,* 507.

14. *Work Diary,* 340.

15. "More Stately Mansions," corrected typescript, leaf 2 (YCAL, O'Neill MS 87).

16. Seymour Peck, "A Talk with Mrs. O'Neill," reprinted in Oscar Cargill, N. Bryllion Fagin, and William J. Fisher, eds., *O'Neill and His Plays: Four Decades of Criticism* (New York: New York University Press, 1961), 94–95.

17. Arthur Gelb and Barbara Gelb, *O'Neill* (New York, Harper and Bros., 1962), 938.

18. Hamilton Basso's report of his interview was printed as a three-part profile in the *New Yorker* (28 Feb., 6, 13 Mar. 1948). The third part was reprinted in Mark W. Estrin, ed., *Conversations with Eugene O'Neill* (Jackson: University Press of Mississippi, 1990), 224–36.

19. Nicholas Gage, *A Place for Us* (Boston: Houghton Mifflin, 1989), 319–21.

20. Quoted in *Floyd,* 222n.

21. YCAL, O'Neill MS 97, leaf 1.

22. See, e.g., *Work Diary,* 351, 459.

23. Equivalent materials in the Yale collection for all O'Neill's non-Cycle plays—including "Billionaire"/"It Cannot Be Mad?"/"On to Betelgeuse," "Robespierre," and "Napoleon's Coronation," ideas of which elements were later taken over for the Cycle—were

published in *Floyd*. Professor Floyd also edited and annotated additional sketches for works O'Neill was planning in the final years of his writing career, "The Visit of Malatesta" (1940), "The Last Conquest" (1940–42), and "Blind Alley Guy" (1940–41), and published them as *The Unfinished Plays* (New York: Continuum, 1988).

24. The account of my involvement with the publication of *More Stately Mansions* is abridged from my *Pigeons on the Granite* (New Haven: The Beinecke Rare Book and Manuscript Library, Yale University, 1988), 291–94.

25. My transcripts of most of the Cycle Papers, typed double-spaced, amount to some fifteen hundred pages. Copies are being deposited in YCAL.

26. *The Calms of Capricorn* was first published in two paperbound volumes in New Haven by the Yale Library in 1981, and in a single clothbound volume in New Haven by Ticknor and Fields in 1982. "O'Neill's Original 'Epilogue' for *A Touch of the Poet*" was printed in the *Eugene O'Neill Review* (Fall 1991 [i.e., Apr. 1992]), [93]–107. The scenario for act one of the second play of the nine-play Cycle appeared in the *Review* (Fall 1992 [i.e., Mar. 1994]), [5]–11.

27. George Jean Nathan, "Eugene O'Neill after Twelve Years," *American Mercury* (Oct. 1946): 462–66. For Hamilton Basso, see n. 18, above; for Elizabeth Shepley Sergeant, see n. 8, above, and n. 40, below.

28. *Letters*, 449.

29. In *Floyd*, the statement is made that "*Long Day's Journey into Night* in scenario, read without a total knowledge of all its autobiographical nuances, seems to have little potential for greatness" (Introduction, p. xviii).

30. Its power was sadly diminished in José Quintero's stage version by cutting and, most seriously, by his casting Ingrid Bergman in the role of Deborah Harford and her insistence on preserving her dignified beauty—immaculately clothed in white—while pretending to be an ugly old woman on the verge of insanity.

31. Carlotta Monterey O'Neill, Diary, 1944 (DCG).

32. *"As Ever, Gene,"* 192. The letter is dated 5 Oct. 1938.

33. *"Cycle/Notes"*, 18 May 1937 (YCAL, O'Neill MS 98, leaf 10).

34. *Letters*, 452.

35. *"The Theatre We Worked For,"* 23.

36. Eugene O'Neill, autograph letter (draft) to Léon Mirlas (YCAL).

37. *"Peninsular War"* and *"Talavera"* (YCAL, O'Neill MS 111, leaves 36, 38).

38. *"7ᵗʰ Play/Notes"* (YCAL, O'Neill MS 99, leaf 6), transcript A.

39. Van Wyck Brooks, *The Flowering of New England, 1815–1865* (New York: E. P. Dutton, 1936), 290–91, [359].

40. YCAL, O'Neill MS 99, leaf 32. O'Neill reported to Elizabeth Shepley Sergeant (interview, 4 Aug. 1946, YCAL) that he "got new light" also from Gustavus Myers's *History of the Great American Fortunes*, 3 vols. (Chicago: C. H. Kerr, 1910).

Matthew Josephson's *The Robber Barons* is the probable source for the two plays' titles. Josephson, in discussing the struggle among Pierpont Morgan, Jay Gould, and James Fisk, Jr., for control of the Erie railroad (pp. 140–41), quotes Fisk as rallying his associates at Pike's Opera House with the exhortation, "Nothing is lost save honor!" That became a tentative title and, with a change of preposition, the final title for Honey Harford's play.

"The Man on Iron Horseback" as title for Jonathan's play seems to have been suggested to O'Neill by a passage (p. 151) in which Josephson writes about celebrations in the autumn of 1870 honoring "the Iron Horse" and "the Vanderbilts, Huntingtons and Fisks who bestrode it."

One of O'Neill's tentative titles probably also came from *The Robber Barons.* Josephson (p. 212) describes the reaction in New York in 1884, during the presidential campaign between James Gillespie Blaine and Grover Cleveland, to the rumor that Jay Gould was playing fast and loose with the telegraphic election returns. He quotes an angry gathering before the Western Union building as singing: "Hang Jay Gould to a sour-apple tree!" "Oh, Sour-Apple Tree" was the original title for the play eventually published as *More Stately Mansions.*

41. Carlotta Monterey O'Neill, Diary, 1943 (YCAL).
42. Travis Bogard, in *"From the Silence of Tao House,"* argues that "There is the outline of James Tyrone [James O'Neill, Sr.] in Con Melody, of Mary Tyrone [Ella O'Neill] in both Nora and Deborah, of Edmund [Eugene O'Neill] in Simon, and, perhaps, Jamie [James O'Neill, Jr.] in aspects of Sara. Enough similarity exists to suggest that in writing the works of historical fiction he [Eugene O'Neill] was somehow caught between the gray reflection of himself and the reality that thrust itself urgently forward in his memory. Was the Cycle a way of disguising a truth which he ultimately gained the courage to present [in the autobiographical plays]?" (p. 150).
43. *The Calms of Capricorn* (1982), 160, 175.
44. *"Notes—Drop Scenes",* Aug. 1937, for the nine-play Cycle (YCAL, O'Neill MS 99, leaves 13–21).
45. YCAL, O'Neill MS 99, leaf 31, transcript B. See also *Work Diary,* 370.
46. *"Cycle as whole,"* Oct. 1941 (YCAL, O'Neill MS +96 [i.e., oversize], vol. 1, leaf 7, 2d count—laid in at end), transcript C.
47. *"Cycle/*11 p[lay].) / (*Notes*)," 1 Oct. 1941 (YCAL, O'Neill MS +96, vol. 1, leaf 5, 2d count—laid in at end of notebook).
48. *"Cycle/Notes (cont.),"* 18 Dec. 1941 (YCAL, O'Neill MS 99, leaf 28), transcript B.

Chapter 1: *June 1931 to January 1935*

1. "Notebook" (YCAL, O'Neill MS 82). The manuscript, called the "1921–1931 Notebook," is published complete in *Floyd,* [37]–222. The Clipper Ship play idea appears on p. 215.
2. "Notebook, ⟨1932–1935⟩" (YCAL, O'Neill MS 83, pt. 3, "Career of Bessie Bowlan," leaf 5), transcript A.
3. *Letters,* 449, 450.
4. *"The Theatre We Worked For,"* 23.

5. "*Calms Of Capricorn series/(General Outline Notes)*" (YCAL, O'Neill MS 103, leaf 20), transcript B.
6. "*Calms Of C[apricorn]. series/Character of Sons*" (YCAL, O'Neill MS 103, leaves 30–31), transcript A.
7. "*Calms Of C[apricorn]./First Play*" (YCAL, O'Neill MS 103, leaf 26), transcript B.
8. "*First Play/Interrelationships/*(men toward Goldie)/ . . . /(women toward Goldie)" (YCAL, O'Neill MS 103, leaf 25).
9. "*Calms Of C[apricorn] series/ Second Play*" (YCAL, O'Neill MS 104, leaf 15), transcript B.
10. "*'Calms Of C[apricorn].' series/Third Play*" (YCAL O'Neill MS. 103, leaves 21–22), transcript B.
11. "*'Calms Of C[apricorn].' series/Fourth Play*" (YCAL O'Neill MS. 103, leaves 23–24), transcript B.
12. "*'Calms Of C[apricorn].' series/Harford & Sara*" (YCAL, O'Neill MS 103, leaf 29), transcript B.

Chapter 2: *January to February 1935*

1. "*As Ever, Gene,*" 192. The letter is dated 5 Oct. 1938.
2. "*Spiritual Undertheme*" (YCAL, O'Neill MS 111, leaf 8), transcript A.
3. "Notebook ⟨1932–1935⟩" (YCAL, O'Neill MS 83, pt. 4, "'*A Touch Of The Poet* [Cycle]'/*Part One*/'*The Hair Of The Dog* [i.e., "A Touch of the Poet"],'" leaves 1–20), transcript C for acts one–four; transcript B for the epilogue.

Chapter 3: *February to April 1935*

1. *Work Diary*, 211.
2. *Letters*, 444.
3. "*Calms Of C[apricorn]. series/*First [*sic*] Play" (YCAL, O'Neill MS 103, leaf 27), transcript B.
4. "Notebook ⟨1932–1935⟩" (YCAL, O'Neill MS 83, pt. 5, "'*A Touch Of The Poet* [Cycle]'/*Part Two*/'*More Stately Mansions*'", leaves 1–27), transcript C.
5. Ibid., leaf 21.
6. Ibid., page facing leaf 1.

Chapter 4: *April to July 1935*

1. "'*The Earth Is The Limit*'/*Outline Notes*" (YCAL, O'Neill MS 104, leaves 27–34), transcript C.
2. Eugene O'Neill, autograph letter (draft) to Lee Simonson [ca. May 1935] (YCAL).
3. "Notebook" (YCAL, O'Neill MS 82), transcript A. The manuscript, called the "1921–

1931 Notebook," is published in its entirety in *Floyd,* [37]–222. The outline for "It Cannot Be Mad" appears on pp. 168–69.

4. Ibid., transcript C. *Floyd,* 169–72, gives a more detailed outline.

5. "*Life Of Bessie Bowen/Act One/*(3rd Outline)" (YCAL, O'Neill MS 66, leaves 19–21), transcripts C and A.

6. YCAL, O'Neill MS 66, leaves 8–11, transcript C.

7. Ibid., leaf 8, transcript A.

8. *Work Diary,* 206.

9. Ibid., 207.

10. YCAL, O'Neill MS 66, leaves 15, 17–18, 21–33, transcript C.

11. Ibid., leaves 10, 14, transcript C. The Announcer's speech is transcript A.

12. Carlotta Monterey O'Neill, Diary, 1935 (YCAL).

13. *Work Diary,* 229.

Chapter 5: *July 1935*

1. *Letters,* 447.

2. " '*Nothing Is Lost But Honor'/Outline* . . . " (YCAL, O'Neill MS 109, leaves 22–41), transcript C.

Chapter 6: *July to September 1935*

1. "*6th Play/Outline*" (YCAL, O'Neill MS 107, leaves 16–19, 1–12), transcript C.

2. "*7th Play/Scene Outline*" (YCAL, O'Neill MS 106, leaves 1–4), transcript C.

Chapter 7: *September 1935 to July 1937*

1. "*Greed of the Meek/Characters*" (YCAL, O'Neill MS 110, leaves 12–13), transcript A.

2. " '*A Touch Of The Poet'/Part One/'Greed Of The Meek'/* . . . " (YCAL, O'Neill MS +105a, leaves 1–3), transcript B.

3. *Work Diary,* 235.

4. Ibid., 236.

5. Eugene O'Neill, autograph letter (draft) to [Dr.] George [Draper, ca. 26 Nov. 1935] (YCAL).

6. *Letters,* 452.

7. "Cycle/Second Play/'And Give Me Death'" (YCAL, O'Neill MS 97, leaves 6–8), transcript C.

8. Elizabeth Shepley Sergeant, typewritten notes of interview with Eugene O'Neill, 3 (i.e., 4) Aug. 1946 (YCAL, MS 3, Sergeant papers, ser. 3, box 16, folder 358, leaf 4).

9. "*Cycle/Notes,*" 18 May 1937 (YCAL, O'Neill MS 98, leaf 10), transcript A.

10. "*7ᵗʰ Play/Notes*" (YCAL, O'Neill MS 99, leaf 6), transcript A.
11. "*2ⁿᵈ Play/1ˢᵗ Scene/* [etc.]", July 1937 (YCAL, O'Neill MS. 110, leaves 1–10), transcript C.

Chapter 8: *July 1937 to October 1940*

1. "*9ᵗʰ Play/Notes*", July 1937 (YCAL, O'Neill MS 99, leaves 7–12), transcripts C and A (for the two speeches).
2. "*Last Play,*" July 1937 (YCAL, O'Neill MS 99, leaf 11), transcripts A and C.
3. "*9ᵗʰ Play,*" 1 Nov. 1937 (YCAL, O'Neill MS 106, leaf 5), transcript B.
4. "Title pages, etc. of first drafts/of two Cycle play[s] destroyed on/Feb 21ˢᵗ [1944] at Tao House (before/moving after we sold [the] place)" (YCAL, O'Neill MS 97, leaves 1–5).
5. "*And Give Me Death/Gen[eral]. Notes,*" Jan. 1940 (YCAL, O'Neill MS 99, leaves 47–48).
6. Eugene O'Neill, typewritten letter to Harry Weinberger, 8 Mar. 1938 (YCAL).
7. "*More Stately Mansions,*" summer 1938 (YCAL, O'Neill MS +96, vol. 1a, leaves 6–7 [numbered by O'Neill "18–19"], transcript A.
8. "More Stately Mansions," corrected typescript (YCAL, O'Neill MS 87).
9. "*Idea Play*", May 1939 (YCAL O'Neill MS. 99, leaf 23), transcript A.
10. *Letters,* 488. The editors date the letter "[June 1939]."
11. "*2ⁿᵈ Play,*" 10 Jan. 1940 (YCAL, O'Neill MS 99, leaf 49), transcript B.
12. "And Give Me Death/*Last Outline—developement*", 21 Jan. 1940 (YCAL, O'Neill MS 99, leaves 44–45), transcript B.
13. YCAL, O'Neill MS 99, leaf 31, Feb. 1940, transcript B.
14. "*As Ever, Gene,*" 207.

Chapter 9: *October to November 1940*

1. *Letters,* 510. The letter is dated 17 July.
2. "CYCLE/(expanded to eleven plays)/*Notes & Outlines/new 1ˢᵗ four plays/*(Oct., Nov. 1940)" (YCAL O'Neill MS +96, vol. 2, leaves 4–9, 22–39), transcript C.

Chapter 10: *November 1940 to November 1953*

1. "*Cycle/*(suggestions—general reconstruction)/(first plays of 9 cycle)," Oct. 1940 (YCAL, O'Neill MS +96, vol. 2, leaf 17), transcript A.
2. "*Cycle/*(notes for rewriting to make it [i.e., the fifth play, *A Touch of the Poet*] one of new Sisters' series)," Nov. 1940 (YCAL, O'Neill MS +96, vol. 2, leaves 10–15).
3. "*Cycle/*(11 p[lay].)/*Notes,*" 1 Oct. 1941 (YCAL, O'Neill MS +96, vol. 1, leaf 5 [2d count—laid in at end]), transcript B. One series of notes, probably of Nov. 1940, refers

to the group of four as the "Sara & the Four Sons series" and "Cornelia & Her Jewels" (YCAL, O'Neill MS +96, vol. 2, leaf 2).

4. "5ᵗʰ Play (Suggestions for rewriting)," 1 Oct. 1941 (YCAL, O'Neill MS +96, vol. 1, leaf 5 [middle], 2d count), transcript B.

5. "*Cycle (new 11 p[lay].)/Notes* . . . ", 1 Oct. 1941 (YCAL, O'Neill MS +96, vol. 1, leaf 6, 2d count), transcript B.

6. Ibid., leaves 6–7, transcript B.

7. "*Cycle as whole (11 p[lay].)/Recurrent . . . aspects*", Oct. 1941 (YCAL, O'Neill MS +96, vol. 1, leaf 8, 2d count), transcript B.

8. "*Cycle /Notes/Recurrent main spiritual theme,*" 18 Dec. 1941 (YCAL, O'Neill MS 99, leaf 27), transcript B.

9. Ibid., leaves 27–28, transcript B.

10. "*Cycle/Notes for whole*", 12 Jan. 1942 (YCAL, O'Neill MS 99, leaf 29), transcript A.

11. "*As Ever, Gene,*" 220. The letter is dated 24 Oct. 1942.

12. "Evan" is O'Neill's mistake for Ethan. He errs again in having Deborah refer later to the Three Sisters as Simon's grandfather's daughters-in-law: they were of course his half-sisters.

13. Carlotta Monterey O'Neill, Diary, 1943 (YCAL).

14. *Letters*, 546.

15. Eugene O'Neill, typewritten letter to Barrett Clark, 29 Aug. 1943 (YCAL).

16. See n. 13.

17. Carlotta Monterey O'Neill, Diary, 1944 (DCG).

18. YCAL, O'Neill MS 97, leaf 1.

19. Nathan, "Eugene O'Neill after Twelve Years," 463, 464.

20. See n. 17.

21. Manuscript note made, presumably, by Lawrence Langner's secretary, Charlotte Watts, on his retained carbon copy of his typed telegram to Carlotta Monterey O'Neill, 8 May 1944 (YCAL, Theatre Guild papers).

22. *Letters*, 556.

23. See n. 17.

24. Ibid.

25. "*As Ever, Gene,*" 228.

26. See n. 17.

27. Eugene O'Neill, autograph letter (draft) to Léon Mirlas (YCAL).

28. *Letters*, 566.

29. Eugene O'Neill, autograph letter (draft) to Frederic I. Carpenter (YCAL, O'Neill MS 118, vol. 3, 4 Feb. to 16 Sept. 1945).

30. Lawrence Langner, typewritten letter to Eugene O'Neill, 2 Aug. 1945 (YCAL, Theatre Guild papers).

31. Eugene O'Neill, typewritten letter to Lawrence Langner [14 Aug. 1945] (YCAL, Theatre Guild papers).

32. "*The Theatre We Worked For,*" 264.

33. Nathan's report, "Eugene O'Neill after Twelve Years," printed in *American Mercury*, was based on letters from O'Neill and on conversations.

34. The blindness of Ernie Ward represents a reversion to an original idea. In her Diary for 25 April 1940 (YCAL), Carlotta writes: "Gene has now decided the present end to 'Bessie Bowen' cannot be used! (Now in *last* play of the 'Cycle')[.] Great pity, for the *blindness* had so much more meaning in Gene's play".

35. Elizabeth Shepley Sergeant, typewritten notes of interviews with Eugene O'Neill, 3 (i.e., 4), 10 (i.e., 11), and 25 Aug. 1946 (YCAL, MS 3, Sergeant papers, ser. 3, box 16, folder 358), transcript B.

36. Nathan, "Eugene O'Neill after Twelve Years," 464.

37. "The Ordeal of Eugene O'Neill" (cover story), *Time*, 21 Oct. 1946, 76.

38. "The Iceman Cometh," typescript (carbon), "original rehearsal copy," with typed explanation signed by Lawrence Langner, 18 Oct. 1946 (YCAL, Theatre Guild papers).

39. Hamilton Basso, "Profiles: The Tragic Sense," pt. 3, in Estrin, *Conversations with Eugene O'Neill*, 229–30.

40. Ibid., 231.

41. Nathan, "Eugene O'Neill after Twelve Years," 463. The only scene of *The Calms of Capricorn* recorded in the *Work Diary* as written (24 May–3 June 1939) is reported there (p. 351) as torn up on 5 June 1939.

42. Dorothy Commins, *What Is an Editor? Saxe Commins at Work* (Chicago: University of Chicago Press, 1978), 74.

43. Carlotta Monterey O'Neill, Diary, 1948 (DCG).

44. Eugene O'Neill, autograph letter to Dudley Nichols (YCAL).

45. Eugene O'Neill, typewritten letter to Winfield E. Aronberg, 4 Feb. 1949 (YCAL).

46. Eugene O'Neill, typewritten letter to Dudley Nichols, 20 Mar. 1949 (YCAL).

47. *"As Ever, Gene,"* 234.

48. Ibid., 236. The letter is dated 27 Aug. 1949 (and was apparently the last one O'Neill wrote to Nathan).

49. Norman Holmes Pearson, in conversation with DCG. Reported also by the Gelbs in their *O'Neill* (p. 905), but without identifying Pearson as the "former Yale associate" of Eugene O'Neill, Jr.

50. Reported by Louis Sheaffer in his *O'Neill, Son and Artist* (Boston: Little, Brown, 1973), 643.

51. Ibid., 649.

Select Bibliography

Books

Bogard, Travis. *Contour in Time: The Plays of Eugene O'Neill.* Rev. ed. New York: Oxford University Press, 1988.

——. *"From the Silence of Tao House": Essays about Eugene and Carlotta O'Neill and the Tao House Plays.* Danville, Calif.: Eugene O'Neill Foundation: Tao House, 1993.

Brooks, Van Wyck. *The Flowering of New England, 1815–1865.* New York: E. P. Dutton, 1936.

Cargill, Oscar, N. Bryllion Fagin, and William J. Fisher, eds. *O'Neill and His Plays: Four Decades of Criticism.* New York: New York University Press, 1961.

Commins, Dorothy Berliner. *What Is an Editor? Saxe Commins at Work.* Chicago: University of Chicago Press, 1978.

Estrin, Mark W., ed. *Conversations with Eugene O'Neill.* Jackson: University Press of Mississippi, 1990.

Gage, Nicholas. *A Place for Us.* Boston: Houghton Mifflin, 1989.

Gallup, Donald C. *Pigeons on the Granite: Memories of a Yale Librarian.* New Haven: Beinecke Rare Book and Manuscript Library, Yale University, 1988.

Gelb, Arthur, and Barbara Gelb. *O'Neill.* New York: Harper and Bros., 1962.

Helburn, Theresa. *A Wayward Quest.* Boston: Little, Brown, 1960.

Josephson, Matthew. *The Robber Barons: The Great American Capitalists, 1861–1901.* New York: Harcourt, Brace, 1934.

Langner, Lawrence. *The Magic Curtain.* New York: E. P. Dutton, 1951.

Myers, Gustavus. *History of the Great American Fortunes.* 3 vols. Chicago: C. H. Kerr, 1910.

O'Neill, Eugene. *"As Ever, Gene": The Letters of Eugene O'Neill to George Jean Nathan.* Transcribed and edited . . . by Nancy L. Roberts and

Arthur W. Roberts. Rutherford, N.J.: Fairleigh Dickinson University Press; London: Associated University Presses, 1987.

——. *The Calms of Capricorn: A Preliminary Edition.* Edited by Donald Gallup. Vol. 1, *The Scenario;* vol. 2, *The Play.* New Haven: Yale University Library, 1981.

——. *The Calms of Capricorn, a Play.* Developed from O'Neill's scenario by Donald Gallup. With a transcription of the scenario. New Haven: Ticknor and Fields, 1982.

——. *Eugene O'Neill at Work: Newly Released Ideas for Plays,* Edited and annotated by Virginia Floyd. New York: Frederick Ungar, 1981.

——. *More Stately Mansions.* Shortened from the author's partly revised script by Karl Ragnar Gierow and edited by Donald Gallup. New Haven: Yale University Press, 1964.

——. *More Stately Mansions: The Unexpurgated Edition.* Edited by Martha Gilman Bower. New York: Oxford University Press, 1988.

——. *Selected Letters.* Edited by Travis Bogard and Jackson R. Bryer. New Haven: Yale University Press, 1988.

——. *"The Theatre We Worked For": The Letters of Eugene O'Neill to Kenneth Macgowan.* Edited by Jackson R. Bryer, with the assistance of Ruth M. Alvarez. With introductory essays by Travis Bogard. New Haven: Yale University Press, 1982.

——. *A Touch of the Poet.* New Haven: Yale University Press, 1957.

——. *The Unfinished Plays: Notes for The Visit of Malatesta, The Last Conquest, Blind Alley Guy.* Edited and annotated by Virginia Floyd. New York: Continuum, 1988.

——. *Work Diary, 1925–1943.* Transcribed by Donald Gallup. Preliminary ed. 2 vols. New Haven: Yale University Library, 1981.

Sheaffer, Louis. *O'Neill, Son and Artist.* Boston: Little, Brown, 1973.

Articles

Basso, Hamilton. "Profiles: The Tragic Sense." *New Yorker,* 28 Feb., 6, 13 Mar. 1948, 34–45, 34–49, 37–47.

Nathan, George Jean. "Eugene O'Neill after Twelve Years." *American Mercury,* 63, no. 274 (Oct. 1946): 462–66.

O'Neill, Eugene. " 'Greed of the Meek': The Scenario for Act One of the First Play of His Eight Play Cycle. Edited and Introduced by Donald

Gallup." *Eugene O'Neill Review,* 16, no. 2 (Fall 1992, mailed Mar. 1994): [5]–11.

——. "O'Neill's Original 'Epilogue' for *A Touch of the Poet:* Developed and Introduced by Donald C. Gallup." *Eugene O'Neill Review,* 15, no. 2 (Fall 1991, mailed Apr. 1992): [93]–107.

"The Ordeal of Eugene O'Neill" (cover story). *Time,* 21 Oct. 1946, 71–78.

Peck, Seymour. "A Talk with Mrs. O'Neill." *New York Times,* 4 Nov. 1956, sec. 2, 1:6.

Eugene O'Neill, The Cycle Papers (YCAL)

The basic materials—written by O'Neill in pencil, unless otherwise specified—are from his files and were received for the Yale Collection of American Literature in 1951 as the gift of Carlotta Monterey O'Neill. Most of those papers were, and in 1997 are still, in folders labeled by O'Neill himself. The order, barring some subsequent accidental rearrangement, is that in which they were received. When O'Neill's original numbering of the leaves does not apply, or when the leaves are without O'Neill's numbers, they have been numbered, in pencil, in sequence. (Some of the set designs, apparently received in 1951 in folder 116, are now filed with the individual plays to which they relate.)

This summary listing incorporates related scripts prepared from O'Neill's manuscripts for *A Touch of the Poet, More Stately Mansions,* and *The Calms of Capricorn.* Folders, notebooks, and scripts appear under the numbers assigned them in the Beinecke Library catalogue. Scripts for *The Calms of Capricorn* follow no. 83, pt. 6 (the manuscript of its scenario); those for *A Touch of the Poet* (nos. 112–115b) are rearranged in the order in which they were actually produced; and those for *More Stately Mansions* follow no. 87 (O'Neill's third-draft typescript).

MS 66   "BESSIE BOLAN"
           Folder containing 25 leaves. 28 cm.
           Contents: leaf 1, *"Career Of Bessie Bolan | A Play | by | Eugene O'Neill"*; leaf 2, " . . . | *Part One*"; leaf 3, *"Characters,"* with none listed; leaf 4, *"Scenes | Part One | . . . | Part Two"*; leaf 5, *"Act One | Scene"*; leaf 6, " *'Career Of Bessie Bowlan' | Part One | Act One | Scene . . . Characters"*, and progression of scenes; leaf

7, " . . . / . . . *Act Two* / Scene . . . "; leaf 8, " . . . / . . . / *Act Three* / Scene"; leaf 9, " . . . / . . . / *Act Four* / Scene"; leaf 10, "*Bessie Bowen* / *Scene—Sound pattern* / . . . / Part (Act ?) One [-Four]"; leaf 11, "*Bessie Bowen* (Borden?) / *Part Two;* leaf 12, " *'B[essie]. B[owen].'*", outline notes; leaf 13, "*The Life Of Bessie Bowen* / *Characters & Interrelationships* 5th; leaf 14, "*The Life* (Career ?) *Of Bessie Bowen* 5th / *Act One;* leaves 15–16, "*Life Of Bessie Bowen* / *Notes*"; leaves 17–18, "*Life Of Bessie Bowen* / *Act One* (Fourth outline)"; leaves 19–21, "*Life Of Bessie Bowen* / *Act One* [*- Three*] (3rd [*sic*] Outline); leaf 22, "*Life Of Bessie Bowen* / *Act One* (*Fourth Outline*) / *Part Four*—Scenes of Youth and Romance"; leaves 23–24, lists of colloquial words and phrases; leaf 25, dates in history of development of American car, "*Motor*", and "*Manufacturing Groups*".

MS 83   "NOTE BOOK / ---- / EUGENE O'NEILL"

Red morocco-bound volume, lettered as above on front cover. 29.5 × 21.5 cm.

Contents: 8 leaves excised, the stubs bearing traces of O'Neill's pencil manuscript, then 2 blank leaves.

Pt. 1, " '*Without Endings of Days* [i.e., *Days Without End*]' / (Tentative Scenario) / . . . / Feb. 10th 1932", leaves 1–6.

Pt. 2, " *'Ah, Wilderness!'* ", 3 Sept. 1932, leaves 1–5.

Pt. 3, " *'Career Of Bessie Bowlan'*", 5 Dec. 1934, leaves 1–5: leaf 1, "*Characters . . . Scenes*"; leaves 2–4, "*Description Of Characters*"; leaf 5, "*Scenes* / *Part One* / *Act One*"; leaf blank save for O'Neill's "6," then 3 blank leaves.

Pt. 4, " '*A Touch Of The Poet* [Cycle]' / *Part One* / '*The Hair Of The Dog* [i.e., *A Touch Of The Poet*]' ", 6–24 Feb. 1935, leaves 1–20: leaf 1, "*Scenes . . . Characters*", with, on verso, outline of "Preliminary scene . . . "; leaves 2–18, scenario, "*Act One*"–"*Act Four*"; leaf 18 (cont.)–20, "*Epilogue*".

Pt. 5, " *'A Touch Of The Poet* [Cycle]' / *Part Two* / '*More Stately Mansions'* ", [10 Mar.–] 26 Apr. 1935, leaves 1–27 [i.e., 28]: leaf 1, "*Scenes . . . Characters*"; leaf 1 verso, "*Prologue*"; leaf 1 [*bis*]–27[i.e., 28], scenario, "*Act One—Scene One*"–"*Act Four—Scene Five*"; leaf 27 [i.e., 28] (cont. to end), "*Epilogue*".

Pt. 6, " *'A Touch Of The Poet* [Cycle]' / *Part Three* / '*The Calms*

Of Capricorn' ", [6 May-] 9 June 1935, leaves 1-17: leaf 1,
"*Scenes . . . Characters*"; leaves 2-17, scenario, "*Act One—Scene
One*"-"*Act Four—Scene Three*"; 5 blank leaves.

DCG   *The Calms of Capricorn.* The Scenario.
        Typescript (original) of transcript made by DCG from
        O'Neill's manuscript (no. 83, pt. 6): 72 leaves. 28 cm.

DCG   *The Calms of Capricorn.* The Play. Developed by Donald Gallup.
        Typescript (original): 103 leaves. 28 cm.

MS 87   *More Stately Mansions*
        Typescript (original): 4 leaves, [279] numbered leaves. 28 cm.
        With extensive manuscript revisions in acts one through three
        (numbered leaves 1-[206]).

        Leaves numbered 16, 83 (1st count) and 14-16 (3d count) are
        missing; leaf numbered 32 (1st count) reproduced in the first
        edition. Repeated or fractional numbers result in 9 extra leaves in
        the first count, 5 in the second count, 3 in the third count, and 3
        in the 4th count.

DCG   *More Stately Mansions* . . . I svensk dräkt av Sven Barthel och
        Karl Ragnar Gierow (Stockholm, Kungl. Dramatiska teatern,
        1962)
        Typescript (carbon) of Swedish translation of O'Neill's third
        draft, omitting only some stage directions: 1 leaf, 251 numbered
        leaves. 36 cm.

DCG   *Bygg dig allt högre boningar (More Stately Mansions)* . . . I svensk
        dräkt av Sven Barthel och Karl Ragnar Gierow (Stockholm,
        Kungl. Dramatiska teatern, 1962)
        Reproduced from typewritten copy: 2 blank leaves, 1 leaf, 192
        numbered leaves, 1 blank leaf. 29.8 cm.

DCG   *More Stately Mansions* . . . (Abridged by José Quintero. New
        York, Elliot Martin; Los Angeles, Center Theatre Group, 1967)
        Reproduced from typewritten copy: 3 leaves, 20, 18, 22, 15
        numbered leaves. 28 cm.
        The script of the play as produced at the Ahmanson Theatre,
        Los Angeles, and the Broadhurst Theatre, New York, 1967.

MS   "CYCLE. | *(expanded to eleven plays)* | *Notes and Outlines* | for
+96,   rewriting 'A Touch Of The Poet' | & 'More Stately Mansions'
vol. 1 (the 3rd | & 4th plays in 9 play Cycle) as 5th | & 6th plays in new

conception, and / continuing the three sisters through both / plays) / (Nov.–Dec. 1940)"

Cover-title of spiral notebook, 35.5 × 21.5 cm., containing 9 leaves (integral), plus 8 leaves, 28–33.5 cm., numbered 1–8, laid in at end.

Contents: leaves 1–7, "*Cycle* / (new scheme—series of Sisters plays) / *6ᵗʰ Play* / 'More Stately Mansions' / [Act] I [–IV] / . . .", Nov. 1940; leaf 8, "*6ᵗʰ Play* New angle for play *Nov. '40*"; leaf 9, "*Cycle Dec. '40* / *6ᵗʰ Play* . . . / . . . Simultaneous scenes, progression"; leaf 1 (2d count), "*Last Five Plays of [7-play] Cycle* / (Notes suggested in writing 1ˢᵗ & 2ⁿᵈ Plays)", Tao House, summer 1938; leaf 2 (2d count), "*Cycle Nov. '40* / *Plays in which Sisters appear / dates & ages of people*"; leaves 3–4 (2d count), "*Cycle* (11 p[lay].) *May '41* / *First Play*"; leaves 5–6 (2d count), "*Cycle* / 11 p[lay]) / (*Notes*) / *Divisions* / . . . / Suggestions for rewriting) / . . .", 1 Oct. 1941; leaves 7–8 (2d count), "*Cycle as whole* [11-play] *October '41*".

MS +96, vol. 1a
" '*More Stately Mansions*'" (notes for revision, Tao House, summer–Dec. 1938)

12 leaves, numbered by O'Neill "2, 4–5, 14, 16, 18–19, 25–26, [27–29]." 33.5 cm.

Originally inserted by O'Neill in YCAL O'Neill MS 96, vol. 1, these are leaves containing at least one uncancelled note. Many other notes are cancelled in pencil, indicating revisions either made or rejected. The leaves missing in O'Neill's numbered sequence contained, presumably, only notes for revisions he had made or rejected.

MS +96, vol. 2
"Cʏᴄʟᴇ / (expanded to eleven plays) / *Notes & Outlines* / new 1ˢᵗ *four plays* / (Oct., Nov. 1940)"

Cover-title of spiral notebook, 35.5 × 21.5 cm., containing 16 leaves (laid in at front), then leaves 17–38 (integral).

Contents: leaves 1–3, "*Cycle Nov. '40* / (New scheme for . . . first [–11th] plays"; leaves 4–5, "*Cycle* / *Nov. '40* / *1ˢᵗ Play* [outline]"; leaves 6–9, "*Cycle Nov. '40* / *2ⁿᵈ Play* [outline]"; leaves 10–13, "*Cycle Nov. '40* / *5ᵗʰ Play* (notes for rewriting to make it one of new Sisters' series) / *'A Touch Of The Poet'*"; leaves 14–16, "*Cycle Nov. '40* / (Sisters carried on into 'A Touch Of The Poet'

& 'More Stately Mansions') (?)"; leaves 17–21, "*Cycle* / (suggestions—general reconstruction) / (first plays of 9 [or 10?– play] cycle)," Oct. 1940; leaves 22–27 (top), "*Cycle Oct. '40* / (new scheme, 1ˢᵗ 3 plays) / *3ʳᵈ Play* [outline]"; leaves 27(bottom)– 38, " . . . *4ᵗʰ Play* [outline]", Oct.–Nov. 1940.

MS +96, vol. 2a   "*Cycle* [11-play. Notes] *April '41* [and undated]"

8 leaves. 17.8 × 10.6 cm. (leaves 1–5); 15.2 × 10.2 cm. (leaves 6–7), in envelope laid in at end of YCAL O'Neill MS 96, vol. 2.

Contents: leaves 1–2, general; leaf 3, "Religious program [plays 1–11]"; leaf 4, "*Quakers*"; leaf 5, "6ᵗʰ [& 5th] Play—dates Nap[oleon]."; leaf 6, [Note on " . . . titles new 1ˢᵗ 4 plays (11 C[ycle])" [and cancelled note on costume technique, dated "Feb. 7 '41)"; leaf 7, "*Quebec Jan. 1ˢᵗ '76* [etc.]"; leaf 8, "2ⁿᵈ Play [Oct.–Nov.? 1940]".

MS 97   [Cycle, 9-play]

Folder containing title pages, "Scenes," and "Characters" for the first drafts of Plays One and Two of the nine-play Cycle, then titled "Greed of the Meek" and "And Give Me Death." 8 leaves. 28–30.5 cm.

On a first leaf, 11 × 17.7 cm., O'Neill has written in blue pencil: "Title pages, etc. of first drafts / of two Cycle play[s] destroyed on / Feb. 21ˢᵗ [1944] at Tao House (before / moving after we sold [the] place)".

MS 98   "CYCLE / *Technique (schemes—outlines—notes)* "

Folder containing 17 leaves of various sizes.

Contents: leaves 1–9, ages of characters in Plays One to Nine; leaf 10, " . . . / *Notes*", on characterization, 18 May 1937; leaf 11, " . . . *The Opposites*"; leaf 12, "*General Notes* / Attitudes Toward Nature, America, of Simon & Sara—Abigail—the sons"; leaf 13, "Quotes," from literature, Plays One to Eight; leaf 14, "*Scheme of Connecting Prologues*", Plays One to Seven; leaves 15–16, " . . . Possible scheme independent *expository preliminary scenes* with newspaper", Plays One to Seven; leaf 17, "*A Scheme For Overlapping Scenes*", Plays One to Five.

MS 99, pt. 1   "CYCLE *(notes)* / *Historical dates—pertinent facts—etc.*"

Folder containing 43 (i.e., 44) leaves of various sizes.

Contents: leaves 1–12, "*Notes*," Plays Three to Nine, June–

July 1937; leaves 13–21, ". . . Notes—Drop Scenes", Plays One
to Nine, Aug. 1937; leaf 22, "Town In Play / *afterwards city*,"
and family names; leaf 23, "*Idea Play* / . . . / Period . . . 1890
[i.e., 1790]–1805", May 1939; leaf 24, "*Notes—Nap[oleon]'s
Coronation*"; leaf 25, "T[ouch of the]. P[oet]. / Note . . . of way
Abigail talks"; leaf 25a, dates, France, 10 Nov. 1799–14 Oct.
1806; leaf 26, " . . . / *Notes for reconstruction*", and progression
of scenes, Plays One to Eleven; leaves 27–28, " . . . / *Notes* /
Recurrent main spiritual theme", Plays One to Eleven, 18 Dec.
1941; leaf 29, " . . . / *Notes for whole*", 12 Jan. 1942; leaf 30,
"Dates—*Utopian movements, etc.*; leaf 31, "*Cycle as whole* /
(mythological background—Sisters as Fates)", Feb. 1940; leaf 32,
"(*General Dope On Empire Builders*)"; leaf 33, "*Data, dates on
Ships, passages, etc.*"; leaves 34–37, typed copy of Ruth Starbuck
Wentworth's letter to her mother, 20 Sept. 1735; leaves 38–41,
typed copy of "Old South leaflets, 7th ser., 1889, No. 8"; leaves
42–43, typed copy of "DECLARATION DES DROITS DE L'HOMME ET
DU CITOYEN".

MS 99, "And Give Me Death"
pt. 2   13 leaves, numbered 44–56, in folder with YCAL O'Neill MS
99 (pt. 1). 28 cm.
Contents: leaves 44–46, " . . . / *Last Outline—development*",
21–22 Jan. 1940; leaves 47–48, " . . . / *Gen[eral]. Notes*", Jan.
1940; leaf 49, "*2nd Play*", Jonathan's returns, 10 Jan. 1940; leaf
50, "*Notes*" of dates, 1794–1803, Jan. 1940; leaf 51, notes,
15 Jan. 1940; leaves 52–56, " . . . *Scenes*", and outline, Jan.
1940.

MS 100 "CYCLE / (Family tree maps—continuance of characters
diagrams)"
Folder containing 7 leaves of various sizes.
Contents: leaves 1–2, Harford family trees, Woods House,
Lafayette, July 1937; leaf 3, later family trees; leaf 4, design for
Jonathan Harford calling card (?); leaves 5–7, continuance of
characters diagrams, 9-play Cycle.

MS 101 [Cycle—Character charts]
Folder containing 5 charts, each 24.2 × 30.1 cm.
Family trees, with the name of each character in ink above a

box in which a detailed description of that person is written in pencil.

MS 102   "Names, dialects, etc."

Folder containing 5 leaves of various sizes.

Contents: leaves 1–3 and 3 verso, lists of Christian and family names; leaf 4, "Lever," lists of colloquial words and phrases; leaf 5, additional words and phrases.

MS 103   " *'The Calms Of Capricorn' * "

Folder containing 56 leaves of various sizes.

Contents: leaves 1–4, " *'Calms Of Capricorn' | Notes for rev[ision].* "; leaves 4 (end)–5, " *. . . | . . . | New [possible] version* "; leaves 6–7, " *. . . | Notes on [for] revision (cont.)* "; leaves 8–9, " *'Calms Of C[apricorn].' | Notes* ", outline for scene of card game eventually in "The Earth Is the Limit"; leaves 10–12, " *3ʳᵈ Play (notes)* "; leaves 13–14, " *'C[alms]. of C[apricorn].' | [Act] Four—[Scene] Four* "; leaves 15–19, " *'C[alms]. of C[apricorn].' | Notes . . .* "; leaf 20, " *Calms Of Capricorn series | (General Outline Notes)* "; leaves 21–22, " *'Calms Of C[apricorn].' series | Third Play* ", i.e., "Nothing Is Lost But Honor"; leaves 23–24, " *'Calms Of C[apricorn].' series | Fourth Play* ", i.e., "The Man on Iron Horseback"; leaves 25–31, " *First Play,* " notes; leaf 32, " *Play Two* ", outline of opening scene; leaves 33–56, notes and set designs.

MS 104   " *'The Earth Is The Limit' * "

Folder containing 34 leaves of various sizes.

Contents: leaves 1–22, " *'The Earth Is The Limit' | Notes* "; leaf 23, " *Calms Of Capricorn series | (General ideas)* "; leaves 24–25, " *'Earth Is Limit' | New Scheme on Wolfe* "; leaf 26, " *'The Earth Is The Limit' | Scenes* "; leaves 27–34, " *'The Earth Is The Limit' | Outline Notes* ".

MS 105   " *'Greed Of The Meek' * "

Folder containing 6 leaves of various sizes.

Contents: leaf 1, " *Dates prior to 1ˢᵗ Play* "; leaves 2–3, outline for "Last Scene . . . [and] *Epilogue* ", 2 Dec. 1937; leaf 4, " *1ˢᵗ Play | [Act] I—[Scene] 1 | (facts [to] look up)* ", Aug. 1937; leaf 5, " *New 1ˢᵗ Play | Epilogue* ", June 1937; leaf 6, " *'Greed Of The Meek' | Part Three—Scene Two* ", set design.

MS   "Note Book / Eugene O'Neill"

+105a   Brown morocco-bound volume containing 8 leaves, the remainder blank. 35 × 23 cm.

Contents: leaf 1, title as above; leaf 2, " 'A Touch of the Poet' / A Cycle of Seven Plays / Scenarios—(continued)"; leaf 3, " *'A Touch Of The Poet' / Part One / 'Greed Of The Meek' / Scenes*", scenes one through three of act one and one of act two only; leaf 4, "*Characters*"; leaves 5–7, " *'Greed Of The Meek'*", scenario for act one—scene one [i.e., act one] only; leaf 8, " *'Greed Of The Meek'* [p.] 4", otherwise blank.

Note: The *Work Diary* would seem to indicate that the "Bessie Bowen" play, now titled "Twilight of Possessors Self-Dispossessed" and eventually "The Hair of the Dog," had become Play Seven before this *eighth* play was thought of—on 7 Sept. 1935.

MS 106   " *'The Hair Of The Dog'* [i.e., Play Nine of the nine-play Cycle]"

Folder containing 11 leaves of various sizes.

Contents: leaf 1, "*7ᵗʰ Play [of 7-play Cycle] / Scene Outline*"; leaves 2–4, " . . . / *Notes*"; leaf 5, "*9ᵗʰ Play / End . . .*", 1 Nov. 1937; leaf 6, " *'Calms Of Capricorn' series* / (General ideas) / Last Play . . ."; leaf 7, " . . . End last play . . ."; leaves 8–11, typed letter signed to Saxe [Commins] from "Joe [Corey?]," Rochester, N.Y., 6 May 1933, enclosing typed copy of Associated Press obituary on Kate Gleason.

MS 107   " 'The Man On Iron Horseback' "

Folder containing 20 leaves of various sizes.

Contents: leaf 1, "*6ᵗʰ Play / Scenes*"; leaves 2–13, " 'Hail, My Columbia!' 'My Gem Of The Sea' / *6ᵗʰ Play / Notes*"; leaf 14, "*Dates for 6ᵗʰ Play*"; leaf 15, "*Dope On Railroads (etc.)*"; leaves 16–19, "*6ᵗʰ Play / Outline*"; leaf 20, "Jonathan (characteristics)".

MS 108   " *'More Stately Mansions'* "

Folder containing 48 leaves of various sizes.

Contents: leaves 1–5, 5a, set designs; leaves 6–8, " *'M[ore]. S[tately]. M[ansions].'* / (Note, possible condensation for future revision)", 22–23 Jan. 1939; leaves 9–10, "*2ⁿᵈ Play (notes)*", 1935; leaf 11, "*Cycle / General Notes*", 1935; leaf 12, "*Notes*", 1935; leaves 13–21, "*More Stately Mansions*", outline, acts three and four, 1935; leaves 22–26, notes; leaves 27–29, "*General Notes*", for insertion as scenario notes, 1935; leaves 30–35, "*Jonathan*", 1935; leaf 36, "[act] 2—[scene] 1 . . . ", outline, 1935; leaves 37–41, notes; leaf 42, "*Play Two* 'Oh, Sour Apple Tree!' " outline of act one, scene two through act two, scene three, 1935; leaf 43, " *'More Stately Mansions' | Notes*", Sept. 1936; leaf 44, " *'More Stately Mansions' | Scenes*", Sept. 1936; leaf 45–48, " *'More Stately Mansions' | (Notes)*", Sept. 1936.

MS 109   " 'Nothing Is Lost Save Honor' "

Folder containing 41 leaves of various sizes.

Contents: leaves 1–3, " . . . Golden Spike Scene", Nov. 1940 and earlier; leaves 4–20, notes; leaf 21, "*Fifth Play 'Nothing Is Lost But Honor' | Notes*"; leaves 22–41, " *'Nothing Is Lost But Honor' | Outline*".

MS 110   " 'Or Give Me Death' "

Folder containing 29 [i.e., 30] leaves of various sizes.

Contents: leaves 1–4, "*2ⁿᵈ Play*", outline and notes, July 1937; leaves 5, 6a, and 6–9, "*2ⁿᵈ Play | Progression Blackouts*", July 1937; leaf 10, "*2ⁿᵈ Play | Epilogue*", July 1937; leaf 11, "Prologue / Notes for revision"; leaves 12–15, "*Greed Of The Meek* [i.e., *'And Give Me Death'*] *| Characters*"; leaves 16–20, notes; leaf 21, "*Act Four—Scene Three 'G[reed]. of the M[eek].' | Notes*", i.e., 4 set designs, 1 of them cancelled; leaves 22–24, notes; leaves 25–29, set designs, with notes on dates on verso of leaf 26.

MS 111   " *'A Touch Of The Poet'* "

Folder containing 63 leaves of various sizes.

Contents: leaves 1–7, notes; leaf 8, "*Spiritual Undertheme*"; leaf 9, "*General Notes . . . | (to be inserted as scenario notes)*"; leaves 10–11, "*Play One | Songs*"; leaves 12–22, notes; leaves 23–31, "*1ˢᵗ Play*", characters; leaf 32, "*1ˢᵗ Play | (7 Cycle)*", notes, 29 Mar. 1938; leaves 33–35, "*A Touch Of The Poet | First Play | Characters*", and outline notes; leaves 36–41, notes; leaf 42, "*Cycle | 'A Touch Of The Poet' | Suggestion Set*", Feb. 1942; leaves 43–47, "*Cycle | 5ᵗʰ Play | Notes For Revision [Re-construction]*", 18 Dec. 1941 and Feb. 1942; leaves 48–49, "A T[ouch]. of the P[oet]. *| Scheme*", July 1942; leaf 50, "T[ouch]. of the P[oet]. /

Act Two / Sequence, scenes . . .*"*; leaf 51, "*A T[ouch]. of the P[oet]. | New Act Two* / Notes for revis[ion].", 17 Sept. 1942; leaves 52–53, "*M[ore]. S[tately]. M[ansions].*", notes; leaves 54–61, set designs; leaf 62, note on reading of literary authors; leaf 63, "Cabin" / 10 × 15", sketch, and notes on Thoreau's log cabin at Walden Pond.

MS 115   *A Touch of the Poet*

First (extant) typescript, with many manuscript corrections, revisions, and additions (totaling 62 leaves): 4 leaves, 32 [i.e., 36] numbered leaves, 1 leaf, 24 numb. leaves, 1 leaf, 28 numb. leaves, 1 leaf, 30 numb. leaves. 28 cm.

With O'Neill's inscription on the first leaf: "(5th play of 11 play cycle as finally planned) / (Last revision—1942—still need cuts & condensation)". Dated at end: "Tao House / Nov. 13, 1942 (Friday!)".

MS 114   *A Touch of the Poet*

Second typescript (original), with extensive manuscript corrections and revisions, incorporating 7 leaves of manuscript of which 2 are versions of the same leaf 76: 5 leaves, 33 numbered leaves, 1 leaf, numbered leaves 34–60, 1 leaf, numbered leaves 61–86, 1 leaf, numbered leaves 87–118 [i.e., 119]. 28 cm.

MS 112   *A Touch of the Poet*

Third typescript (carbon): 4 leaves, 88 numbered leaves. 28 cm.

Prepared from 114, incorporating its manuscript changes.

MS 115a   *A Touch of the Poet*

Another copy. Given by O'Neill to Lawrence Langner of the Theatre Guild in 1944. With Langner's typed statement, signed, 7 Sept. 1960. Gift of Mr. Langner to the Yale University Library, 1960.

MS 113a   *A Touch of the Poet*

Final typescript (original), prepared by Hart Stenographic Bureau, New York, N.Y.: 3 leaves, 40, 30, 30, 39 numbered leaves. 28 cm.

Used as setting copy for the first edition (New Haven, Yale University Press, 1957).

MS 113   *A Touch of the Poet*

Another copy (carbon).

MS   *A Touch of the Poet*
115b   Galley proofs for the first edition.
MS 116 "Sets"
      Folder containing 30 leaves of various sizes.
      Set designs, with occasional notes, for plays of the
      Cycle.

Other Manuscript Materials

O'Neill, Carlotta Monterey. Diary, 1935, 1940, 1943 (YCAL).
———. Diary, 1944, 1948 (DCG).
O'Neill, Eugene. *The Iceman Cometh.* "Original rehearsal copy."
      Typescript (carbon): 3 leaves, 65, 45, 37, 40 numbered leaves.
28 cm.
      With typed explanation signed by Lawrence Langner, 18 Oct.
1946, bound in (YCAL, Theatre Guild papers).
———. Letters to various correspondents.
      Some of these, given or acquired for the O'Neill collection, are
filed, with the call number "Za (YCAL) O'Neill *to*,"
alphabetically by correspondent. They include letters and drafts
of letters to Winfield Aronberg, Dr. George Draper, Léon Mirlas,
Dudley Nichols, Lee Simonson, and Harry Weinberger. Other
drafts of letters are contained in a series of three stenographic
notebooks (Za. O'Neill. 118, vols. 1–3); most of them have ink
notations by Carlotta Monterey O'Neill of the dates on which she
typed them for mailing.
      Letters to Barrett Clark are filed in YCAL with the Clark
papers (listed at the Beinecke Library). Those to Theresa
Helburn and Lawrence Langner are filed with the Theatre Guild
papers (not yet catalogued as of 1997).
YCAL,   ———. Notebooks, etc., containing ideas for plays.
O'Neill   These were transcribed, annotated, and published in *Floyd.*
MSS 78, Nine leaves excised from notebook 82 when it was used as an
80, 82,   exhibit in the Lewys-O'Neill plagiarism case were still laid into
84, 85,   notebook 80 when both manuscripts were received at Yale in
86   1942. Those leaves were restored in January 1979 to their proper
      places in MS 82.

YCAL, ——. Notes, chiefly on books read. 23 leaves. Various sizes.
O'Neill   Most of these were removed from O'Neill library books offered
MS 158   to YCAL in 1954 but returned to Carlotta Monterey O'Neill as
not needed. (She subsequently gave the books to John H. G. Pell,
who eventually gave them to the library at C. W. Post College.)
Each card bears my note of the author and title of the volume
from which it was removed.

YCAL,   Sergeant, Elizabeth Shepley. Typewritten notes of interviews with
MS 3   Eugene O'Neill: 3 (i.e., 4), 10 (i.e., 11) and 25 Aug. 1946.
(Sergeant papers, ser. 3, box 16, folder 358).

Index

Permissions